Criminal Justice

Recent Scholarship

Edited by
Marilyn McShane and Frank P. Williams III

A Series from LFB Scholarly

Being Real
The Student-Teacher Relationship and African-American Male Delinquency

Camille Gibson

LFB Scholarly Publishing LLC
New York 2002

Copyright © 2002 by LFB Scholarly Publishing LLC

Library of Congress Cataloging-in-Publication Data

Gibson, Camille, 1971-
  Being real : the student-teacher relationship and African-American male delinquency / Camille Gibson.
      p. cm. -- (Criminal justice)
  Includes bibliographical references and index.
  ISBN 1-931202-31-1 (alk. paper)
  1. African American teenage boys--Education (Secondary)--New York
(State)--New York--Case studies. 2. Teacher-student relationships--New
York (State)--New York--Case studies. 3. African American juvenile delinquents. I. Title. II. Criminal justice (LFB Scholarly Publishing LLC)
  LC2803.N65 G53 2002
  373.1829'96'073--dc21

                                    2002005602

ISBN 1-931202-31-1

Printed on acid-free 250-year-life paper.

Manufactured in the United States of America.

Table of Contents

List of Tables and Figures

Acknowledgements

This study was facilitated by the feedback and support of many senior faculty, colleagues, relatives and friends. Special thanks to Warren Benton, David Brotherton, and Basil Wilson plus - my ready prayer warriors, my church family at Agape Christian Ministries in Paterson, New Jersey and most of all my Heavenly Father, my Lord and Savior Jesus Christ and my Counselor, the Holy Ghost. This is dedicated to the students of the Bronx, New York and the well-meaning teachers and staff members who labor among them.

CHAPTER 1

CAUSE FOR CONCERN

Over the past two decades many juvenile justice practitioners have expressed a desire to reduce the over representation of African-Americans[1] in the juvenile justice system. Nevertheless, the best way to accomplish this is likely to remain elusive until policy-makers understand how this over representation has been created and sustained.

While it is commonplace to identify factors behind delinquency, understanding how these factors operate is yet, unclear. This study explored the school context as an element in delinquency. School parallels the juvenile justice system in an over representation of African-Americans who do not fare well academically or behaviorally. This is significant because while poor academic performance is not an independent risk factor for delinquency (Famularo et al., 1992; Lawrence, 1985), it is a stronger predictor of delinquency than socio-economic status and peer relations (Cernkovich & Giordano, 1992). On a larger scale, about 75 percent of all inmates are functionally illiterate (Smith, 1995). Such micro manifestations of structural failings began centuries ago. Yet, legally mandated desegregation (1968) was to have been the start of a better education for blacks. Indeed on paper, this appears to have been the case. Nevertheless, the present study reveals that many inner city teachers today seem just as perplexed about the ethnically different students before them as teachers in 1968. Shirley Brice-Heath's (1983) described the immediate post-desegregation anxieties this way:

> A group of mill personnel who felt the need to know more about how others communicated: why students and teachers often could not understand each other, why questions were sometimes not answered, and why habitual ways of talking and listening did not always seem to work....They brought a central question: What were the effects of pre-school home and community environments on the learning of those

language structures and uses which were needed in classrooms and job settings? Answers to this question were important for black and white children who were unsuccessful in school, and for their parents who were frustrated in their interactions....

This work examines the enigma of minority over-representation in poor school performance and incarceration rates. Are these effects connected – the result of a subtle marginalization of African-Americans from legitimate opportunities to economic success? A social reproduction of poverty? Has education failed to be the great equalizer? This work proposes a model for examining how a home-school discontinuity might contribute to ego effects in students that pre-disposes them to delinquency. The focus is a group of African-American male high school students in New York – how they perceive their teachers; how their teachers perceive them and, how perceptions on both sides influence their relationship and in turn, the performance and behavioral outcome of the students.

New York, has long been one of the most difficult places to gain access to delinquents for research purposes. Thus, much of the research on delinquents in the northeast are conducted in nearby states like New Jersey and Pennsylvania. For some reason, prior to entering the field, it did not fully hit me just how unappealing the title of my study would be to potential teacher participants. Nonetheless, it hit me soon enough and I kept the title to myself while in the field. The title seems to suggest that yet again teachers are blameworthy not only for failing schools but crime as well. Yet, no such determinations had been made before hand. While the researcher entered the field with a slightly critical perspective for the most part the study was approached with a constructivist paradigmatic orientation. As such the study was described to the teachers as an effort to hear from the subjects themselves - teachers and students about what is happening in New York City public schools. Due to various bureaucratic delays in getting the many approvals necessary to conduct the study, both school were not observed during the same semester. The comprehensive school observations and interviews occurred from April to June spring 1999. Data collected three years earlier at this school site was also utilized in the data analysis (since many of the same teachers remained in place in place). The alternative school observations and interviews occurred from the beginning of the fall term - September 1999 and ended in early January 2000.

At the comprehensive school, a deep distrust of school administrators made the teachers most paranoid about doing the study. This was not surprising to me. I had observed over 40 different teachers in action and interviewed both teachers and students three years earlier as part of another research effort on gangs at this same school. The principal and most of the teachers remained largely unchanged by time. They were still paranoid and highly critical of the administration. If anything, the paranoia had increased. Nevertheless, the school itself was far more pleasing to the eye having gone through extensive renovations since the last time that I had been there.

Since my primary interest was the student experience of schools, my initial research design stated that I would solicit student participation and then approach those students' teachers about sitting in on classes. However, at my first site, the comprehensive school, I was assigned to the vice principal for security. She thought that getting teacher participation first would be a more effective way to proceed. She was right. The vice principal helped to distribute the teacher consent forms (which included a description of the study) to the teachers, with assurances of confidentiality, anonymity and requesting their voluntary participation, absent any penalty for their decision. Only a few teachers volunteered for the study and they were unable to garner sufficient student interest from their students. I suggested, and eventually went in to speak in their classes about the study. I told the students that they would be part of a book, the study would be anonymous and they would get a $30.oo honorarium for their troubles. Yet, few students volunteered. Most of the interest expressed was from female students. The boys struck me as largely unengaged. I was getting nowhere.

Things changed when I ran into a guidance counselor while waiting by the assistant principal's office one morning. We began to chit-chat about what I was attempting to do. She offered to assist in any way that she might. I do not think that she expected me to take her up on her offer, because when I approached her for assistance a few days later, her demeanor seemed more paranoid than the teachers had been. She introduced me to the assistant principal for special education who, after clearing my presence with security, proceeded to introduce me to some teachers. She stressed to them that they did not have to do the study. From there, one teacher introduced me to other teachers in other departments who might be interested. Thus, through snowballing, I got my teacher participants. One of the teachers, a black female stated that she was doing it because she really wanted to help "a sister" (meaning me) out, but she refused to have anything tape recorded. Another teacher who volunteered was simply good at her job and she knew it – so why hide. The third teacher was very passionate about her job but dismayed over the performance of her students. She was willing to participate in an effort that might improve things. The other teachers who volunteered but were excluded because of low student interest, had volunteered either because they knew they were effective teachers and hence, were unthreatened by observations or they had taken pity on me for they had relatives who also had a challenging time doing research in graduate school. They wanted to help me graduate.

I had done a pilot study in New Jersey which indicated that mailing consent and assent forms home, then awaiting their return by mail would be a huge time waster. I would have also lost time (and did initially), by asking school personnel to distribute the forms and then awaiting their return. Instead, gaining student participation was a factor of: a) allowing potential student subjects to become comfortable with me before even mentioning my interest in interviewing them, b) handing them the assent and consent forms myself and asking them to return them if interested and c) explaining the permission forms to the subjects at the time that I handed it to them. The legalese of the permission and consent forms as recommended by my academic institution's review board had made the documents a deterrent in themselves. For example, the term "participation fee" on the assent forms made it sound as if I was charging the subjects $30.oo to participate instead of giving them $30.oo.

The parent consent form included a section that requested a precise ethnic description of the subject - that is, whether of direct African, Caribbean, South-American or African-American descent (meaning the descendants of those who had been African slaves in America). Black youths who are not African-American (as defined for this study) were to have been screened out. However, it turns out that many of the black males in New York City public schools are not African-Americans as herein defined. Many who are called "blacks" are of Caribbean descent including Hispanic descent. In particular, many of the "blacks" in the two schools were dark skinned Dominicans, Jamaicans, or other islanders or they had an immigrant parent or parents. Since these were the black males in New York's Bronx public schools, these were the blacks included. Note, that in other parts of the city (such as Brooklyn) many direct African and Haitian immigrants are represented. Largely out of a desire for the $30.oo honorarium and partly because influential others had decided to do the study, students began to volunteer. Unfortunately, the females were turned away, although, I used the opportunity to also interview a few Hispanic males.

Initially, the students and teachers seemed to behave either a bit better or worse in my presence. But by about my third week in each setting, both teachers and students seemed to fall into what appeared to have been their regular routine.

The Plight of African-American Males

Empirical realities suggest that there are racial differences in schooling that may be responsible for the different levels of delinquency involvement between blacks and whites via a self-fulfilling prophecy: higher drop-out rate of black compared to white adolescents (England et al., 1988); charges of racially biased testing (Cernkovich & Giordano, 1992: citing Ogbu, 1988); classification and tracking (England et al., 1988; Epstein, 1985); negative teacher attitudes toward black students and lower teacher expectations for black than white students (Aaronsohn, et al., 1995; Cernkovich & Giordano, 1992: citing Ogbu, 1988).

While the dropout rate of African-Americans has declined, the quality of the public education that many of them in central cities receive has also declined. What has risen substantially since the 1970s is the number of African-American males represented amongst those who are officially recognized as "delinquents" (McGarrell, 1993). African-American youths without a subsequent record are six times more likely to be incarcerated than Caucasians similarly situated. Indeed, between 1988 and 1997 the number of white youths processed in juvenile court increased 39 percent while the number of blacks processed increased 68 percent. Hence, the case rate for black youths became 124.1 per 1,000 in 1996 as opposed to 51 per 1,000 for whites (National Criminal Justice Association citing a National Council on Crime and Delinquency report (1998)). In 1997, white youths were involved in 59 percent of juvenile court cases, and 35 percent were waived to adult court. However, African-Americans were 39 percent of those petitioned in juvenile court but 63 percent of them were waived to adult court. Indeed 58 percent of the youths in the adult system are black. Black juveniles also serve longer sentences than white youths in state facilities (an average of 254 days for blacks, 305 days for Latinos and 193 days for whites), (National Criminal Justice Association citing a National Council on Crime and Delinquency 1998).

By 1997 about 79 percent of juveniles were white and 15 percent were black (Stahl 1997). However, blacks constituted 31 percent (535,500) of those handled by juvenile courts while whites constituted 66 percent (1,162,700) (Stahl 2000). Plus, the person offense rate for blacks is three times that for whites; the property offense rate is double the white rate for blacks. Indeed, blacks were processed primarily for person offenses (37%); then public order offenses (33%) followed by drug violations (32%) and finally property offenses[2] (26%). For whites the main offenses were property offenses (70%); then public order offenses (64%), drug offenses (66%) then finally person offenses (60%) (Stahl 2000). Overall, largely reflecting blacks, detention increased for person offenses[3] 97 percent and for drug offenses 89 percent between 1987 and 1996. When education diminishes as an avenue to financial security, activities such as drug dealing may appear more appealing in a context where survival includes employing violence when threatened.

Relatedly, African-Americans are also over-represented as violent crime victims. In 1992, at 12 percent of the population, African-Americans were 50 percent of homicide victims (Messner & Rosenfeld 1997). Indeed, homicide is the leading cause of death of young African-Americans. The likelihood of homicide victimization is 1 in 26 for black males but 1 in 170 for white males, (Messner & Rosenfeld 1997).

Nevertheless, even though African-Americans are arrested for more serious crimes than whites, self-reports indicate few differences between the offending rates (Huizinga & Elliot 1987; Tracey 1987). The disproportionate numbers could reflect a combination of system biases and poverty effects (Bishop & Fraser 1989; Dannefer 1982; Duster 1987).

Indubitably, the violence and the drug offending are a micro context manifestation of a macro stronghold - the immense poverty of many African-Americans. Over a decade ago, when drug related crimes were still at their peak in America, nearly 42.7 percent of black youths under 18 years lived below the poverty line (Census 1987). Then, the national unemployment rate was 6 percent, but for black youths it was an alarming 34 percent (Gibbs 1988).

African-Americans are approximately 12.7 percent of the United States' population (Census Bureau, 1998). Yet, they account for 41

percent of juveniles in detention facilities (Snyder & Sickmund, 1999).
Defending present criminal justice policies some would argue that
black youths commit serious offenses more often than non-blacks,
hence their over-representation in the juvenile justice system. The over
representation has also been attributable to a <u>combination</u> of factors.
Most often mentioned are: discriminatory arrest practices (McCarthy &
Hoge, 1987; Sampson, 1986); inadequate parental or guardian support
(Jenkins, 1995; Simons et al., 1994; Veneziano & Veneziano, 1992);
the poverty of many Blacks (Figuiera-McDonough, 1993; Morash &
Rucker, 1989); the location in which the delinquency occurs (Peeples &
Loeber, 1994; Sampson, 1986); the mistrust that many African-
Americans have of large institutions (Biafora et al., 1993; Stanton-
Salazar, 1997) and a strain between attempts to acquire academic
success and the actual attainment (Agnew, 1985; Cernkovich &
Giordano, 1992; Greene, 1993; Tygart, 1992). The present study is an
effort at deciphering a piece of the minority over-representation
enigma. The over-representation has long been high and increasing
over the past two decades. Is such a result of a subtle (if not overt)
marginalization of blacks from mainstream legitimate opportunities to
economic success? A social reproduction of poverty? Since education
is supposedly the great equalizer in the United States, herein is an
examination of schooling effects for possible contributions to a cycle of
poverty which feeds the attractiveness of delinquency from generation
to generation.

Of course, black America recognizes the value of and is desirous
of a good education for its children. In line with this recognition, the
dropout rate for high school age blacks (14-24) declined from 23.8
percent in 1960 to 13.2 percent in 1984 (Gibbs 1988 discussing the
College Entrance Exam Board findings of 1985). Yet, many black high
school students cannot fill out a job application because they are
functionally illiterate (Gibbs 1988) - victims of social promotion[4].
Additionally, eighteen percent of black families with incomes of over
$20,000 "have had at least one child suspended from school." It has
also been established that the problems of inner city children include
"poorly prepared teachers, inadequate education facilities, low teacher
expectations, ineffective administrators, and chronic violence," (Gibbs
1988). The result is the alienation and institutional mistrust of black
students from their schools (Gibbs 1988). Additionally, the glowing
numbers on the decrease of the black dropout rate are less remarkable

in urban settings were the rate exceeds the national average by 50 percent or higher (Luster & McAdoo 1996).

Tracking Continues

Another poison to the academic advance of blacks is tracking. Nowadays, "tracking" is rarely called by its name. Instead, it is often "academically suitable placement." But suitable for whom? A common placement for African-Americans is the special education track. Herein, blacks are over-represented (Caribbean Life 2000). Recently, various scholars have noted that claims of such placements being objective are highly suspect since blacks are largely over-represented in only the more subjectively diagnosed disabilities. The National Medical Association found that hyperactivity disorders are over-diagnosed in the black community and thus, black children are over-represented in special education classes. African-Americans constitute 28 percent of special education students. According to the1998 Annual Report of the Federal Office of Special Education Programs blacks were placed in special education at twice the rates of whites from 1980 to 1990. For Hispanics the numbers were worse with a 53 percent increase in placement compared to a six percent increase for whites, (Caribbean Life, 2000). Overall, in the present technological age, this course towards substantial educational deficiency amongst people of color will lead to a social devastation that society can ill afford (Swanson & Spencer 1991).

Although researchers have examined possible reasons for this connection between school and delinquency, there has been little research on the relationship between teachers and individual African-American students. This is examined here.

CHAPTER 2

WHAT WE KNOW AND DON'T KNOW ABOUT URBAN EDUCATION

What Students Bring into the Student-Teacher Relationship

High school students bring into the student-teacher interaction mental constructs of classroom roles based on their ascribed or achieved status (Cohen, 1955). The ascribed status is defined by the status of the student's family (social position, income and values) (Cohen, 1955). This status determines the quality of the school that the student attends and how the student initially adjusts to school life (Garner & Cole, 1986; Tygart, 1992; Wilson & Wilson, 1992).

Adjusting to school may be easy or difficult depending on whether the family equips the student to successfully navigate the school system (Stanton-Salazar, 1997). Simply communicating that education is important is not enough for success. Being socially equipped for school means being able to demonstrate competence in the classroom. Such competence contributes to self-efficacy (a perception that one can achieve and advance). This in turn produces resiliency (Rutter, 1990) against delinquency.

Significantly, most delinquents are from low-income families (Peeples & Loeber, 1994) and blacks are over-represented amongst the poor (Census Bureau 1998; Nettles & Pleck, 1994). Forty-five percent of black children live in female-headed households, of these 70 percent are poor, (McLoyd, 1990). Significantly, while the poverty rate has declined for African-Americans over the past 40 years (to 26.5 percent), (Census Bureau 1998) juvenile offending rates remain high. Of course, poverty itself does not cause delinquency, it increases the risk of offending when it exists in conjunction with family dysfunctions such as: the criminal history of a family member (Rowe et al, 1992;Veneziano & Veneziano, 1992: citing Bahr, 1979; McCord & McCord, 1959; West & Farrington, 1973; Wilson, 1980), the mental illness or active substance abuse of a family member (Bryan, 1992) and/or child neglect by a parent or guardian (Crouch & Milner, 1993; Veneziano & Veneziano, 1992). All of these factors reduce the likelihood of a child attaining school success or its protective effects.

Additionally, juveniles with learning disabilities are over-represented amongst delinquents. Five percent of school-age children have learning disabilities, (American Psychiatric Association, 1994). Yet, delinquents with learning disabilities represent 32-36 percent of those adjudicated delinquent (Simpson et al., 1992). However - "learning disabilities" is a very elusive concept. Its operationalization varies with jurisdiction. Thus, a student may be "cured" of a learning disability by moving from one state to the next.

Another predictor of delinquency is hyperactivity (Jefferson & Johnson, 1991 citing: Borland & Heckman, 1976; Cantwell, 1978) (Peeples & Loeber, 1994). In the absence of socially acceptable means of stimulation hyperactive students may misbehave to increase their arousal (Jefferson & Johnson, 1991). Such behavior may also negatively affect the student-teacher relationship (Glass et al., 1993).

These ascribed status disadvantages, create obstacles for gaining a high achieved status (the prestige that an adolescent earns through academic or athletic excellence) (Cohen, 1955). If the student's ascribed values differ from the teachers', that student may initially do poorly in school - in conduct (Gutierrez et al., 1995b) and in academics (Ingram-Willis, 1995). This initial "lack of fit" sets up a trajectory for continued school failure (Taylor, 1991).

What Teachers Bring into the Student-Teacher Relationship

Some of the most important traits of successful teachers of students who are at-risk to become delinquent include: positive classroom interactions; making quick responses to students' problems; listening to individuals; flexible instruction; coaching students on matters of interpersonal relations and social skills; pushing students in specific tasks at which they can succeed and encouraging persistence at tasks (Peterson et al., 1991) and having a positive regard for each student (Aspy et al, 1972, citing: Prescott, 1957). This study will use these criteria as some of the indicators of a positive student-teacher relationship in its observations of classroom interactions.

Usually, teachers (regardless of race[1]: Washington, 1982), bring mental constructs of school roles based on middle class values from their middle class training into student-teacher interactions (Aaronsohn et al., 1995; Bollin et al., 1995; Cohen, 1955; Scott, 1995). A middle class-oriented person emphasizes deferred gratification, conscious planning, upward social mobility, control over feelings to be physically aggressive, and the mastery of certain speech and gestures befitting success (such as, the "ability to make friends and influence people") (Cohen, 1955).

The Student-Teacher Relationship and Delinquency

When many teachers see that initially a student's performance is poor, they may attribute this to an insurmountable deficiency (per stereotypes). These views about specific students may be passed on from teacher to teacher, from year to year. Indeed, McCarthy & Hoge (1987) found that black pupils received greater rates of punishment than other groups based on teacher rumors of students' past academic and conduct record.

Additionally, teachers tend to interact with, call on, intellectually challenge and praise white male middle-class students most, whereas African-American males are usually reprimanded the most (Rios 1993: citing Sadker & Sadker, 1985). Blacks are suspended more than three times as often as white students although self-report measures suggest only small differences between groups (McCarthy & Hoge, 1987). Plus, black males are less likely to be submissive than other groups - a trait that most teachers (black and white) find unfavorable in students of any race (Borduin, Pruitt, Henggeler, 1985). The present study examines whether or not teachers contribute to situations that increase the self-derogation of African-American students. Kaplan's self-derogation theory (1978) proposed that when individuals are persistently exposed to negative evaluations from others, they may eventually internalize these evaluations. When internalized, these evaluations can produce negative feelings about the self (self-derogation). These individuals who feel derogated are more likely to be delinquent to boost their self-perceptions.

Thus, students who teachers view as failures might then begin to see themselves as failures and become more of a failure with time according to Ross & Jackson, (1991) supporting the work of James Coleman in the 1960s. Significantly, this self-fulfilling effect often does not occur unless the student perceives the negative treatment to be differential treatment (Wittrock, 1986). For low income students who tend to evaluate themselves (and be evaluated) by more external than by internal measures this process occurs easily (Bowler et al., 1986; Garner & Cole, 1986).

These messages can flourish when teachers engage in silencing (efforts to eradicate uncomfortable talk - often about matters that differ from the teacher's position) (Fine, 1991). Avoiding differences may lead students to feel misunderstood and to perceive that their culture is less valuable than the dominant culture (Ingram-Willis, 1995). In response some students may create an underlife (Gutierrez et al., (1995b). This refers to activities for distancing oneself from a situation. Such actions may be constrained (passive) or radical (active). If this feeling of being misunderstood persists the student is likely to become disengaged from school (Chevalier, 1995; Ingram-Willis, 1995).

Significantly, the weaker a student's commitment to school becomes, the more likely it is that the student will violate rules and regulations (Thornberry et al, 1991; Hirschi 1969). According to Coie (1992), children usually have strong bonds to conventional individuals. However, when bonds to the teacher (who represents conventionality) are weak, bonds to conflicting unconventional peers increase (Myer-Kester, 1994) and delinquency becomes more likely (Thornberry et al., 1994).

According to self-derogation theory (Kaplan, 1978) delinquency may be self-protective for individuals who find conventional activities self-derogating (Wells, 1989). Regardless, culture is important in understanding behavior. It is plausible that African-Americans have adopted intra-group comparisons over any inter-group comparisons as a protective process (Fordham 1996; Bowler, et al., 1986).

These intra-group comparisons may well be expected since African-Americans in the United States have endured a history of segregation. Indeed, this segregation continues for "truly disadvantaged" blacks (Wilson 1987). It is a segregation fueled by a gradual capital flight from major northern cities as businesses move elsewhere for cheaper labor and operation costs. With the migration of industry to cheaper manufacturing areas, the primary job market with positions offering employment stability and benefits became a secondary job market with unstable employment, and low wage positions without job benefits. Under these circumstances community deterioration is inevitable. The effect on local education – the quality of which reflects the local economy, has been a subtle continuation of "separate but unequal."

The Prior Works

The present research design involves an adaptation of the methodology in works like Paul Willis (1977) *Learning to Labor*, Shirley Brice Heath (1983) *Ways with Words: Language, life, and work in communities and classrooms*, Annette Lareau (1989) *Home Advantage: Social class, and parental intervention in elementary education*, Michelle Fine (1991), *Framing Dropouts*, Jay MacLeod (1995) *Ain't No Makin' It: Aspirations and attainment in a low income neighborhood*, Signithia Fordham (1996) *Blacked Out: Dilemmas of Race, Identity, and Success at Capital High* and a series of New York school ethnographies by David Brotherton (1997; 1996) and qualitative studies by Kris Gutierrez and colleagues (1995) on student-teacher interactions.

Willis'work (1977) is an often-cited example of high quality qualitative research. His study explored whether school was indeed "the great equalizer" thus, leveling the training of all students towards upward social mobility. To this end, Willis spent over a year observing and interviewing working class boys, their teachers and parents. He compared their school experiences to that of middle class boys. His conclusion was that both the arrangement of the larger social structure and the individual interaction processes between teachers and students operated in conjunction to reproduce the working class status amongst working class children. This was largely by not exposing these children to the knowledge capital, behaviors and ways of thinking necessary for their social advance. Willis' study was of white English boys. So, the question herein, is whether or not a typical inner city comprehensive high in the Bronx operates similarly to reproduce low-income secondary market laborers from the children of secondary market laborers. America is very different from Willis' England in that the American culture has a greater emphasis on materialistic pursuits. Such being the case, if the public school estranges low-income students from legitimate avenues to success, it is no wonder that some of these students in the American context may empathize or even supplement their existence through illegitimate means. The present study attempts to capture both the nature of the school and the type of students it produces and the perspective of low-income African-American juveniles on how their school experiences have influenced their outlook. This information has significant juvenile justice implications because although poverty in itself does not cause offending, it is correlated with street crimes.

Michelle Fine's book *Framing Dropouts* (1991) offered a comparison to what the present study is attempting to accomplish in understanding the effects of schools on the lives of New York public school students. Indeed, the researcher benefited from the input of Michelle Fine in preparing the present study's research design. Michelle Fine's study of a New York City public comprehensive high school indicated that the school indeed reproduced the low income status of its students by various acts of silencing (where discussions of differences between the lives of teachers and students are avoided if they are raised in the classrooms), offering an overall low quality education, and by taking no steps to retain its students. Indeed, the quality of the education and the atmosphere of the school were so low that Fine suggested that dropping out was probably no worse a move than staying in. Nevertheless, Fine did not examine in great detail the actual interactions between students and teachers and the students' response to these interactions. The present study does. The present study also offers a gauge to determine just how transferable Fine's findings are to the typical New York City comprehensive high school.

To this end the researcher also benefited from the assistance of nationally recognized gang researcher David Brotherton in designing the present study. In the mid-1990s Brotherton and his team of researchers did extensive qualitative research in both New York and California high schools. Brotherton examined schools as possible instruments of social class reproduction and thus, a mechanism of marginalization which fosters the development of subcultures from which youth gangs emerge and exist. Brotherton's work (2001) is an excellent analysis of how the larger social context of many public schools foster deviance. However, like Fine's work, the exact role of teacher interactions was not examined specifically in relation to African-American males as is the case in the present study.

Brice-Heath (1983) also looked at student-teacher interactions. Brice-Heath, a long time professor of anthropology and linguistics at Stanford University adapted the qualitative methodological approaches of Bambi Schieffelin, Elinor Ochs, Ann Peters and Patricia Causey. Brice-Heath carefully examined the effects of social structure shifts regarding desegregated housing and schools and diminishing factory employment on the citizens of two towns that she called Trackton and Roadville in rural South Carolina from 1969 to 1978. Understanding the impact of changes in the social structure meant collecting archival data - a technique also utilized by the present study. Brice Heath observed and interviewed students, teachers and various other community figures for her in-depth examination of how cultural differences in communication between blacks and whites may have been detrimental to the educational outcome of black children. The necessary social capital[2] to successfully navigate mainstream routes to success included language. Post-1968 this, amongst other things was still lacking amongst the newly desegregated people of color. The present study is an examination of whether a home-school discontinuity in language and topics that are of interest to African-American students are still at odds with the language and topics that teachers embrace. It will also describe any evidence of change in terms of the once exiguous resources of social capital available in schools 30 years ago versus that available today.

Building on this linguistic approach, the present study also utilizes the theoretical model of Kris Gutierrez and colleagues in isolating patterns of spoken and unspoken student-teacher interactions and related student deviance. Gutierrez's (1995) model states that teachers communicate with their students according to the rules of a "scripted pact." This pact is an unspoken expectation of how student-teacher interactions should proceed. Students unfamiliar with their expected role in the pact are likely to violate it especially if they sense that they are in some way being marginalized from the classroom routines. Students may also feel devalued or excluded when the teachers "silence" student-initiated discussions on specifics about their (the students') lives. Such marginalization of student interests may result in various forms of passive or active resistance to teacher-initiated communications. Gutierrez and colleagues recorded classroom student-teacher interactions, noting student responses to subtle classroom marginalizations for Latino students in California. Thus, the present study examines whether the results hold true for African-American males in the Bronx. Are their lives, interests and curiosities discounted in the school context? If it is, does this lead to their feeling marginalized, derogated and eventually disengaged to the point of not participating, getting expelled for misbehavior or playing truant from school? The literature suggests that the problem may simply be that teachers have not infused popular culture techniques into their teaching. Nevertheless, the present study was open to the possibility that the problems were somewhat deeper than teaching technique. The present study posits that eventually, students who actively resist the teachers' expectations are likely to become disengaged from school, targeted by the school for further exclusion, or voluntarily depart. Thereafter, they may succumb to temptations beyond the bounds of the law.

Another study, by Jay MacLeod (1995) examined a group of African-American delinquents called "the Brothers." He contrasted their lives with a similarly located group of white juveniles called "Hallway Hangers." Macleod followed these individuals from teenage years (1981) into adulthood (1991). Much of his book however, focuses on the boys' lives as teenagers - their perceptions of school and their prospects for the future. MacLeod called the African-American males in his study "atypical" because they subscribed to a number of mainstream values such as education as the great equalizer and a belief that racism had declined significantly over the past few decades. Therefore, if African-Americans work hard enough, they could advance materialistically without significant difficulty. Nevertheless, in the event of failure, a person may mentally placate him or herself by blaming racism. The researcher of the present study posits that such is not the case for African-American public school students. While Macleod's study was largely a between group comparison of black versus white teens, the present study is a within group comparison of law-abiding versus non-law-abiding African-American males similarly situated.

Signithia Fordham's (1996) qualitative study of "Capital High" a Washington D.C. public school also involved within group comparisons of African-American males. Her findings included a belief that when African-Americans juveniles excel in academia many of their same-race peers view this as a rejection of their "blackness" and an effort to "act white" - suggesting that upward mobility via education was the exclusive realm of white folks. The present study is an effort to examine whether or not this holds true for some New York African-Americans. The comparisons here should be interesting since New York City and Washington D.C. are both major metropolis areas - where images of both wealth and poverty (relative deprivation) abound.

Relatedly, Annette Lareau (1989) examined class differences. Lareau spent months in two schools - one serving low-income students and another serving largely middle class students. She noted how the social context from which students came affected their school experiences. She concluded that within group differences in academic success were related to an exposure to the cultural capital of those with means and to the investment of that capital. Thus, a possible explanation of the poor academic performance of even middle class African-American students is not the absence of cultural capital but a failure to invest it. The present study is an effort to determine the extent that the student-teacher interaction affects the impartation of cultural capital and whether or not that cultural capital ever becomes social capital which the students then investment towards their upward social mobility.

After reviewing the recent literature, the researcher created a conceptual model of two general life trajectories: 1) towards delinquency and, 2) towards conformity. The model has five major conceptual grouping: 1) cultural, family and demographic traits, 2) individual traits, 3) school factors, 4) interaction factors and, 5) outcomes (delinquency versus non-delinquency and academic success versus academic failure). As discussed above, the status or life circumstances into which a child is born will affect that child's sense of self. When the child begins school, the school climate may be such that it either nudges the student towards conformity or pushes the student into an alternative lifestyle of offending. The quantity and quality of these interactions may then contribute to outcomes of either delinquency or conformity.

The study was such that the researcher was able to examine major and minute occurrences that influence behavioral outcomes - a task that quantitative studies rarely permit. Therefore, findings are transferable in a limited fashion to youths similarly situated. Admittedly, much of the common generalizeability of quantitative research was sacrificed for the authenticity of qualitative research. The effort revealed hypotheses for further testing. Also, this study went beyond the norm in juvenile justice research of a focus on delinquents only. Herein, the lives of non-delinquents provided a contrast.

The researcher (a black female), approached this project with what Denzin and Lincoln (1994) called constructivist lens which were not mutually exclusive of a critical-ethnic worldview. As such, the interpretation of the data reflects a subjective sensitivity to the debased status of many African-American males. Significantly, the researcher is both a psychotherapist and a criminologist which made her a rare, yet highly skilled instrument for the task.

CHAPTER 3

A RESEARCHER INVESTIGATES PUBLIC EDUCATION IN THE BRONX

Theoretically Speaking: A Model for Studying Juvenile Experiences in School

The theoretical model was largely developmental with an emphasis on how macro contextual factors influence micro level behavioral choices. The interdisciplinary nature of the model captured variables from criminology, sociology, psychology, (social-personality, educational, developmental and clinical) and public administration. From these disciplines, the researcher isolated a few variables that held substantial predictive possibilities regarding delinquency. Nevertheless, the study is an effort to understand and explain, not predict. The interdisciplinariness of the model and the knowledge of the various literatures it represents is a primary strength of the study. The other is its macro-micro rapprochement in examining behaviors in light of the larger social context. Particularly important is that it addresses a psychological component in connecting how certain thoughts may emerge from certain experiences and how those thoughts produce different types of behaviors. In particular, the study isolates the "black box" of student-teacher interaction effects on deviance as it pertains to low-income African-American males in Bronx, New York.

The model consisted of five major sections. The sections came largely from the following theories:

- Cohen's subculture theory (1955): is a discontinuity between the traits that teachers bring into the classroom and those that students

bring into the classroom a primary determinant of whether a student takes a delinquent or a conforming trajectory? (Sociological)
- Gutierrez' scripted pact model (1995): what is the nature of the student-teacher interaction and how does it motivate behaviors? (Sociological / Psychological)
- Kaplan's self-derogation theory (1978): is feeling self-derogated in the school context a risk factor for delinquency? (Sociological / Psychological)
- Bourdieu and Passeron's cultural capital or social reproduction theory (1977): is the student's community (in particular, the school) reproducing delinquency in some way? (Sociological)

Figure 1: The General Theoretical Model

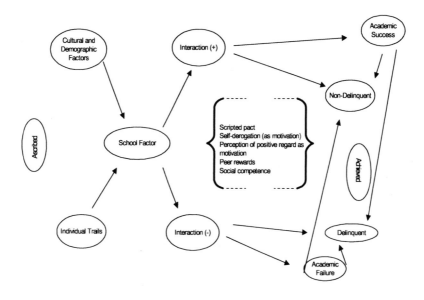

Expected Findings

The expected findings were:

I.   The greater the level of stress in the students' environment outside of school (family and neighborhood), the more likely the student is to be both a poor student and a delinquent.

II.   The greater the volume of positive interactions that the student has with teachers (that is the more the student cooperates with the teacher's scripted pact) the less likely the student is to be a delinquent.

III.   If the student performs poorly academically and/or behaviorally early in the semester, the teacher's positive regard for the student (if it ever existed) would ebb for the rest of the semester.

IV.   The w~~~~   ~~~~her has for a student,
    ~~   ~~n school.

    ~~~~ilar to that for

    ~~~~dents from
    ~~~~ncy more
    ~~~~se would
    ~~~~capable
    ~~~~ademic
    ~~~~urther
    ~~~~d to
    ~~~~tire

f   , enduring
it   unattached and
un~   ~n so desirous of material
pos~   ~etermination to resist the life of
pove~   ~umb to illegitimate avenues to success
(Jank~

The Framework of the Present Study's Theoretical Model

Given the amount of data that the present study was expected to generate, the theoretical model served as a framework for data reduction (Miles & Huberman 1994). The first two categories of the model are, (i) the child's ascribed status[1] or social context and (ii) the child's individual traits.

The ascribed status that a child inherits will be that of his or her family. This status will either reflect a more working class or middle class orientation to the world. The middle class ascribed status endorses the following ideas: ambition as a virtue, effort as important towards outstanding performance, planning, control of physical aggression, respect for property, individual responsibility, delayed gratification, courtesy and constructive recreation (Cohen 1955). On the other hand the working class culture is weak in its endorsement of the above ideas.

The Typical Positive Juvenile Social Context

Presence of an accumulation of positive life experiences
Stressors – if present, are not perceived as such (e.g. family mobility, health problems, etc.)
Significant exposure to mainstream cultural and social capital
Ethnic socialization to mainstream prescriptions for upward social mobility.
Household composition effects – e.g. positive father involvement
Socio-economic status – above the poverty level
Strong formal and informal support systems
Family cohesion
Active religiosity
Parent-child fit
Positive parent/guardian-child communications are common
Parental school involvement
Parent/guardian consistent in monitoring and supervising child
Parent/guardian are not a risk/liability to the child (e.g. associates with active criminals)
High emphasis on materialistic pursuits
Mother has high educational skills (at least high school completion)
Strong educational press in the home
Parents'/guardians' aspirations for the child are consistent and high
Attributions of academic success to effort
High neighborhood collective efficacy

The Typical Negative Juvenile Social Context

Presence of an accumulation of positive and/or negative life experiences

Stressors – if present, are perceived as such (e.g. family mobility, health problems, etc.)

Insignificant exposure to mainstream cultural and social capital

Not ethnically socialized to mainstream prescriptions for upward social mobility.

Household composition effects – e.g. negative, if any father involvement

Socio-economic status – below the poverty level

Weak formal and informal support systems

Family discord

Non-religious

Parent-child misfit

Negative and/or absent parent/guardian communication

Parental school non-involvement

Parent/guardian inconsistent in monitoring and supervising child

Parent/guardian are a risk/liability to the child (e.g. associates with active criminals)

High emphasis on materialistic pursuits by any means

Mother has weak educational background (often, less than high school completion)

Weak education press in the home

Parents'/guardians' aspirations for the child are low and/or inconsistent

Attributions of academic success to innateness

Low neighborhood collective efficacy

Herein, regarding their impact on the student-teacher relationship, the social context points under examination aree:

• *Presence or absence of an accumulation of positive life experiences* (especially in early school life).[2] The literature indicates that an accumulation of positive life experiences serves as a mental reserve from which a child may build a positive self-concept and otherwise draw strength to overcome future challenges (measured by interviews with teachers, parents, school staffers; interviews with juveniles) – *(See Appendix D: 2B and Appendix D: 3C # 27-46).*

• *Stressors that are perceived and experienced as such.* The juveniles were asked about their life circumstances - for example, experiences with the death of a loved one, family exposure to various effects of poverty, et cetera. If students indicated that these common stressors had occurred in their lives, they were then asked to describe how the events affected them. The questions were adapted from the Life Events Checklist (Johnson & McCutcheon, 1980 and the DSM IV 1994. *(See Appendix D: 2C, # 27-46)*

• *Exposure to mainstream cultural and social capital* (values, meanings, messages and capabilities necessary for legitimate upward social mobility. Cultural capital refers to a participation in mainstream culture such as exercising an interest in mainstream music and sports while social capital refers to a knowledge of cultivating social relationships that may facilitate upward social mobility (Bourdieu & Passeron, 1977). The students were asked about their exposure to various types of music, literature and mainstream cultural activities such as attendance at fine arts events like the opera, the theatre, et cetera. (*See Appendix D: 2C, # 20-26; 75-82; 92*) This was also measured by the researcher spending time in the schools observing and asking questions about the exposure to social capital offered at, or facilitated through the school. The literature indicates that mere exposure to cultural capital is not enough for success. The cultural capital must be activated such that the child will invest it to work for him or her. Indeed there are middle class people who have cultural capital at their disposal, but they are not particularly "successful" because they have not invested their cultural capital (Lareau 1989).

• *Ethnic socialization* regarding a person's ethnic identity and culture. For African-Americans the ethnic identity may prescribe one or a combination of the following postures: 1) racelessness, 2) biculturality, 3) oppositional or 4) diffused or passive. "Culture": refers to meanings, values and pleasures which are peculiar to a group of people. (Fiske, 1994). These are manifested in behavior (Geertz, 1983). These meanings, values and pleasures that influence behavior were subjectively identified by the researcher. To gauge the accuracy of these interpretations of behavior, the subjects were asked about the meanings, values and pleasures that they associate with their behavior. Regarding socialization to an ethnic identity *See Appendix D: 3C, # 1 and 26.*

• A related concept to ethnic socialization is *"double talk."* Margaret Beale Spencer who published extensively in the early to mid-1990s on African-American social and educational outcomes encouraged the further examination of "double talk" a concept developed earlier by John Ogbu. Beale Spencer suggested that double talk might explain some of the variance involved in the gulf between the high aspirations of African-American parents and the infrequent realizations of those aspirations by their children. "Double talk" occurs when a parent or guardian encourages a child to aspire to a profession, while also inadvertently sabotaging this message by describing society as not permitting people of color to advance. Macleod (1995) described a similar situation when he noted that the parents of the African-Americans in his study were very careful about not aspiring too highly for their children, lest the realities of life disappoint them with unrealized dreams as the parents themselves had been. The present study examined any such effects. *See Appendix D: 2B, # 32-33, Appendix D: 3C, # 1, 26.*

• *Household composition effects* (number in home, single parenthood, father' presence, economic status). Economic circumstances were determined by asking if the students qualified for school lunches. "Student eligibility for free lunch means that the child's family income is "below 130 percent of the federally determined poverty level," (Census Bureau 1994). For a family of four in 1998 the poverty threshold was $16,588 (adjustable for family size), (Census Bureau 1999).

⊁• *Formal and informal support systems* (for psychoimmunization from minor cumulative stress[3] and/ or major stressful events). "Formal support system": refers to the availability of assistance from school or other agency personnel such as pastors, or youth leaders in problem solving and social skills) as indicated by self-report. "Informal support system": friends or family members from whom an individual may readily receive assistance with academics and social concerns (for example, problem solving skills), as indicated by self-report. Such support systems encourage and reinforce coping efforts (Garmezy 1985). *See Appendix D: 3C, # 50-55.*

• *Family cohesion, absence of discord* and, *level of religiosity.* The literature indicates that non-delinquents come from more cohesive families with little household conflict. Additionally, cohesiveness is more common in religious households (Brody et al. 1996). Significantly, boys are more likely than girls to manifest behavioral disturbances when exposed to considerable family discord (Rutter 1987). Indeed, parents are more likely to argue in front of boys than girls. In turn, boys are more likely to behave oppositionally. Thus, boys solicit more negative parent responses than girls. Rutter (1987) went on to note that if one child must experience institutionalized placement, the boy is usually selected - (possibly because they are assumed to be the stronger gender), *See Appendix D: 3C, # 14-19.* In addition to items 64 and 65 *Appendix D: 2C* subjects were asked "do you get along with the people in your household?"

•   A related concept is *family resilience*. This refers to the support and coping response (or lack thereof) in times of trouble. It also refers to whether or not the family as a unit is in pursuit of goals that involve family advance. *See Appendix D: 3C, # 47-55.*

•   *Parent-child fit* refers to how well the parent or guardian's temperament matches that of the child and vice-versa. This does not mean that the parent and child have the same personality but that whatever their personalities they get along, especially where communication is concerned. Evidence of a parent-child fit includes a child's report of positive communications with a parent or guardian and a report that that person also renders the right amount of affection. *See Appendix D: 2C, # 56-61, 64-65, 87.*

•   *Parental communication* is an indicator of parent-child fit. Quality communication holds the potential of mediating delinquency involvement. In instances of conflict, the child's pattern of responding also holds insight into the child's resiliency threshold. The juveniles who maintain communication through conflict are generally more resilient than those who withdraw. *See Appendix D: 3C, # 56, 64-69, 103, 106.*

•   *Parental school involvement* The literature indicates that a child's school performance is positively related to parental school involvement. For many children from low-income families, parental school involvement is minimal. This study presents an opportunity to inquire about the nature of involvement. *See Appendix D: 3C, # 70-74.*

•   *Parental monitoring and supervision* refers to the presence of consistent adult monitoring of a juvenile's behavior. This includes an awareness of the juvenile's whereabouts and a familiarity with the juvenile's peers. Such will be indicated by student responses, *see Appendix D: 3C, # 62-63, 68-69, 85-86.*

•   *Parent as risk / liability* this refers to situations where a parent possesses traits or acts in a manner that may potentially harm the juvenile. Such may include parents with criminal sympathies or associates. *See Appendix D: 3C, #. 27-39, 44-46.*

•   *Materialism* refers to how satisfied parents are with their material status. Parents with a strong desire for material possessions are likely to impart this to their children. Depending on the opportunity structure immediately available a student may subscribe to legitimate or illegitimate means of securing funds. The latter becomes particularly attractive if legitimate avenues to success, such as school are considered off limits. When illegitimate means are highly visible and readily accessible, the mediating factors may be religion, having children of one's own, or a firm embrace of the "Protestant work ethic."

• *Mother's educational level* (the literature indicates that the educational level of the mother has a more significant impact on the child's academic outcome than the father's educational level (Marjoribanks 1984). More educated mothers are more inclined and capable of preparing their children for higher education in terms of the expectations they declare for their children and the education press that they facilitate (Jenkins 1997). *See Appendix D: 3C, # 5-6.*

• *Education Press* refers to a parent or guardian imparting the importance of education to a child often by emphasizing things like care in doing homework well and the importance of communicating in Standard English (Marjoribanks 1984). This was expected to be largely a function of the mother's educational level irrespective of the father. *See Appendix D: 3C, # 67-69, 72-74.* Note: #20 on the original instrument was changed to "growing up, did your parents emphasize speaking standard English?"

• *Parents' academic aspirations versus expectations for their child.* "Parents' academic aspirations" for their child refers to the amount of education that parents desire for their children. While aspirations indicate hope, parental expectations indicate what parents' perceive their children's reality will be. The difference is important because despite what parents state as aspirations, children pay attention to subtle or overt messages about expectations. Thus, based on what the subjects had to say, the researcher inquired whether or not the student was aware of his parents making provisions for any future education. This according to the literature is a good indicator of parental expectations as opposed to mere wishes. *Appendix D: 2B, # 24, 32-34.*

• *Attributions of academic success* (effort versus innateness). Where students attribute their performances to effort, they are more likely to be academically successful than those who attribute their performance to innateness. Performance attributions will be measured by student report - see *Appendix D: 2B, # 7.*

• *Neighborhood collective efficacy* (an examination of community cohesiveness versus criminal opportunities). When low-income adolescents are chronically exposed to violence their common response is rage, hopelessness and distrust (Greene 1993). A healthy transition to adulthood involves a sense of safety, security and hope. Yet, a third of

New York City's children under 19 years live below the poverty line. Of these, 44 percent are African-American (Greene 1993). This study examined community collective efficacy adapting items from the work of Sampson and Earls (1997) - see *Appendix D: 3C, # 45-46, 118-121.*

Individual Juvenile Traits

The second set of components in the first part of the model is the juvenile's individual traits. The variables reflect points from the literature which have empirical support or significant recommendations for further examination. Arguably, some of these traits may be present from birth, but many of them are formed through nurture. They represent the juvenile's level of resiliency.[4]

Positive Juvenile Traits

Fit/match (possesses traits favored by parents/guardians)
LD and/or ADHD etc., if present is under control
Belief in the mainstream prescribed opportunity structure
Clear cause orientation (dream/goals)
Attributions of success to effort
Religious
High self-concept/self-efficacy – cognitive, social, physical
Sense of control
Sense of humor
Social competence (includes Bourdieu's cultural capital and Stanton-Salazar's social capital)
Personal insight, emotional regulation, independence of spirit
Tendency to cut out non-supportive others
Ethnic identity – e.g. raceless, bicultural
Materialism
Sports or other extracurricular involvement
Employment out of need and / or desire

Negative Juvenile Traits

Misfit/match (possesses traits not favored by parents/guardians)
LD and/or ADHD etc., if present is not under control
Doubt in the mainstream prescribed opportunity structure
Unclear cause orientation (dream/goals)
Attributions of success to innateness
Low religiosity – if any
Low self-concept/self-efficacy – cognitive, social, physical
Low sense of control
Low sense of humor

Low social competence (includes Bourdieu's cultural capital and Stanton-Salazar's social capital)
Lacks personal insight, emotional regulation, independence of spirit
Tendency to associate with non-supportive others
Ethnic identity – e.g. oppositional, diffused or passive
Low materialism
Not involved in sports or other extracurriculars
Employment out of need and / or desire as a priority over school

• *Parent-child fit* How well the child's temperament matches that of his/her parent or guardian (Anthony 1987). Resilient children "elicit positive reactions from teachers" are more likely to be the favored child in the family and have positive self-perceptions, (Radke-Yarrow & Brown, 1993). This does not mean that the parent and child have the same personality but that whatever their personalities they get along - they communicate. Evidence of a parent-child fit includes a child's report of positive communications with a parent or guardian and a report that that person also renders the right amount of attention. *See Appendix D: 2C, # 56-61, 64-65, 87.*

• *Presence of a disability that affects school behavior* (for example, childhood depression, learning disabilities, attention deficit hyperactivity disorder, a co-morbidity of the two, et cetera.). "Hyperactivity": refers to poor concentration, impulsivity and restlessness. Such was measured by the researcher's classroom observations (adapting DSM IV guidelines), and by interview reports. "Learning disability": a developmental disorder where a person achieves lower than would be expected given his or her intelligence (categories of the disorder include: dyslexia (reading disorder), dysgraphia (writing disorder), dysphasia (speech disorder). *See Appendix D: 3C, # 34.*

• *Belief in the mainstream opportunity structure* affects academic aspirations and in turn the effort invested into achieving school success. *See Appendix D: 2B, # 36.* A related concept is a *mistrust of societal institutions* such as schools. See *Appendix D: 3C, # 113-116.*

• *Cause orientation* (dreams versus goals or aspirations versus expectations). "Cause orientation": is a protective trait against deviance; "a personal dream [which] simplifies life, makes it manageable, and gives meaning to goals." (Richardson & Nixon, 1997). Also, aspirations are strongly related to adolescents' eventual academic attainment (Marjoribanks, 1984). However, they do not emerge on their own but are shaped over time largely through significant others and academic performance (Walker & Sutherland 1993). *See Appendix D: 2B, # 24-25; 3C: 95-100.*

- *Religiosity* and its effects on life-style.[5] Religiosity contributes to household harmony and possibly to individual resilience. *See Appendix D: 3C, # 14-18.*

- *Self-concept/self-efficacy* in the cognitive, social and physical arenas (an example of the physical arena would be notable accomplishments in sports). "Belief in self-efficacy": a fusion of self-cognitions with one's regulation of behavior (Sylva, 1994). A student's belief in his or her own efficacy or capabilities to achieve academic goals (Zimmerman, 1995). In this study, belief in self-efficacy was indicated by student-report about the extent of their efforts towards realizing their goals; and the efforts which the researcher observes in the classroom that seem to support the students' stated goals. *See Appendix D: 2B, # 4, 7, 15-16.*

- *Sense of control* An "Internal locus of control" refers to perceptions of control over one's own life circumstances (Luthar, 1991). *See Appendix D: 3C, # 98-100* (Hughes & Demo 1989).

- *Sense of humor* is a commonly identified protective trait (Rutter 1987) *See Appendix D: 3C, # 87-90, 105.*

- *Social competence,* good decision-making (Richardson & Nixon citing Benard 1991) and social problem-solving are traits of resilient children (Rutter 1985). This was measured by the researcher's observations and collection of opinions from teachers and staff.

- Other common individual protective traits in the literature include-S*trong sense of self-preservation* or a commitment to self (Kobasa 1979) including a tendency to eliminate non-supportive peers from one's life *independence of spirit or an ability to restore self-esteem, introspection / personal insight, and emotional self-regulation* (a cognitive skill manifesting social competence). *See Appendix 3D: 2B, # 36, 3C, # 8-13, 26, 54-55, 66-67, 87-91, 101-112.*

- *Ethnic identity* (African-Americans as raceless or bicultural, et cetera). "Ethnic identity" or an "awareness of the group to which one belongs and the perceptions and feeling that accompany such membership," (Brookins, 1996). *See Appendix D: 3C, # 1,26.*

- *Bicultural identity:* one well socialized into the mainstream who also strongly identifies with his ethnic group (Clark, 1991). *See Appendix D: 3C, # 1, 20-26.*

- *Acting white:* referring to blacks or African-Americans who behave according to mainstream Caucasian norms while denying identifications with being "black." *See Appendix D: 3C, # 26.*

※ • *Oppositional social identity*: one who resists mainstream socialization; does poorly in school; rebels against authority figures; sees school as a place of oppression; and, who may pretend cooperation to protect his self-esteem (Clark, 1991: citing Ogbu, 1988). *See Appendix D: 2B, # 4-7, 30-31, 87-91* and, *AppendixD:3C, # 26.*

• *Raceless identity*: when one is oblivious to racism as a barrier; lacks closeness to African-Americans while endorsing mainstream values (Clark 1991: citing Boykin, 1986; Fordham 1988). *See Appendix D: 3C, # 1, 26.*

• *Materialism* the child's perceptions of wealth and the channels for obtaining it versus present material satisfaction. The literature indicates that students who do well academically and behaviorally are more materialistic than their less deviant peers. This implies that the drive for material possession may be so strong that it drives juveniles to pursue property via the means that are readily accessible to them. For some groups of students an ongoing marginalization from legitimate means like school, normalizes illegitimate financial networks. *See Appendix D: 3C, # 95-100.*

↜ • *Involvement* refers to the students' involvement in sports or other extra-curricular activities. Students who are more involved in school are more likely to be bonded to school and thus, less likely deviant according to the literature (largely Hirschi 1969). Involvement when utilized in a comprehensive school offers an opportunity for teacher - student bonding. This dynamic and its effects were measured by student interviews. *See Appendix D: 3C, # 92-94.*

• *Employment* (its effects on the juvenile - whether done out of necessity or simply a desire for extra spending money). The literature indicates that employment often fosters disengagement from school (Steinberg, 1996). After all, work is often more exciting than school and it offers more immediate rewards for the effort invested, *see Appendix D: 3C, # 7.* In some cases it is the responsibilities at home that offer a substantial alternative to the boredom of school. *See Appendix D: 2B, # 37.*

School Factors

<u>Positive School Environment</u>
Instructional leadership from the principal
Orderly environment
Quality instruction (grading practices) good
School climate – welcoming, warm, inclusive

School size – small (thus, encouraging active, not passive student involvement)

Negative School Environment
Lack of instructional leadership from the principal
Disorderly environment
Poor instruction and grading practices
School climate – unwelcoming, cold
School size – large (thus, encouraging passive, not active student involvement)

The third component of the model refers to the nature of the school context in which the student-teacher interactions occur. The focus here is the influence of historical, social, political, and economic factors in shaping the school contexts of New York's truly at-risk students.[6] The initial model contained the points below:

• *Instructional leadership from the principal* The researcher subjectively measured the caliber and quantity of instructional leadership from the principals. These are described in detail.

• *Extent of orderliness in the school environment* The researcher subjectively measured the caliber and extent of orderliness in the school environment. These are described in detail.

• *Quantity and quality of instruction (including the school's grading practices)* The researcher subjectively measured the caliber and quantity of instruction. These are described in detail.

• *School climate* The researcher subjectively measured the nature of the school climate. This is described in detail.

• *School size*

• *School ecology:* refers to both the geographic location of the school and the nature of life therein. This addresses school type: public, private, Catholic, secular, relationship to the community et cetera.

In addition to the above points a number of other factors about the school context emerged from the data.

Student-Teacher Interactions

The fourth component of the model is student-teacher interactions. To measure this, the researcher first observed how students and teachers behaved in the classroom. Then she interviewed them for insights on the behaviors that she had seen. This yielded both knowledge and understanding of the school histories of individual juveniles as they had come to shape the students' present behavior. The researcher was well aware that student-teacher interactions could not be measured effectively solely in one semester's observations, after all - the effects of student-teacher interactions are processual - and thus, not likely to be terribly revolutionary over one semester.

This fourth component of the model is divided into three parts: A, B and C.

Part A: Teacher Traits

Part A consists of teacher traits that are predictive of positive school outcomes for truly at-risk urban students per the literature. Teacher traits were measured subjectively via researcher observations and interviews.

Attributes of an Effective Teacher to At-Risk Students

Teachers
High expectations
Sincere caring
Unconditional positive regard
Quick responses to student problems
Listening to individuals
Flexible instruction
Coaching students on matters of interpersonal relations and social skills
Pushing students in tasks at which they can succeed, encouraging persistence
Closely monitors student progress
Communicates effectively with parents about child's progress and school programs

Attributes of an Ineffective Teacher to At-Risk Students

Teachers
Low expectations
Lack of caring
Conditional positive regard
Slow, if any responses to student problems
Not listening to individuals
Rigid instruction methods
Disinterest in coaching students on matters of interpersonal relations and social skills

Fails to push students in tasks at which they can succeed, fails to
encourage persistence
Fails to monitors student progress
Fails to communicate effectively with parents about child's progress and
school programs

- *High expectations of students:* the researcher looked for things
such as a communication from teacher to students that college would
be a part of the latter's future. The teachers were asked how they
thought various students in the study would turn out in life.
- *Sincere caring* could be evidenced in various words and deeds.
These signs emerged from the data. They were largely evident in how
the teachers spoke of the students and how they interacted with them
in the classroom. Teachers were asked about their thoughts regarding
each student targeted as primary subjects in the study.
- *Unconditional positive regard for students* (maintaining a belief
that students can and will learn) as evidenced by words and deeds.
- *Quick responses to student problems* measured through
classroom observations.
- *Listening to individuals* measured through classroom
observations.
- *Flexible instruction* measured through classroom observations.
- *Coaching students on matters of interpersonal relations and
social skills* measured through classroom observations.
- *Pushing students at tasks in which they can succeed* measured
through classroom observations.
- *Encouraging persistence* measured through classroom
observations.
- *Closely monitors student progress* measured through classroom
observations.
- *Communicates with parents/ guardian* about student progress
and school programs. This was measured through teacher interviews.

Part B: Student -Teacher Interactions

Part B is the student-teacher interactions component. It refers to the
communicative behavior - verbal (e.g. back channels[7] and reprimands)
and non-verbal (for example, eye contact, smiles, gazes, gestures and
frowns) between students and teachers and the meanings that each
attaches to such exchanges. Such will be observed and recorded during

classroom observations and inquired about during interviews. The Coker Scale was used as a guide in the observations. The process also involved recognizing and understanding the scripted pact between student and teacher as it relates to classroom deviance (Kris Gutierrez and colleagues, 1995). It also meant understanding Howard Kaplan's theory on how feeling self-derogated may lead a person to behave deviantly. The factors included are:

Positive Psycho-Social School Interaction Effects

Kaplan
No signs of internalized self-derogation as motivation to deviance
Gutierrez
Home-school continuity such that both student and teacher are operating from a scripted pact of how each will behave and what is expected from both parties in their relationship with each other.

Negative Psycho-Social School Interaction Effects

Kaplan
Signs of internalized self-derogation as motivation to deviance
Gutierrez
Home-school discontinuity such that the teacher's script is at odds with the students' leading to: Counterscript - when students resist the teacher's script (whether actively or passively).

- *Self-derogation*: signs of an internalized negative self-evaluation of one's cognitive, physical or social skills based on a perception that significant others hold such views of oneself (Kaplan, 1975). The researcher interpreted these subjectively from classroom observations and inquired about self-derogation in interviews - *see Appendix D: 2B, # 4-7, 11, 23, 27, 36.*
- *Self-derogation* could also manifest in violations of the teacher defined *scripted pact* operating in the classroom. Such were noted after carefully reviewing audiotapes of classroom dialogues between teachers and students.
- The *scripted pact:* an unwritten contract between student and teacher about how to relate to each other. Evidence of this contract is most noticeable when it is broken. For example, if a student speaks out of turn, a teacher may scold that student, thereby magnifying the fact that speaking out of turn violates classroom procedure. Measured largely through classroom observations.

- *Teacher script*: teacher's assumptions about how students and teachers should relate to each other. Measured by classroom observations and interviews.
- *Student's Counterscript:* differing from the teacher's script, it is a student's oppositional assumptions about how students and teachers should relate to each other.
- *Underlife constrained*: passive resistance to the teacher's script .
- *Underlife radical:* active resistance to the teacher's script e.g. making witty, irrelevant comments during serious classroom moments.
- *Third Space:* when teachers and students are communicating successfully.
- *Silencing:* Efforts by either student or teacher to avoid discussing issues that appear to be uncomfortable topics for either party, for example, racial prejudice might be an uncomfortable for some white teachers to address with minority students.
- *Positive regard*: refers "an active and sincere valuing of each child at all times" (Moustakis, 1966) and a belief that each child can learn, albeit differently. This was measured via classroom observation and teacher interview, *see Appendix D: Teacher Interviews..*
- *Institutional-mistrust*: refers to a student's belief that no matter how hard he/she tries to do well in school, such will not happen because of external factors. *See Appendix D: 2B, # 7* and *Appendix D: 3C, # 26, 98-100, 113 - 117.*
- *Peer influence*: refers to a subjective and objective measure of the extent to which a subject's behavior is influenced by interactions with school peers. This will be measured by self-report from the interviews and from classroom observations. *See Appendix D: 3C, # 8-13, 79-84.*
- *Prejudice*: a pattern of verbal and/or nonverbal reactions to an event, a person(s) or a situation, which indicate fear, mistrust and / or hatred directed against the interests of a particular person and/or group. Subjectively identified by interviews and observations within the school context.
- *Stereotype*: conclusions or generalizations about an individual based on a knowledge of a group with which one associates that individual (this is without regard for the individual's uniqueness). Such were indicated by statements from the subjects.

Part C: Record of Student Educational Experiences

Part C of the model's interactions' component refers to the educational experiences that the students have had up to their present point in high school as manifested by the following:

Elements of a Positive Educational Experience

Experiences of academic success after investment of effort, thus, building academic self-concept

Engagement in school (belief in school, commitment to school, active involvement in school)

School conforming conduct

Orderly environment

Peer influences to achieve academically

Formal support for academic achievement (e.g. tutoring, teacher availability outside of classroom)

Informal support for academic achievement (i.e. in wider community, e.g. from relatives)

Elements of a Negative Educational Experience

Experiences of academic failure after investment of effort, thus, fostering a low academic self-concept

Disengagement from school (rejection of school as a viable opportunity for success; passive involvement or non-involvement in school)

Resistance to school manifested in misconduct

Disorderly environment

Peer resistance to academic pursuits

Lack of formal or informal support for academic achievement

• *Presence of home-school discontinuity* refers to a school *modus operandi* that defers from that to which the student is accustomed from home. For example, if the school fosters individualism and competitiveness and the child has been raised with an orientation to group dependency and external performance attributions, such differences would mean a home-school discontinuity such that the child is at odds with the school's expectations of him. This was measured by observations and interviews.

• *Experiences of academic success or failure.* "Poor academic performance" refers to having a "D" average or below as the final grade in two or more classes (according to the literature "D" indicates performance slightly below average [Agnew, 1985]). This was measured by student self-report in response to questions about the grades that they were presently getting and their grades prior to their present high school.

• *Conduct record* "Poor school conduct": as evidenced by at least one incident of in-school or out-of-school suspension, expulsion or notes sent to a parent or guardian in regards to a child's misconduct. This information was obtained by student self-reports and teacher reports. For the delinquents additional information came from staff reports.

- *Belief in school* refers to the child's belief in school as an avenue to opportunities for material success or other legitimate pursuits, *see Appendix D: 2B, # 36, Appendix D: 3C, # 95-100.*

- *Commitment to school* refers to the investment that the student makes into doing well at school in terms of conduct ratings and academic performance (adapted from Hirschi's, 1969). Such will be measured by self-reports and teacher interviews.

- *Involvement in school* (active, passive or non-involvement). "Involvement" extent of student involvement in extracurricular activities. The literature suggests that for African-American males, being involved in an organized sport activity fosters resilience. Also, sports offers an arena for building achieved status regardless of academic performance. Measured by observation and, *Appendix D: 92.*

- *Exposure to orderly school environments* prior to the present setting as measured by student-self report about prior school experiences.

- *Peers influences to achieve:* The educational psychology literature indicates that peer influences to succeed academically are highly predictive of academic success. See *Appendix D: 3C, # 79-84.*

- *Peer influence towards deviance* Amongst delinquents peer deviance or peer introduction to deviance is common. *See Appendix D: 3C, # 8-13, 79-84.*

- *Formal* (from school personnel) and *informal support* (family and friends) for academic achievement. As measured by observation and self-report, *see Appendix D: 3C, # 66-78, 106-109.*

Model Outcomes

Finally, the sixth piece of the model is the student outcome (behaviorally and academically). The possible outcome combinations are:
- *Non-delinquent and academically successful*
- *Non-delinquent and academically non-successful*
- *Delinquent and academically successful*

- *Delinquency and academically non-successful*

"Non-delinquency" is not a behavioral absolute. It refers to those who have not been officially labeled "delinquent" by the juvenile justice system, regardless of whether or not they claimed that they had committed an offense. "Delinquents" refers to those who have been so labeled by the juvenile justice system whether or not they have admitted to having committed the offense. "Delinquents" are individuals charged with committing an offense which, had it been done by an adult would have been deemed "criminal." Thus, the focus of the present study is not status offenders. Signs of risk for delinquency include early school failure, history of trauma, special education placement and mental health problems (Hsia & Beyer 2000). Developmental signs of risk for delinquency include poor decision-making, poor judgment in weighing the consequences of behavior, impulsivity, past trauma, school failure and substance abuse (Hsia & Beyer 2000). Delinquency may also result from ego-defenses. Examples of ego-defenses include assertion, negation, withdrawal and counter-aggression (Brookins, 1996).

"Academic success" refers to students making at least a "D" average in most schools. Herein, to capture those who are disengaged from academia but who may be the "beneficiaries" of social promotion, the present study uses "C" as an "academic success" minimum. Note that some bright children may also evidence maladaptive motivational responses that result in underachievement, (Ablard & Mills 1996 discussing: Heyman & Dweck 1992; Licht & Dweck 1984). One reason for negative behavior in school is boredom (Ablard & Mills 1996 discussing: Rimm & Lovance 1992; Sisk, 1988) which occurs when students are under-challenged.

Other Outcome Descriptives Include:
- *Deviance*: (for the purposes of this study) refers to actions that constitute a violation of a law (be it a status or delinquent offense).
- *Juvenile:* refers to a person who is under 18 years of age.
- *Non-delinquent*: refers to a youth who has never been arrested (as indicated by self-report, and any available official records) and who claims that he or she has not engaged in behavior that if done by an adult would be considered criminal (Note: study excludes status offenses).

- *Recidivist*: one who has been arrested two to four times for deviant behavior (status or delinquent in nature), as indicated by self-report and any official available records.
- *Chronic recidivist*: one who has been arrested five or more times for deviant behavior (Tracy, Wolfgang & Figlio, 1990), indicated by self-report and any available official records.

The initial hypothesis is that students who are academically unsuccessful are more likely to be delinquent. Thus, it is also posited that the trajectory to school failure will be very similar to the trajectory for delinquency adjudication.

Cohen's theory is more valuable for its psychological assumptions of classroom deviance than for its sociological predictiveness of gang involvement. The study herein discusses the psychological aspects of the theory in terms of a clash of cultures where the culture of black and Latino students are often at odds with that of their often monocultural mainstream teachers. The wider social context in which this clash occurs fosters a cycle of marginalization of the minority cultures. This marginalization makes the minorities more prone to experiencing the ravishes of the law (Black 1976). Thus, while the opportunities for minority advancement exist in the United States the problem is that the truly at-risk lack the knowledge or social and cultural capital necessary for accessing these opportunities. Normally, this information would come through formal education (the great equalizer), but for the most part, it does not.

Admittedly, the theoretical model herein would not explain all African-American male juvenile delinquency. The theory is an effort at explaining and presenting promising areas for innovative research on the specific social context of New York City public schools. It is not a model that would explain faux delinquency (situations where an adolescent is tricked into offending), nor is this an effort to explain the actions of truly antisocial psychopathic youth. The subjects herein are humane and feeling students who seemed to have fallen prey to their circumstances. The present study examined the extent to which teachers might provide protection against a trajectory to delinquency. Since teachers function according to how their context permits them, this was also examined.

Kaplan's theory implies that poor self-esteem predisposes a person to delinquency (Leung & Drasgow 1986). The self-esteem motive is "the personal need to maximize the experiences of positive self-attitudes and to minimize the experience of negative self-attitudes," (Kaplan 1980). Since blacks generally have a high self-esteem, the present study posits that self-esteem is not problematic for African-Americans but rather a low self-concept regarding individual academic ability. Some schools can and have destroyed the academic self-concept of many students of color.

Kaplan's (1980) general theory of offending focused on self-attitudes and deviance. His theory stated that self-attitudes or self-feelings were "the affective or emotional responses of individuals to themselves upon perceiving and evaluating their own attributes and behaviors." They "vary in intensity and range from positive...to negative..." Negative self-attitudes could indicate "a predisposition or motivation to deviate, or the absence of motivation to conform, seeking out deviant behaviors."

Deviant behaviors refer to a change in the person-group relationship. It is doing other than the norms prescribed to a group member as perceived by both the member and the group. The new behavior may be the result of some motivation to deviate or an otherwise diminished motivation to conform. Behaviors would not be deviant if the person had not internalized the behaviors of the group or if such expectations were new to a person. "Membership in a group is evidenced by a pre-deviance conformity to group norms and the application of group norms expectations to the individual, " (Kaplan 1980).

Deviant behavior emerges as a protective response to damaged self-attitudes which are the result of: i) self-perceptions of failure to possess personally valued attributes or to perform personally valued behaviors; ii) "self-perceptions of failure as objective of positive attitudes by personally valued others," iii) "failure to possess and employ normatively defined self-protective response patterns that might preclude the occurrence or mitigate the self-devaluing effects of such experiences." The probability of the above outcomes is influenced by one's placement in the social structure as affects a disjunction between goals and the access to the goals and the extent of stigmatizing experiences.

Yet, why would a person adopt the values of significant others initially? A need for self-approval which is satisfied when significant others accept the subject's attributes. This begins in childhood as infants depend on adults for sustenance. Eventually, the infants become "extremely sensitive to the very presence" of significant adults and these people's behaviors towards them (Kaplan 1975). Kaplan called this drive for approval a "self-esteem motive" which may be observed in the prevalence of positive self-descriptions" in the early years. An individual will tend to develop negative self-attitudes if he has in balance a history of perceiving and interpreting the behavior of highly valued others as expressing negative attitudes toward him in general or toward personally valued aspects of him," (Kaplan, 1980)

When a person perceives the self as having devalued traits and behaviors, hence the object of rejection by valued others, the response may include: i) an alteration of one's perception of the situation, or, ii) giving higher priority to, or adopting new values that permit the individual to re-evaluate self-attributes and behaviors in a more positive light (rejecting one group's values for another that yields a more favorable report of the self). Here, deviance "facilitates intrapsychic and interpersonal avoidance of self-devaluing experiences associated with the pre-deviance membership," (Kaplan 1980).

As self-devaluing consequences outweigh self-enhancing ones, persons will experiment with various forms of deviance (Kaplan 1980). These may be active (hostile - such as critical or suspicious looks and a lack of identity with others) or retreating (for example, denying reality or avoidance behaviors) (Kaplan 1975: discussing Washburn 1962). In a study of high school students Rosenberg (1965) found that students presumed to be sensitive to self-devaluations were more likely to daydream and to "express preferences for occupations that leave them free of supervision and involve little or no competition - and indicate that it is less important for them to get ahead in life than subjects with higher esteem scores," (Kaplan 1975). Kaplan (1975) cited a study of university student behaviors by Dosey and Meisels (1969). They found that people increased their spatial distance from people who threatened their views of themselves. Similarly, some of the subjects in this study seemed to cut classes or school to avoid the threatening nature of the context. Another possible response is a re-ordering of values where less value is placed on the traits one lacks and more value is placed on the traits one possesses (Kaplan 1975 citing Ludwig & Maehr 1967). The third possible response is a devaluation of the source of the negative evaluations with comments indicating things like: the source misjudged them; the source was not serious; the source used different measures, the source did not know them well (Kaplan citing Harvey 1962). The data herein support this.

The Subjects

The subjects came from two schools in the Bronx, New York. One school was a typical comprehensive public high school and the other was an alternative public high school. Both schools served students who were similar in demographics (such as socio-economic status, household composition, neighborhood, school histories, et cetera). However, five of the research subjects lived in Brooklyn, one lived in Manhattan and the others lived in the Bronx. The alternative school had sites in different locations. Data were collected from students in two of these locations. The primary research subjects were 16 delinquent and 8 non-delinquent African-American males, ages 14-19 years. The 8 non-delinquents at the comprehensive school were in 10th grade classes. The 16 delinquent students at the alternative school were largely in ninth grade classes.

In both settings the students who volunteered for the study might be described as "at-risk" for delinquency. The comprehensive school had a history of gang activity and related violence some years before. Since then, the school had implemented a series of delinquency intervention programs run by community groups. The alternative school was established specifically for delinquents whom it was expected would be poor academic performers coming in. As such the alternative school programming was designed to arrest delinquent behavior and assist students in catching up as much as possible academically. One major way of accomplishing the later involved teaching fewer subjects – largely variations of the basics (Mathematics, Science, English, Computers, Global Studies and Gym) in double period sessions. The offenses represented amongst the subjects included assaulting teachers, staff, or students, vandalism and gun possession in or near a school. Each delinquent was officially involved in the justice system and serving a minimum one-year superintendent's suspension from a regular high school.

Table 1: The Subjects

DELINQ.	AGE	ETHNICITY	BOROUGH	EMPLOYMENT
Russell	15	African-American	BRONX	3 to 6 hours per week
Roger	15	African-American	BROOKLYN	Summer job
Vinny	15	African-American	BROOKLYN	No (young)
Steven	15	Jamindian (Jamaican & Indian)	BRONX	No (young)
Malcolm	14	Black/African-American all the same	BRONX	
Lunch	15	West Indian	BROOKLYN	
Trevor	15	Black	BROOKLYN	Summer job
Peter	16	Black	MANHATTAN	Yes – spending money
Player	15	African-American	BRONX	Yes – mother wants me to learn to earn
Jaoquan		American	BRONX	Yes – presently, to stay off streets
Roderick	15	Caribbean	BRONX	No
Marty	17	African-American	BRONX	Yes – for extra money
Jerome	17	Caribbean	BRONX	Yes – summer job with church
Tyrone	17	African-American	BRONX	Yes – 20 hours per week to avoid trouble
Roshaud	16	Jamerican (grandmother from Jamaica)	BRONX	No
Mutt		Mutt (parents are from different countries) or black	BROOKLYN	Yes – in the past for spending money
NON-DEL				
Bugsy	18	Black or African-American(doesn't matter)	BRONX	Tried to get one once but didn't
Mike	17	Black	BRONX	Yes – 8 hours per week
Anthony	19	African-American	BRONX	Yes – 16 hours per week
Bobby	14	(names Caribbean country)	BRONX	Want to but can't get one (young)
Evan	17	Black or African-American	BRONX	Yes – after school for extra money
Barry	16	African-American	BRONX	No
Ross	18	Caribbean	BRONX	Yes – 30 hours/wk (after sch & wkends)
Devon			BRONX	No

Table 2: The Subjects' Deviance

NAME	PRESENT OFFENSE	TIME	JUST	PRIOR TROUBLE
Russell	Jumped a kid	7 mts	Y	None
Roger	Robbery			Yes – fighting school trouble
Vinny	Fight over gold teeth	4mts	Y	Yes – fighting, suspended
Steven	Gun in school	1 yr. 8 mts	N	Yes – suspended a lot for fighting because of gangs
Malcolm	Stabbing a kid	1yr	N	Yes – fights at school, arrest for stolen car
Lunch	Assault-security guard	9mts	N- really	Yes – suspended (about 20 times) for fighting and taling in school
Trevor	Vandalism	6mts	N	Yes – suspended twice for fighting and cutting; arrest for robbery
Peter	Pellet gun in school	1 yr.	N	Yes – cutting school
Player	Threatening girl w/knife	1 yr.	N	None
Jaoquan	Pushed teacher	1yr. 7mts	N	Yes-kicked from 2 schools for fighting; falsely arrested for sexual offense against female
Roderick	Gun outside school	8mts	Y	Suspensions
Marty	Robbery	1 yr +	N	Twice – robberies
Jerome	Jumped someone	7 mts	Y	Yes – frequent suspensions, expulsion for fighting, two arrests for attempted robbery
Tyrone	Assault elderly teacher	1yr 2 mts	N	Never
Roshaud	Hit teacher w/ bottle	10 mts	Y	Yes – robbery, weapons
Mutt	Gang-related fights	1st day	Y	Yes – suspended frequently(fighting), cutting; almost arrested when with peer in stolen car
NON-DEL				
Bugsy				No.
Mike				Truancy (picked up by the police a short distance from school & returned – angry about it)
Anthony				No.
Bobby				Yes – suspended in 5th grade (accused of threatening to hit a teacher)
Evan				No.
Barry				No.
Ross				Tickets (blocking subway staircase; jumping turnstile), suspended for hitting a teacher
Devon				No.

Data Collection

For optimum authenticity, the procedures involved a methodological triangulation (observations, one-to-one and group interviews) and a data source triangulation (juveniles, teachers and parents). The primary items of analysis for capturing student-teacher relationship effects were the interviews with the subjects about their school histories and the present teachers' perceptions of what their students' school histories might have been. It was not expected that a semester's worth of classroom observations would yield much on the effects of student-teacher relationships, but that the present observations would merely indicate markers about the students' past about which the researcher could inquire. Interviews and observations from spring 1996 at the comprehensive school were also included in the present analysis. For each semester that observations were conducted the researcher spent at least two days on site. For spring and fall 1999, this was on Tuesdays and Thursday mornings and early afternoons (usually 8:20 a.m to 12:30 p.m. at the alternative school and 8:20-2:00 p.m. at the comprehensive school. Interviews were conducted individually mostly during breaks in the school day at the subjects' convenience.

For all of the observation sessions, the researcher made detailed notations of 1) Artifacts: for example, colors in the room; the structure and contents of the room, seating arrangement, presence of windows, lighting, temperatures, noise, etc.; 2) Behaviors (a) what occurs in the classroom (for example, how students enter, how they leave, their verbal and body language, various student-teacher exchanges) and (b) thoughts on the meanings of such occurrences; 3) People: descriptions of appearances and mannerisms. The classroom sessions were audiotaped for accuracy where teachers and students consented. The audiotape was kept out of sight to reduce possible Hawthorne effects. Initially, the researcher's presence altered student behaviors. A large part of this was her profuse note taking. Thus, the researcher learnt quickly how to consolidate her note taking while keeping her descriptions thick. Quickly, students in both settings resumed their normal behaviors as the researcher became more of a regular classroom fixture.

To give the subjects time to get comfortable with the researcher before administering the rather prying interview questions, the researcher began the interviews after being at the comprehensive school for a month during fall 1999. At the alternative school, with trust being a greater issue, she waited two months to begin the interviews. Nevertheless, from day one she utilized as many opportunities as possible here and there to ask non-threatening questions about various aspects of the school experience. For the most part student interviews were completed at one sitting but on occasion the interviews with teachers and other staffers were done in parts as their breaks permitted. These semi-structured questions covered the subjects' thoughts and feeling about past and present school experiences. The teacher interviews were also semi-structured (*see Appendix*). Such was an attempt to gain insight into the teachers' perceptions of, attitudes towards, and beliefs about the students.

Examining the Expected Findings

What I longed for most from this qualitative enterprise was novel information (or emic revelations) - pointing to fresh directions for research on student-teacher relationship effects and delinquency. This being the case the expected findings were both expressions of the theoretical model and a framework for data reduction.

I.   The greater the level of stress in the student's environment outside of school (family and neighborhood), the more likely the student is to be both a poor student and a delinquent.

The stressors were measured through interviews with the juveniles as indicated by items in the Appendix D. Additional information came from informal interviews with teachers and staffers.

II.   The greater the volume of positive interactions that the student has with teachers (that is the more the student cooperates with the teacher's scripted pact) the less likely the student is to be a delinquent.

The volume of positive interactions was measured in a two-fold manner. In one sense it was a measure of the student-teacher interactions that the researcher herself noticed twice per week. Since a researcher can only focus on some stimuli at any given moment, tape recording the classroom sessions helped to capture aspects of the classroom interactions that the researcher sometimes missed while taking notes. The observations were substantiated by interviews with the students about their experiences with teachers past and present and with interviews of the present teachers about the classroom interactions with their students be they delinquents or not.

.
III. If the student performs poorly academically and / or behaviorally early in the semester, the teacher's positive regard for the student (if it ever existed) will ebb for the rest of the semester.

This was measured by my observations of the student-teacher interactions over the course of the semester.

IV. The weaker the positive regard that the teacher has for a student, the more likely that student is to be disengaged from school.

To measure this I isolated words and phrases from the teachers in the context of their renderings on specific students. The teachers were also asked about their perceptions of specific students. Changes in regard from early in the semester to the end of the semester were noted. Student disengagement was measured according to cues given in the literature - such as students who are uninvolved with classroom activities, students with heads on the desk and no work being done, students walking about the room, engaging in activities other than the prescribed school work.

V. The trajectory to academic success is very similar to that for non-delinquency.

Protecting the Subjects

Anyone interviewed for the study was informed of the confidentiality and anonymity of the data. They were also informed that while their communications were not privileged, it would not, under any circumstances be revealed in any identifying manner to anyone other than my methodologist - and, this only for his academic input. Additionally, since the researcher is a nationally Certified Rehabilitation Counselor (C.R.C.) before each interview session she reminded the subjects that if they led her to believe that they or anyone under 18 years was the subject of abuse by another person I would be obligated to report it to the appropriate authorities. Thereafter, the researcher mentioned that this obligation did not apply to any other offenses. From the pilot study, it became clear that questions of abuse would dissuade participation. Thus, these items were omitted from the study.

Herein, pseudonyms are used for the subjects and identifiers were erased from audiotapes and notes within hours of collection. Subjects were informed that they need not answer every question and that they may terminate their participation in the study at any time without negative repercussions. Subject approval was requested before audiotaping. Subjects were also offered the opportunity to review the completed tapes. All files and audiotapes have been secured per Human Subject Review Board conditions.

The parent or guardian interviews were not conducted as initially proposed because it became evident that such would have been an unnecessarily repetition of data collection. One parent of a delinquent was interviewed. For other information about parents or guardians beyond that rendered by the juveniles, a more significant source was the teachers and staffers. Thus, these persons were interviewed about the juveniles' family contexts. Indeed, at the alternative school, staffers made home visits and thus, they could say a great deal about the parents. The interviewer was also able to observe some of the parents in action as they visited the schools.

For a complete picture of the school settings and the interactions therein, the researcher interviewed all available administrators and staffers. For the most part these interviews took the form of informal chats during breaks. In addition to the teachers whose classes were observed through the semester, all available teachers at all the school sites involved were asked questions at their convenience.

Data Analysis

The study yielded several pages of data. The initial plan was to transcribe the data within a few hours of collection. However, the volume of information was such that much of the data was actually transcribed weeks after collection. Nonetheless, prior to transcription, the researcher examined and made notations about the data promptly. There were three main coding categories: 1) descriptive 2) pattern, and 3) thematic codes. The researcher noted how her perceptions of the subjects, their teachers and parents changed during the data collection and how this affected the data analysis. The researcher also made both within and between group comparisons of the subjects as she collected the data. She was able to identify and decipher key processes as only qualitative analysis allows.

Classroom observation data was not meticulously coded using the Coker Chart for Classroom Observations (Wiersma, 1985). With so many things going on in the classroom at the same time, it would have been impractical to use the Coker without videotaping. Thus, the Coker Chart became a mere guide for elements that may have been significant in the classroom observations. Such coding facilitated the production of descriptive statistics. These codes were examined for patterns and correlations between student and teacher behaviors and the students' academic and behavioral outcomes.

From these classroom observations the researcher also looked for patterns of the "scripted pact" (the Gutierrez concept referring to subtle, often unspoken rules of a student-teacher relationship that are most visible when violated). The researcher examined the Initiation, Response and Feedback patterns of the student-teacher interactions and how this related to conforming or deviating patterns amongst the students. Understanding these interactions involved an examination of the motivation's literature in educational psychology and the communication's literature in social personality psychology. Key to this study was understanding how student-teacher dynamics may or may not affect a motivation to deviate and perhaps eventual delinquency. Since such relationships do not occur in a vacuum, the contexts from which both students and teachers emerged and the contexts in which they operated were also considered. For accuracy, and since human instruments tend to subjectively focus on some environmental stimuli to the exclusion of others, wherever possible, interactions and interviews were audiotaped.

It was expected that various scripted pact episodes would indicate specific self-derogatory thoughts. Isolating those thought patterns was a matter of recognizing key words and phrases from the juveniles' mouths. This involved doing data reduction. From the theoretical model the researcher already had broad etic categories of concepts into which the data were expected to fit. This was also another useful means of data reduction. Nevertheless, the researcher remained sensitive to the emic voice of the subjects and the categories that they had defined for their own experiences. Thus, to the researcher's initial etic codes, new codes emerged from the data. This process revealed not only patterns, trends, and novelties, but also their meanings and themes.

I used the Non-numerical Unstructured Data Indexing Searching Theorizing (NUD.IST) software program in the analysis effort. NUD.IST 4.0 was an excellent program for qualitative text base management. It facilitated the coding and retrieving process of words and phrases. It also generated basic charts which made it easy to see where data to specific items were missing. NUD.IST also has a strong theory building function that allowed me to formulate and test hypotheses given the data entered. Much like hierarchical regression in quantitative research, with NUD.IST it was I who decided initially what the most potent variables might be. Thus, the researcher is also able to create tree indices (visual representations) of expected relationships among variables based on the literature and then check to see whether or not those relationships held up with the data. NUD.IST also facilitated cross-case comparisons - another way of indicating the strength of conceptual relationships. NUD.IST also allowed me to adjust the tree indices accordingly to explore emerging hypotheses. The program also recorded any major changes in the database thus, providing a log of the progression of the analysis. Much of the analysis involved the process of memorizing, that is, repeatedly going over written transcripts of data and making notations relevant to various variable measures and the literature towards understanding the data. The research results were considered in relationship to the wider society utilizing summary statistical reports from the New York City Planning Division on the nature of the communities that the schools served and otherwise directly impacted.

Limitations of the Study

Limitations of the study include the subjectivity of the researcher as a measurement instrument. To address this the researcher attempted to be as objective as possible. She kept a journal to monitor the effects of the research process on her as instrument. Another limitation is the lack of data generalizeability. Nevertheless, the findings are transferable to juveniles similarly situated. Thus, the authenticity of the work compensated for the lack of generalizeability. Also problematic was the effort to capture school effects largely through retrospective reports. There was the possibility of error of recall, or selective recall given maturation. Nevertheless, the research model is largely interpretive and less about the actuality of the experience (Galbo & Demetrulias 1996). Plus, juveniles could have had difficulty verbalizing their experiences precisely. It was also logistically challenging to observe both sets of juveniles in their different schools in different semesters. This made it difficult to gauge exactly how the nature of spring itself may have affected the behaviors of the students observed during the spring semester versus the nature of fall on the students observed during the fall term. To address this the researcher made thick descriptions on everything from the sounds, the appearances, the temperatures, the lighting, the dominant news items of the day, holiday effects, et cetera on the changing dress and behaviors of both students and teachers as a way of deciphering how such things may have influenced fluctuations in mood and energy.

CHAPTER 4

THE SOCIAL, POLITICAL AND ECONOMIC CONTEXT OF THE SCHOOLS

The larger historical, social, political and economic macro contexts from which students and teachers come shape the traits and preconceptions of the other that each party brings into the school relationships. Along the joint trajectory of the student-teacher relationship, there are opportunities to mediate the path. The present study finds that effective teachers need not be from the "same walk of life" as their students, but they must be willing to make an effort to understand and value difference. As such, there are policy implications herein for pre and post-teacher training.

For students from a truly at-risk background, school interactions can be potentially mediating against delinquency and other forms of social service dependency. This can happen when teachers present plausible legitimate avenues to material success and prepare their students to access those avenues.

African-American Students: All "black" ain't the same "black"

A major problem in the criminal justice literature is a failure to recognize the within group variations of "blacks" in the United States. Indeed, blacks represent a cultural smorgasbord. Nowhere is this more true than in New York City. The differences are extremely significant. Different cultures mean different social contexts as people from different cultures may vary in their perceptions of the same situation. What may be an "open door" to one black man may be a "closed door" to another based on culturally learned ways of responding to circumstances. Say a middle class black male from the English speaking Caribbean applies for the same job as a black American male.

The former's accent (colored with a tint of a British tone) and demeanor of boldness amongst whites (having grown up in a culture that taught that there was little to fear from the white man) may appear more attractive to a mainstream employer. The black American male however, is often easily identified by his accent. It is not novel and his demeanor in the presence of whites may seem evasive - the marks of a mind seared with the realities of lynchings and "colored only signs" barely 30 plus years ago in American history. He continues to live under the suspicion of his "blackness." Such has been his experienced reality. Thus, these two men may perceive and thus experience, the same prospects differently.

Unless the black immigrant family determinedly holds on to its original culture, with each generation, the original culture fades. With this "the blacks" become far less distinguishable. Nevertheless, New York City is unique in many respects as a continual point of disembarkment for a wide range of peoples and cultures. Thus, certain pockets in the core of the city (especially Manhattan, Brooklyn, and the Bronx) are much like the central zone[1] in Shaw and MacKay's (1942) social disorganization theory. Yet, remarkably most of the comprehensive schoolteachers seemed to know very little about the different cultures represented in their classrooms. More shocking, they did not appear interested in rectifying their ignorance - yet, many claimed that they wanted to be effective in teaching. The result? An attempt at monocultural impartation as opposed to a multicultural examination. The result is that "the other" becomes marginalized as this lack of interest by the immediate authority figure - the teacher suggests that their culture is of lesser worth. While this does not refer to all of the comprehensive schoolteachers observed in this study, it refers to the majority of them. The standard explanation for the "disinterest" was that they had been instructed by the administration to proceed thus in order to complete their curricula.

Hispanics Amongst the Ranks of the Disadvantaged

Hispanics are one of the United States' fastest growing ethnic groups. They are important to mention in an examination of African Americans and schools because for the most part, African-Americans share their urban public schools classrooms with Hispanics (in the Bronx these are largely Dominican immigrants). The dark complexion of many

Dominicans means that they are often the recipients of the same treatment as African-Americans.

Nonetheless, Hispanics have additional strikes against them: 1) language and 2) poor parent-teacher relationships (Bates & Doob 1999). According to the National Statistics for Education statistics only 57 percent of Hispanics finished high school in 1993. Thus, they represented 30 percent of high school dropouts 16-24 years old and only 3.9 percent of those earning bachelors degrees.

Many Hispanics are recent immigrants. Thus, at the comprehensive high school, bilingual education for these students meant that classes were taught in Spanish. Initially, the researcher's reaction to this approach was that it shortchanged the students from learning English - a vital piece of capital that would enable these students to realize their "American dreams." Nonetheless, a friend of the researcher who tutors immigrants noted that for older children (unlike their elementary counterparts) learning a new language is difficult. Thus, for the sake of at least communicating academic content, classes are conducted in Spanish. The justification makes some sense after all.

The second shortcoming is the student-teacher relationship. At the comprehensive school, Hispanic teachers mentioned that for the most part they had no problems communicating with the parents of their Hispanic students. However, the white teachers complained about parents being unresponsive to their contacts. The problem? Many of the less effective teachers used a standard approach to reaching out to all parents (mail, or telephone during business hours). The inflexibility was unproductive. For example, one white bilingual teacher mentioned that at times she was invited by her students to visit their families. She refused believing such would be improper. But would this perspective have been the same if the students she taught (largely blacks and Hispanics) did not constitute "the other?" The teachers who were effective in reaching parents were not all Hispanic, but they all took the time to figure out which means of contact worked with which sets of parents. For example some parents worked long hours, but welcomed calls at work. The result was more successful parent-teacher alliances on behalf of the student.

A third dilemma for many Hispanic students was special education placement. Possibly unfamiliar with the American educational system, these parents succumbed to school requests to have their child tested -

resulting in special education placement. Teacher interviews indicated that even students with minor language deficits could find themselves in special education classes.

Given these circumstances Hispanics lead in New York's dropout rates. Indeed, Puerto Ricans still had the highest dropout rates and the lowest SAT scores in New York City (Bates & Doob 1999 citing Fuentes 1994 and the *New York Times* staff respectively). Additionally, Latinos are three times more likely than white youths to be incarcerated (National Criminal Justice Association (1998): citing National Council on Crime and Delinquency). In addition to the 24 African-Americans herein discussed, five non-delinquent Hispanics and two delinquent Hispanics were also interviewed and observed. The findings indicated a similar, if no worse condition than their African-American counterparts. Amongst most of the Hispanics observed in the comprehensive school the risk factors largely involved their parents who were incarcerated and/ or substance abusing, inconsistent monitors and welfare dependent).

West Indians

Over a third of the delinquents (and a quarter of the non-delinquents) identified themselves as being of Caribbean descent. In some cases, the juveniles were born in the United States to at least one parent who was a Caribbean immigrant. For one delinquent, Roshaud, the closest West Indian was his grandmother. Amongst the delinquents it appeared that these reaches for an identification beyond mere "American" were efforts to be more visible than simply "black." On the other hand, the identity reach may be largely a solicitation for machismo status endorsement. In the projects of America it is commonly believed that those from the islands (especially Jamaica) are not to be toyed with given their high propensity for violence demonstrated largely during the crack epidemic and its aftermath from the 1980s into the early 1990s. Nevertheless, many of the working class Caribbean immigrant students were being exposed to the same environmental endorsements of deviance as their African-American peers. Without a quality education, their chances at social mobility were also threatened.

Contextual Effects: Being a "Truly At-risk" Child

Household Composition

The present study included family background as a social factor because the context in which a child lives is important in determining the child's thinking and thus his or her actions towards academic achievement, (Marjoribanks, 1987). Presently about 62 percent of African-American students are being raised in single parent headed households (Census Bureau 1998). The poverty rate for single parent families is about five times that for two-parent families. Indeed, in large families (4 or more children) there is often less time for the parents to attend parent-teacher meetings, check schoolwork, respond to discipline problems or supervise the children adequately. When such happens older siblings and peers often become more influential to a child (Jenkins 1997 discussing: Hirschi 1969; Leflore 1988; Myers et al., 1987; Nye 1958 & 1973; Tygart 1991). A failure by parents to communicate clear standards of behavior to their children through consistent reinforcement or discipline, plus inadequate monitoring and supervision predicts later delinquency and substance abuse, (Capaldi & Patterson 1996; Hawkins et al., 1995; Loeber & Stouthamer-Loeber; Gove & Crutchfield 1982). Most of the subjects - delinquent and non-delinquent lived with a single mother and more than one sibling.

Poverty

School meals were free at 1.3 times federal poverty guidelines and subsidized for families with incomes 1.85 times federal poverty guidelines (a factor of family size and income), (Alexander et al., 1994). All of the delinquents except one qualified for school lunches. At least a half of the non-delinquents also qualified.

Welfare

None of the subjects had been homeless. Amongst the delinquents, four (Malcolm, Trevor, Peter and Player) had been on welfare in the past. Amongst the non-delinquents only Mike had been on welfare. From both sets, the juveniles spoke of this memory nonchalantly as a detail that they would rather forget. Welfare status was a secretive thing, a shameful thing, not a routine aspect of life. Of course, more of the subjects may have been on welfare at some point in their early lives but they might not have known it.

Table 3: Household Composition

DELINQ.	PARENT MARITAL	HOUSEHOLD COMPOSITION
Russell	Divorced	Mom+ 2 older and 2 younger siblings
Roger	Never married	Mother, little sister
Vinny	Never married (brother)	Brother (approx. 23 years old)
Steven	Never married	Foster care w/ grandmother, 2 sis., 1 bro.
Malcolm	Never married	Mother, 16 yr. old sister
Lunch	Divorced	Mother, little brother and 18 yr. old bro.
Trevor	Widowed	Mother, 18 yr. old sister, 4 yr. old bro.
Peter	Divorced	Mother, little sister
Player	Never married	Mother, 21 yr. old cousin, 5 brothers
Jaoquan	Divorced	Mother (grandm. & older bro. Across street)
Roderick	Never married	Mother
Marty	Married	Father, mother, 3 brothers., 1 sister
Jerome	Never married	Mother, younger sister
Tyrone	? (Grandmother)	Grandma, sis., little bro. (older bro. Elsewh)
Roshaud	Never married	Foster mother, 4 brothers, 4 sisters
Mutt	Married	Step-father, mother, sis., little bro., older bro.
NON-DEL		
Bugsy	Divorced	Mother, brother, sister
Mike	Never married	Father
Anthony	-	Mother
Bobby	Married	Father, mother, 1 sister (8 siblings elsewh)
Evan	Seperated	Mother (siblings elsewhere)
Barry	Divorced	Mother, 1 sister
Ross	Married	Father, mother, 1 sister
Devon	Married	Father, mother, 5 brothers (1 older)

Context: Parenting Effects

Fathers

The absence of a father in the home threatens family stability (Children's Defense Fund 1986). Nevertheless, ethnographic research indicates that many black fathers remain involved in their children's lives even if they are not living in the home. Yet, a noted deficit in most of the delinquents' lives was the absence of a father or father figure. Seventy-five percent of the delinquents mentioned having no relationship or hardly a relationship with a father. In two cases the father was dead or presumed dead (having abandoned the family). In the latter case, Vinny's 23-year old brother played the father and mother role. In two cases the father was away (one "down south," the other overseas). Only two delinquents (Marty and Mutt) lived with parents who were married to each other. Marty was also the only delinquent who was above poverty and he was the rare former honor student in the group. On the other hand, Mutt's parents were both Caribbean immigrants. His mother was married to his stepfather.

Of all those who stated that their father was involved - whether he lived in the home or not - only one delinquent described the relationship as close. In another case the father (who lived in the home) had a crack problem. On occasion, this man obtained his crack supply from his teenage son who not only dealt drugs himself but also used it. The mother was reportedly unaware of these activities under her roof. These details of family dysfunction came not from the juvenile himself but from a teacher and a staff member with whom the teen had built a trusting relationship. In the case of another high-risk delinquent, a teacher reported that the student became particularly troublesome whenever his father was around. Recently, this teen's father had been released from prison. Apparently, the relationship between father and son was strained because of how the father related to the mother. The son in response became his mother's volatile protector. This protector role was common amongst the delinquents. It extended beyond their mothers to black females in general. In another case, the father, a Caribbean immigrant was a violent man. He had threatened to kill his son and had raped his 11 year-old daughter. The later act resulted in the dissolution of the family with the children entering foster care.

Clearly, the absence of a father as a risk is relative. From an economic perspective, the benefits of a double income could mean many positives including the ability to move away from a community with criminal opportunities and violent victimizations. Yet, a mother may be a risk factor if she exposes her children to the "wrong" sort of man. The family research team at the University of Arizona (1998) found that the odds of delinquency increases with the exposure of a child to delinquent father figures to the point that delinquency becomes certain with significant exposure to at least four criminal men. A surprising finding in the present study was the infrequent mention of stepfathers (once).

The situation was only slightly more positive for the non-delinquents. Three out of eight of them had parents who were married to each other. Two of these students seemed well adjusted, but Ross (who had a delinquency record) also had married parents. Of course, Ross was a West Indian immigrant and that may have been significantly compounding. In all, five out of eight non-delinquents had a good relationship with their fathers. Exceptions were the non-delinquent Anthony whose father was deceased and Bugsy who had seen his father only once.

Single-Parent Homes

Delinquency is more prevalent in mother only households (Steinberg 1987; Dornbusch et al., 1985; Gove & Crutchfield 1982). Such is largely an effect of a lack of economic and psychological support which leaves little time for parents to effectively supervise their children or be actively involved in their schooling (Jenkins 1997). These are important because a crucial determinant in a juvenile's trajectorial outcome is the extent to which he or she is consistently monitored (Capaldi & Patterson 1996; Hawkins et al., 1995; Gove & Crutchfield 1982). Herein, the reality was that for the most part the students were from single parent homes. However, only one parent was on welfare (for a disability).

Regarding warmth in the home, intimacy does not thrive in environments where having a low-income makes survival a constant pressure (Greene, 1993). Nevertheless, 87 percent of the subjects (7 non-delinquents and 14 delinquents) stated that their parents or guardians gave them the right amount of affection. Indeed, many children from single parent homes turn out very well. According to McCord (1983), "the absence of parents is less important than domestic tranquility in predicting delinquency.

Hence, as Emery (1982) concluded students from homes characterized by interpersonal conflict are at greater risk of involvement in delinquency than are students from broken but harmonious homes or intact households." Some of the alternative school teachers believed that three delinquents (Roderick, Malcolm and Jaoquan) were particularly moody on days when they had had conflicts with their mothers. Often these conflicts were over the mothers' adult male interests. Also, children who lack strong affectionate ties or identification with stepparents may care much less about embarrassing or hurting them by their conduct (Jenkins, 1997). Of similar significance are parent-child separations which occur before the child reaches age 10. The literature indicates that such separations are correlated with violent behaviors. The delinquent Roshaud's life supports this finding. A classic crack baby, he maintained a relationship with his biological mother although he was bounced about in foster care. His present offense was hitting a teacher with a liquor bottle.

Sixty-nine percent of the delinquents lived with a mother as head of household. In one case, the mother was a foster parent. Two delinquents were under the charge of a grandmother; one was under the charge of a 23-year old brother and only two were from two-parent homes. The non-delinquents had greater father input. For the most part the father was either in the home or regularly involved in their lives. In one case a non-delinquent was shifted from his mother to his father's care when the boy reached pre-teen years.

Conditional Affection

Cohen (1955) stated that working class parents were more inclined to render their children unconditional affection after they had strayed from a parent prescribed path more so than middle class parents. Middle class parents exercised a more powerful control over their children by raising them on conditional love - threatening to withhold their affections if their children strayed. In the present study students were asked to respond to the statement: "one of the worst things that could happen is to find out that I let my parents down." Seventy-one percent of the subjects (5 non-delinquents; 12 delinquents) agreed or strongly agreed with this rough measure of conditional affection. Supporting this perspective, in response to the statement "my parent gives me the right amount of affection" 7 non-delinquents and 13 delinquents agreed or strongly agreed with the statement. Among the delinquents who disagreed, Malcolm thought his sister gained more affection. Plus, Steven who lived with his grandmother felt constantly persecuted by her. Both of these adolescents were from highly dysfunctional backgrounds. The former lived in a high crime area, and had conflicts with his father. The latter had a father who had raped his 11-year old sister.

Family Criminality

What of parents who endorse criminality? Baker and Mednick (1984) found men 18 to 23 years old with criminal fathers to be 3.8 times more likely to commit violent crime. Farrington (1989) found boys with parents who had an arrest before the child's 10th birthday were 2.2 times more likely to commit violence. Three quarters of the delinquents had a relative who had been involved in criminality. The offenses were as severe as attempted murder. Amongst the non-delinquents only 37 percent had a relative who had been apprehended for a crime.

Table 4: Family Criminality

DELINQ.	FAMILY CRIMINALITY
Russell	Younger brother – fighting; older brother arrested
Roger	Parent crack habit
Vinny	Brother serving 5 years for stealing a chain
Steven	Father raped daughter, cousins beat up someone, three uncles for drugs, grandma arrested
Malcolm	Father served time
Lunch	Me – fighting
Trevor	Brother – life for attempted murder; brother for defending me; sister – shoplifting
Peter	Cousin – drugs
Player	Two uncles, one arrested for weapons possession – a cabbie who carried it for protection
Jaoquan	Father served time
Roderick	Cousin " for little things like driving without a license"
Marty	Brother – assault
Jerome	Cousin of similar age – "for fighting, drugs, weed and stuff"
Tyrone	Brother
Roshaud	Cousin – selling
Mutt	Step-father
NON-DEL	
Bugsy	-
Mike	Cousin robbed armored truck; sold drugs
Anthony	Brother – drug dealing
Bobby	Uncle was arrested – don't know for what
Evan	No
Barry	No
Ross	Father mistaken for burglar after trying to get in his house after accidental lockout.
Devon	-

Significantly, amongst both groups the adolescents empathized with offenders who committed crimes for income - such as drug dealing. A common perception was that such persons were only doing what was necessary to secure needed funds. Immersed in such rationalizations for criminality it was clear that these juveniles were engaged in weighing the costs and benefits of various deviant behaviors - beyond the scope of the law. For example, Vinny spoke of stealing a gold chain as not worth risking a five year prison sentence. Also, non-delinquent Mike spoke of getting into trouble with the law to protect a younger sibling as "worth it." Indeed, these juveniles had been socialized to accept the tenets of an alternative cultural capital in relating to the world.

Perceptions and the Experience of Commonly Identified Risk Factors

The literature carries the assumption that some events are inherently stressful (for example, the presence of marital discord, loss of significant others, parents hostile or neglectful behavior, financial and health disruptions (Radke-Yarrow & Brown 1993)). However, human responses vary. For example, the present study indicated that family mobility was not experienced as stressor for the juveniles in this study - including instances of national migration. Instead, migration from the "third world" was almost a totally welcomed event. Death was also common, but it was often experienced as merely a part of the life course and not a major disruption (except when a primary breadwinner was lost).

Substance Abuse

The children of parents with a favorable attitude to substance abuse are more likely to use illicit drugs (Peterson et al., 1994). This being the case, the delinquent Jerome was at serious risk. His mother, a very busy working woman was described as largely unaware of her son's doings and otherwise only nonchalant about his closeness to a heavy "weed" smoking cousin. Another delinquent juvenile, was actively selling and using cocaine. He lived at home and on occasion supplied his crack-addicted father. Yet, this case was one out of sixteen delinquents. It is suspected that young African-American males are refraining from the use of hard drugs such as crack-cocaine from having observed the destructiveness of drugs. Nonetheless, the perceptions of substances like marijuana as virtually harmless remains strong. Few (5 out of 24) subjects indicated having a relative with a substance abuse problem. Some of the delinquents indicated that their relatives occasional drinking and "weed smoking" were not particularly problematic. However, many of the youths knew people who sold drugs. They viewed dealing as simply a way to secure funds, albeit, not the most desirable way.

Residential Mobility

The juveniles perceived the effects of residential mobility to be short-term. Few students had made major re-locations, moving largely within boroughs. Even national re-location was not problematic (from the "third world" to the "first world"). Everyone had done some moving. The sole person suffering grave consequences from moving was the delinquent Steven. His frequent re-location from one state to another led to his being held back a grade. He did not go into any details about the effect of having been held back. Such was in keeping with his pattern of idealizing his mother – the person whose repeated discordant choices led to the frequent re-locations.

Mental Illness

Another risk factor common in the delinquency literature is parental mental illness. The dynamics that such creates in a home can lead to delinquency. Only one delinquent, Trevor indicated having a parent (mother) who had had psychiatric depression and who was also a recovering alcoholic. The drinking and depression had a distinct trigger (the death of a child from AIDS). While ill, she had sent Trevor to live with an aunt until she recovered. The researcher met this mother and spoke with her at length. A devout woman, she seemed fully recovered and a model parent in terms of her sacrificial attentiveness to her children. This mother traveled for about two hours each way on public transportation, after leaving work to attend each parent-teacher conference. Determined in her efforts to safeguard her children she was presently executing plans to re-locate to suburbia in another state. She had been particularly concerned about the presence of negative peers in gang - laden Brooklyn. She truly feared for her children's safety. Despite her efforts, her children had already tasted corruption (a son adjudicated delinquent; another son serving life for attempted murder and a daughter arrested for shop-lifting). What else was she to do? Granted, her present attentiveness might have come too late. Trevor's mother looked like a woman in her forties, so much so that many of the teachers and staffers thought she was his grandmother. The norm was mothers who looked as if they had given birth in their teens.

Physical Illness

Another risk factor for delinquency common in the literature is the physical illness of the child and / or parent. One delinquent (Roshaud) indicated having a sick mother (cancer). Others however, noted having other relatives with illnesses that are not uncommon in the African-American community namely diabetes, sickle cell, HIV and asthma. Only three subjects indicated having health problems themselves (Malcolm, Mutt and Bugsy) - migranes and asthma. Overall, the juveniles did not perceive either their illnesses or those of their relatives to have been of any significant impact on their behavior or achievement. However, health problems amongst secondary labor market families can have stark economic consequences as "sick leave" is not available to many who are amongst "the last hired." Only one delinquent had a primary caregiver on disability. Then there was Vinny - mother deceased, father missing - being raised by a 23 year old brother. Might Vinny's behavior be largely a result of an interaction effect between poverty and inconsistent parenting?

Social Context Effects on the Juveniles' Individual Traits

Individual Risk Traits: Learning Disabilities, Attention Deficit and Crack Babies

At both the comprehensive and the alternative schools the teachers identified students whom they believed to have learning disabilities and/or attention deficit disorder. While largely positive about working with these students, the teachers at both sites felt restricted in their ability to assist them. This seemed to be a common feeling of teachers who cared in general. There was a realization that they spent a substantial amount of time with their students and given the chance -

they might actually be able to do more. The teachers noted a need for better diagnosis procedures, possible medication administration, better monitoring and special academic programs for students who needed it. Alas, in poor school districts such as these, desires long remained simply thus - desires.

Beyond the teachers feeling restricted were deeper economic and political issues. At the comprehensive school, the researcher noted that the special education students were largely Hispanics. The researcher suspected that this may have been a result of a lack of familiarity with the educational system. The African-Americans in special education seemed more in need of those services, though such was not always the case. The teachers noted that some African-American parents distrusted the system to the point that they would not permit their children to be tested for potential special education services, lest the child is mislabed negatively. Significantly, many of the Hispanic students in special education were from highly dysfunctional backgrounds with welfare dependence, substance abuse, and parental criminality.

However, a surprising finding was the teacher reports of the emergence of crack-addicted babies now teenagers. At both schools some teachers indicated strong suspicions that certain students who seemed unusually hyperactive had been born crack-addicted. In some cases the teachers had more information about the student's background to validate their suspicions. The effective teachers maintained their positive regard towards these students while maintaining anger at the students' biological mothers. Roshaud is an example of one such student. His present offense was striking a teacher with a bottle. His physical features were consistent with that of a child born substance addicted. He was very hyperactive - sitting only for about 15 minutes or so before pacing his classroom. His artistry was much lauded by the teachers and he seemed a very likeable fellow. The alternative schoolteachers and social workers had been successful in getting him limited therapy. The funds were apparently not available to sustain his treatments and the juvenile had begun smoking marijuana in conjunction with his medication - a dangerous mix. Roshaud was a part of a six children foster home and his foster mother seemed incapable of monitoring his medication or other activities. Most would agree, Roshaud's future seemed beyond his control and likely to continue on that negative path although he possessed many redeeming traits. Regarding his behavior Roshaud noted that it was out of his control - some days were good, others were not.

Peer Risk Traits - Delinquent Peers

Four of the non-delinquents acknowledged having delinquent peers. Surprisingly, the "non-delinquent," Ross denied having delinquent peers. Although his own delinquent behavior (such as blocking a subway staircase and jumping a turnstile) leave his denial in question. Indeed, when asked about things like gang activity, some non-delinquents seemed evasive. Apparently, the school has had a history of national and ethnic-based gang conflict. Presently, there was social distance (not necessarily hostility) between the Puerto Rican and the Dominican students. From eavesdropping on some students the researcher learnt that some believed that there were gang informants in the school. Thus, discussing delinquent group associations was largely taboo. Indeed, as the students left the campus in the evenings, some of them then displayed various gang paraphernalia such as beaded chains for the Latin Kings.

For the delinquents, juvenile gangs were very much a part of their reality especially in Brooklyn. There were several gangs around - according to Mutt and others. In Trevor's area there was the unpredictability of the Bloods, the Crips and the ABGs (Anybody Get It). Roger had also been attacked by Bloods. One substantial risk that came from a neglect to address the predominance of gangs was that students armed themselves with deadly weapons. Indeed, Vinny noted that repeated complaints to the teacher were useless when under siege. Not only were students subject to attack from gang members outside of school, but they were also subject to the attacks of other students. Guns were everywhere - including in the schools. After all, they had brought them in themselves repeatedly for a while before getting caught. Thus, while Roderick offered no justification for his gun possession near his school, Steven stated that his gun possession in school was necessary for his protection. Not surprisingly, many delinquent instances involved or began at the urging of peers.

The literature indicates that peer influence is very important to academic success. Six non-delinquents had close friends who were getting what they considered "good grades" (65 and above), interested in school, and attending classes regularly. Among the delinquents, only 36 percent (6) indicated having a close friend who was invested in school as evidenced by regular attendance and good grades (80 and above). But are positive peers readily available? Oh yes! Such peers exist. However, given school segregation in New York by not only ethnicity, but also social class - such access has been severely curtailed to places like the subways.

Table 5: Risks or Stressors – Delinquents and Non-Delinquents

DELINQ.	RISK or STRESSORS				Death of Friend or Relative	Re-Location	Welfare	Victimization of Self or Relative	Homelessness
	FamilySickness	Self–Sickness	Relatives Drink/Drug	Relatives Mentall Ill					
Russell	None				Grandmother – scared, scared, cried a lot				
Roger	None				Aunt – cancer; cousin murdered – took it badly	MOST		Sliced, jumped by Bloods	NONE
Vinny					Mother – pneumonia; father-left; uncle, grandpars.	MOVED		Robbed at gunpoint	CLAIMED
Steven	None				2 year old sister	LOCAL-		Sister (11) raped by father	HOME-
Malcolm	Diabetic		YES		Grandmother	LY	Yes-past	Sister	LESS-
Lunch	None		YES		Grandmother	SO.			NESS
Trevor	Asthma, bronchitis	Yes-dk,dr			Sister from AIDS, father, uncle	NO	Yes-past	Theft, battery	
Peter	Sickle cell				Uncle, friend playing Russian Roulette	PROB-	Yes-past		
Player	None				None	LEMS	Yes-past		
Jaoquan					Grandfather (took it well)	EXCEPT		Burglary	
Roderick	None	Yes			None	FOR			

DELINQ.	RISK or STRESSORS								
	FamilySickness	Self - Sickness	Relatives Drink/Drug	Relatives Mentall Ill	Death of Friend or Relative	Re-Location	Welfare	Victimization of Self or Relative	Homelessness
Marty	AIDS	Yes			2 friends (1 cancer, 1 shoot-out)	Steven			
Jerome	None	Yes			Aunt – cancer	who was			
Tyrone	None				Mother	Held			
Roshaud	Diabetes, cancer				Friend an older man – AIDS	back as		Yes	
Mutt	Asthma	Yes-social	YES		Female friend – raped & murdered	a result		Burglary; father assaulted	
Evan	None	No	None	No	No				
Barry	None	No	None	No	2 cousin in car accident but we were not close				
Ross	None	No	None	No	Grandmother when I was 14 – I didn't fret				
Devon	None	No	None	No	Friend – kid who was high fell between subway				

Table 6: Peer Effects

DELINQ.	REGARDING	YOUR	BEST	FRIENDS	
DELINQ	Gets good grades	Interested in school	Attends classes regularly	Plan to go to college	*Friends who have gotten into trouble with the law?*
Russell	NO	-	YES	NO	Dumb stuff –vandalism, stealing
Roger	YES (85, 90)	YES	YES	YES	-
Vinny	YES	YES	YES	YES	YES – try to stop them
Steven	KINDA	NO	YES	DON'T KNOW	LOTS-guns, cutting, fights, beat up vendor
Malcolm	DON'T KNOW	DON'T KNOW	YES	DON'T KNOW	NO-(contradicts staff reports)
Lunch	NO	NO	NO	WANTS TO	Suspended for playing around with me
Trevor	NO	NOT REALLY	NO		YES-stupid stuff, e.g. stealing
Peter	YES	YES	YES	YES	YES-robbery
Player	YES	YES	YES	YES	NO
Jaoquan	YES	YES	YES	DON'T KNOW	YES – drugs, guns
Roderick					NO
Marty	DON'T THINK SO		DON'T KNOW	YES	NOT REALLY
Jerome	SOMETIMES	SOMETIMES	SOMETIMES		YES – fighting drugs
Tyrone	YES		YES	SOME	YES – robbery, shooting
Roshaud			DON'T KNOW	NO	
Mutt	HONOR ROLL	YES	YES	YES	YES: Gang people – fighting, shooting
NON-DEL					
Bugsy	YES (70 or 80s)	YES	YES	YES	YES – friends
Mike	"Don't have one	-	YES	YES	NO
Anthony	YES – finished sch.	-	-	Finished college	YES – attempted murder; perjury
Bobby	-	YEAH	Often	No – work	YES – selling drugs (need quick money)
Evan	YES	-	YES	YES	NO
Barry	65, 70, 75	YES	YES	YES	Yes – but not friends acquaintances
Ross	YES	YES	YES	YES	No
Devon	YES (80 +)	YES	YES	Don't know	Yes – smoke weed, drink, cut school

Another opportunity where students may interact with positive peers would be extra-curricular activities. Indeed, most of the subjects stated an interest in extra-curricular activities, but their schools offered none or very little of this. Most of the subjects wanted to participate in sports, but unless they made the basketball or football team - (which most did not) - that option was closed to them. The comprehensive high school in question had a tennis team - but none of the students herein were interested in that sport. Peers were also kept apart after school as security guards promptly shooed them off campus. Class transitions also kept them apart (3 minutes) and lunch times varied for various students.

Students wanted the opportunity to mix with others. Such seemed a part of the natural curiosity of youth. Of course this could be done - if only school personnel cared enough to facilitate it. The words of the delinquent, Jerome expresses a common sentiment of a desire for exposure to a larger world:

R: Ahh, aamm what do you enjoy the most about school?

JEROME: About school? The people, you know, the friends you meet. Like here, I never you know, here I never, people, I never used to meet nobody from Brooklyn until I came here. I know people from Queens you know....

R: Ummhuh.

JEROME: Now I go to they, their boroughs and chill with them, you know.

The peer experiences of the delinquents at the alternative school may be summed up in the words of Vinny:

R: Aaammm do you get along well with the students here?

VINNY: Yeah, they cool, main cooler than the people that's at my regular school. I think that, I think this school is better than at a regular school, 'cause at a regular school you get in more trouble. In this school kind of more relaxed, know what I'm saying. People here you can, faa, they feel more

like kinda family, not family but, know what I'm saying, like
we mad cool.

R: Ummhuh.

VINNY: I kind do be trusting them. People at my old school
I can't really trust them like that. 'Cause they smile in your
face one minute then one minute they turn their back on you.
Know what I'm saying?

R: You're talking about friends? Students? Or students and
teachers or?

VINNY: Students.

Then, there were the many teachers who believed that excluding
the ill-prepared or mischievous would solve their classroom problems.
But, exclude these students to what? Might Gutierrez and Kimberly
Gordon be right - the mischievous behavior is an act of rebellion in the
face of self-derogation and marginalization from the classroom
context? The perceptions of the delinquents about their school
experiences would certainly support such a premise. Indeed, even
teachers at the alternative school noted that when the work seemed too
challenging to some students they then become mischievous - talkative
and boisterous to divert attention from their failing academics reflecting
Gutierrez and colleagues' scripted pact. The alternative school
however, made it a point to foster closeness between both students and
staff despite student efforts to escape a stressful classroom situation.

Criminal Victimization and Alternative Cultural Capital

Show time. That was my constant struggle and perpetual
fear: that I'd cross some cat who hates his own skin and
takes it out on me because I look like him; that I'd
inadvertently bump into some dude willing to put his
devalued life on the line to prove a foolish manhood point.
                                                    - Nathan McCall

A surprising finding was that many of the juveniles did not realize
when they or their relatives had been victimized. Nor did they always

realize when they had criminally assaulted someone or even committed a robbery themselves. For example, the delinquent Trevor accompanied a friend who playfully took a ring from another boy and then pawned it. Trevor and his friend were then arrested for robbery. The charge seemed to have sincerely surprised Trevor - whom from the classroom observations seemed more like a follower than a leader, yet capable of holding his own. In large part, being assaulted or battered by others their age or older was a part of life. So too was being robbed at gunpoint or being the victim of a theft. They had made it through such instances alive and that was all that seemed to matter. Thus, when asked if they or a family member had been the victim of a crime, many subjects said "no" - but at other points in the interview they proceeded to describe being the subject of criminal attacks. This suggests that these New York African-Americans were more inclined to see themselves as survivors of their circumstances not victims of them. Being attacked was something that they had grown used to from their elementary years and living in the projects. It was to be expected.

A positive survivalist perspective? No, not totally - not to the extent that these juveniles found it necessary to arm themselves for protection as in the school setting where such could have meant expulsion (even though for these delinquents expulsion turned out to be a good thing - given the high caliber of education that expulsion brought them). These teenagers also calculated the costs of their actions. The delinquent Jerome and an African-American female student told one of their teachers that if attacked in an empty subway car by an ungunned bandit "someone would be going on the tracks." Plus, the delinquent Vinny suggested that some things might be worth risking five years incarceration - but stealing a gold chain as his brother had done was not one of those things. He also stated that when he had had a gold chain stolen at gunpoint - resisting had not been worth it. The teenagers had a reverence for a crook with a gun. Matching that power was how some (like Steven and Roderick) chose to respond to threats.

In the words of Vinny:

> VINNY: I wish people would stop telling me that 'cause once somebody tell me they goin' shoot me I take that to the heart. I feel that you put my life in danger. The next time I see you that's just forcing me to do something negative to you. If you don't want that to happen just - the fight is over

it's des...??? you win some, you loose some. I mean, it don't
make no sense like goin' "I'm goin' shoot you," 'cause you
tell me you goin' shoot me; I'm goin' get you first. I mean,
'cause I don't wanna loose my life; I don't wanna get shot.
So, I'm gonna have to do you in first before you get to me.

It was generally acceptable for an older relative to commit battery
in response to an attack on a juvenile. So, what of the police?
According to these juveniles, it seemed the police only make matters
worse if they choose to intervene at all. For example, when non-
delinquent Ross' father was mistaken as a burglar after locking himself
out of his house, or when non-delinquent Mike was picked up a few
feet from school and returned in a police cruiser causing him great
embarrassment, or when the delinquent Steven's family was split up
when his father sneaked in the house and raped his 11- year old sister.
Particularly for the boys from Brooklyn, gangs were a serious threat,
but the police were not considered a source of refuge. The police just
did not get it. Hence, Roger was sliced by Bloods, Vinny robbed at
gunpoint, Malcolm's sister victimized, Steven's little sister raped,
Trevor assaulted and the victim of theft; Peter stabbed, Joaquan's home
burglarized, Roshaud victimized, Mutt's father assaulted and their
home burglarized. Among the non-delinquents four had been
victimized (theft and assault).

Protection: Resiliency Traits in the Face of Risks

Resilience is "a process, capacity or outcome of successful adaptation
despite challenges or threatening circumstances," (Masten et al., 1990).
Resilience is not fixed. Even the most resilient of persons can have
setbacks (Radke-Yarrow & Brown 1993). Certain specific procedures
that are protective at a certain time and place may be risk traits at
another time or place. For example, the confrontational posture of some
African-Americans when threatened may be protective from various
predatory others in a low-income context, but not fitting when
addressing conventional authority figures such as teachers or law
enforcement.

Community Collective Efficacy

Community collective efficacy refers to "a sense of trust, caring, common values, and cohesion in neighborhoods" where residents are willing to intervene in the lives of children to stop truancy, graffiti and hanging out. Such flourishes in settings where people own their homes and have been long time residents. This fosters a "sense of engagement and ownership of public space," (Butterfield 1997 discussing the work of Felton Earls and Robert Sampson in 343 Chicago neighborhoods). According to Earls and Sampson neighborhood criminality is not simply about race or poverty but the relationships among people in a community. Some items from Earls and Felton study were used to measure neighborhood collective efficacy in the present study – *see Appendix D: 3C, # 118-120.*

Again, all of the non-delinquents lived in the Bronx. Only one (Anthony) did not feel safe in his neighborhood. Only four perceived their neighbors to be helpful and five thought the neighbors were close-knit. However, for the most part, there was little trust of the neighbors. For the delinquents (10 in the Bronx; 5 from Brooklyn; 1 in Manhattan) the findings were fairly similar except more of the delinquents (50 percent) thought their neighbors were trustworthy. Overall, Brooklyn was the more dangerous borough with substantially active and violent gang activity.

It bears noting how unique a city New York is. It is, perhaps the nation's immigration capital. As such, there are many mobile, low-income renters therein. Often, the landlord or owner of a premis lived elsewhere. Thus, many city dwellings are not as well maintained as they might be. Other neighborhoods are more stable as rent-stabilized apartment dwellers rarely re-locate in a fiercely tight real estate market. Overall, the juveniles indicated that neighbors often stuck together though not necessarily by ethnicity but more often by national origin. While people seemed familiar with their neighbors, the collective efficacy was not particularly strong. Such is in keeping with Marvin Krohn's (1986) network analysis model. Krohn (1986) claimed that were multiplexity is low and density great, the informal controls that might rein in deviant behavior are weak. Multiplexity refers to overlapping interactions in the same settings with the same people - for example, if one ran into the same people at church, school, or in recreation - their opinions would begin to matter. Density refers to the number of people in an area. The more people there are, the denser the population and the less likely it is that neighbors will know each other. This severely diminishes the power of informal control.

Table 7: Protective Factors -Delinquents

DELINQ.	EXTERNAL PROTECTIVE FACTORS		BEST	FRIENDS			
	Mother's Education	*Religion*	*Family Pride*	*Household Harmony – Dis-Agreements?*	*Cooking Skills*	*Approval Expressed*	
Russell	High School	Used to – Kingdom Hall	YES	Once in awhile	-	Mother – basketball	
Roger	High School	Every week (CLC)	YES	Once/week	Can't do anything, against Mom	Parents, friends – test, classes, basketball	
Vinny	Bro. some college	No	YES	Never – similar		Brother – classes, karate	
Steven	9 or 10th grade	Only crusades	YES	Daily stress	Argue	Mother – report card	
Malcolm	Forgot	Used to – Baptist	?	Twice/ month	Go to room, play music	Mother – school, etc.	
Lunch	2 yrs. College	Used to – Kingdom Hall	YES	Not much	Walk away	Coach – football	
Trevor	High School	Yes – at least weekly	YES	On weekends	Walk away or we sit and talk	Mother, teachers – grades	
Peter	Some college	Used to – Baptist	YES	Yes+w/litt.sis.	We still talk	Parents, teachers – school	
Player	Some college	Daily – Catholic	YES	Yes w/ sibling	Keep to myself	-	
Jaoquan	Don't know	Once in awhile – Baptist	YES	Once in awhile	Keep mouth shut	Mother – grades, bkball., staying off streets	
Roderick	Finishing college	Twice per month	YES	Once in awhile	Go to room, or sit and talk	? – report card	
Marty	In college	Once in awhile	YES	Once in awhile	-	Parents – achieving	
Jerome	High School	Twice per week + Lutheran	Of course	Once in awhile	Argue with everything she says	Mother, grandmother – report card	
Tyrone	Can't recall	Every Sunday – Baptist	M.Definitely	We get along	-	-	
Roshaud	?	Used to	YES	1 in blue moon	Leave the house	No	
Mutt	Two years college	Once in awhile – Baptist	?	-	-	Parents, 4th grade teacher	

Table 8: Protective Factors –Non-Delinquents

NON-DELINQ.	EXTERNAL PROTECTIVE FACTORS		BEST	FRIENDS		
	Mother's Education	Religion	Family Pride	Household Harmony – Dis-	Cooking Skills	Approval Expressed
Bugsy	High School	Every Sat; mother too		-	-	Mother – attending plays and church
Mike	Don't know	Used to – now working		Often, when in	We still talk and I stay by myself	Parents and gran.-behavior & school
Anthony	Junior yr. high sch.	No, and rarely in the past		Once in awhile	Stop talking	Mother and grandmother
Bobby	High School	Almost weekly – Baptist		Never	Not talk	Parents and teachers for grades and pass
Evan	Don't recall	No – can't say it's important		Hardly	We still talk	Going to school
Barry	Some college	Not in 3 or 4 years		Less than wkly	We still talk	
Ross	College graduate	No-but it's important		Hardly	I throw stuff	Boss & parents for job performance
Devon	Some college	Twice per month – Baptist		Not often	I always talk to them	

Herein, only Jerome spoke of a nosey neighbor:

> JEROME: Ohh, I got this one neighbor downstairs, she's so annoying, she's always calling the cops, and talking about, you know, my cousins. You know, they smoke weed a lot in the building. So, he comes, my cousin comes to see me, you know and I can't tell him don't come 'cause that's my cousin. So, she always calling the cops talking 'bout they smoking weed and all that. And so, you know, my mother gets real mad about it. so, I don't like her a lot....???

For the most part in the neighborhoods represented in this study, anything could happen.

> VINNY: It's like wherever I go, I never feel safe. Never, 'cause you don't know what can happen to you.

> R:Ummhuh.

VINNY: There are certain people that feel too safe....

R: Ummhuh.

VINNY: .....wind up getting hurt. Like, you walk the streets, I don't really feel safe. I'm always looking over my shoulder. Like if I hear somebody walking up behind me....

R: Ummhuh.

VINNY: ....I turn around real fast, because I don't trust nobody in the street, nobody.

R: Mummmm...

VINNY: 'Cause the sweetest person could be that person waiting for you, schemimg on you, that's waiting to clap you in the head.

R: Mummm...

Parent-Child Fit

Parent-child fit refers to a match in the temperament of a parent with the temperament of the child (Anthony 1987). Childrearing is not a static activity. How the child behaves towards the parent influences how parents behave towards the child. For example a child prone to temper tantrums is likely to evoke hostility from parents, thus feeding a reciprocal cycle, (Sampson & Laub 1997). Very poor parent-child relationships are predictive of delinquency (Gove & Crutchfield 1982). Most of the students reported that they had a good relationship with their parents or guardians, but at various points most indicated having some conflicts with their parents though perhaps no more than might be expected in the teenage years. According to the juveniles most of the conflict involved household responsibilities, keeping curfew, conflicts over purchases and delinquent juvenile companions. More indicative of a misfit were Roshaud and   Malcolm. Roshaud lived with a foster mother who was responsible for at least six children and Malcolm claimed that his mother favored his sister not him. Significant? Perhaps for these two were on some of the most troubling life trajectories in terms of a future delinquent outcome from the viewpoint of teachers. Regarding both students, the teachers viewed this as a function of family-related dynamics. A case could well be made that parent-child attachments matter but for some African-American males - violence is a part of environmental survival and drug and property crimes the available avenues for securing property.

The teachers also suggested other cases of a parent-child misfit for Jaoquan and Roderick. In both cases the students seemed somewhat moody and immature to the teachers. They reported that these students had serious conflicts with their mothers over the mothers' active dating life.

Ethnic Socialization

Ethnic socialization shapes ethnic identity. "Ethnic socialization entails the intergenerational transmission from parent or guardian to child of certain messages and patterns that relate to personal and group identity, relationships between and within ethnic groups, and the ethnic group's position in society," (Marshall 1995). As such it is important for navigating the larger society. On the other hand, ethnic identity refers to the accurate and consistent use of an ethnic label based on the perception and conception of themselves as belonging to an ethnic group," (Rotheram & Phinney, 1987, pp. 17).

Regarding race, some parents socialize their children as "black Americans," not simply "Americans" (Peters 1985). Others minimize race differences and yet others emphasize pride in ethnic and racial background while engaged in a pursuit of mastering the mainstream culture (biculturality).

The socialization is done primarily by parents or guardians, but also by teachers, peers and the media. Given the negative stereotypes and discrimination that African-Americans too often experience in America, ethnic socialization is very important in how or whether or not one weathers these strikes against oneself, (Peters & Massey, 1983; Spencer 1982). Sheree Marshall (1995) looked at ethnic socialization amongst middle income African-Americans attending predominantly white schools. She examined three variations of ethnic socialization. First, an emphasis on cultural experience. This was generally not done beyond the parents' personal experience (Marshall: discussing Thornton et al, 1990). Second, there was an emphasis on the minority experience. This was a focus on the race struggles that children encountered. Finally, there was the mainstream experience.

In Thornton and colleagues' study (1990) the African-American parents who were older, more educated, female, and in the Northeast were more likely to ethnically socialize their children. Parents who were never married did less socialization than their married counterparts. This reflected a proxy effect to overall family circumstances such as family condition and family relationships.

Why even examine ethnic socialization? The academic achievement of African-American adolescents depends in part on their social identity and their support networks (Clark, 1991). Of course, the family is but one aspect of that network - though by no means an insignificant part. African-American parents can help their adolescents to develop techniques related to coping with a subordinate racial or class status, (Clark, 1991). Their socialization patterns can also influence their children's academic achievement (Clark, 1983; Ford & Harris, 1994). Bowman & Howard (1985) did a national study on African-American ethnic socialization effects. They found that what parents communicated to their children about their race and it's societal barriers affected children's aspirations and achievement. Successful ethnic socialization was high on emphasizing ethnic pride, an awareness of racial barriers and egalitarianism. Students who were not socialized about societal barriers had the lowest academic achievement. Not surprisingly then, many of the students in the present study - both delinquent and non-delinquents lacked effective ethnic socialization in the home as evidenced by the interview responses below:

R: Aammm has your family given you any special advice about being a black person in America?

RUSSELL: Ahhh, let me think, let me think. Well recently, my...??? before she just tells me that if you don't go to school and do your work, it's not hurting her: it's hurting yourself.

R: Umhuh.

RUSSELL: She tells me to do good in school, do what I'm supposed to do, etc.

++++++++++++++++++++++++

R: African-American all right. Aaahh, your parents or other relatives have they given you any special advice about being a black person in America? African-America person in American?

ROGER: Yeah. But. I don't remember it.

R: Don't remember it.

...
++++++++++++++++++++++++

R: No, has your family given you any special advice about being a black person in America? Your brother? Like what sort of...?

VINNY: Like, being like hearsay I have 3 strikes....

R: Unnhuh.

VINNY: And I already have one taken away from me and that's the color of my skin....

R: Humm...

VINNY: ...and he be like "I can't tell you what to do but I can give you a word of advice like 'make something out of yourself.'" Like past relatives in the family they didn't really do anything with they self and they on welfare. And he like "I don't wanna see you on welfare. I wanna see you doing good like me." And, that's my role model so I'm trying to live up to what he do.

++++++++++++++++++++++++++++++++++++

R: Aaamm has, your folks have they ever given you any special messages about being a black person in America? Life as a black?

STEVEN: No, they just say "life is bad when you black...???

R: I'm sorry?

STEVEN: They just say "life is bad when you're black, life is worser."

R: Tougher. Did they give you any advice about how to deal with that?

STEVEN: They tell me go to school. Get an education. That's the only way you can probably like beat the system.

++

R: Ok, how do you identify yourself ethnically? Do you consider yourself Black? African-American, what, what do you....

MALCOLM: [*He chuckles*]. They both like the same.

R: Both the same so it really doesn't matter?

MALCOLM: Yeah.

...

R: You do. That's a form of poetry. Has your mother or maybe any other relative told you anything special about being a black person in America?

MALCOLM: [*Hisses teeth*] Naaaw.

Malcolm was one of the youngest subjects, only 14 years old. This may explain some of his lack of introspection on his ethnic identity. Indubitably, Malcolm qualified as "truly at-risk." Teachers indicated that he appeared in need of special education services - not necessarily for a disability, but perhaps tutoring to catch up academically. He lacked substantial social and cultural capital. Instead he had had a school background that endorsed social promotion - something he came to depend on. He was also from a dysfunctional family background (that is, conflicts with mother and an ex-convict father). In addition, he lived in a high crime area in which it seemed he had become very comfortable (according to the staffers).

++++++++++++++++++++++++++++

R: You're not, ok. Has your family given you any special advice about being a black person in America? Special advice?

LUNCH: What like...?

R: Anything at all.

LUNCH: That, you gotta be very careful out there because they want us in jail and stuff.

R: Who said that?

LUNCH: Family members, police, like the, the co. Growing up you'...??? to understand and - that's true.

R: That's...

LUNCH: Guiliani trying to get us locked up.

Lunch's response reflected a common theme in the ethnic-related advice that students claimed to have received from their families - on one hand, an encouragement to pursue education and on the other hand - an urge of caution. What is different about this caution is that it involves a distrust of that very system and people designated to protect and serve. Even quality education was a rare treat.

R: All Americans, ok. Has your family given you any special advice about life as a black person in America?...??? about that?

TREVOR: Just get through school.

R: Just education?

TREVOR: Get all the education you can get.

R: No. Has your family given you any special advice about life as a black person in America?

PETER: Yeah.

R: Like what? Give me an example.

PETER: You have to work hard in life, but you have to work even harder because you're black.

R: Has your family given you any special advice about being a black person in America?

PETER: (Indicates "no").

R: Has your mother or your brother or anyone else in your family given you any special advice about being a black American? What it means to be a black person in America? Anything like that?

JAOQUAN: Not really. They've just given me information about go to school and do that, and all that. They don't really talk about being an African-American...

R: Or anything like that.

JAOQUAN: About being yourself.

++++++++++++++++++++++++++

R: No. Have your folks given you any advice about being a black person in America? Special advice?

RODERICK: Just, do the right thing. That's it.

++++++++++++++++++++++++++

R: No. Okay. Has your family given you any special advice about being a black person in America?

MARTY: It's hard being a black man in America.... have to be on my toes.

++++++++++++++++++++++++++

R: Ok, have your parents - your mother or grandmother given you any special advice about being a black person in America?

JEROME: Of course.

R: Like give me an example.

JEROME: She tell me like aaamm she want me to grow up and make her proud or something, do something for the black people you know. Like let them know that black people...she like when I got arrested she was really mad because you know, she saying black peoples already being looked at as the bad race already, you know and that just makes us look worse - that I keep getting arrested. So...

+++++++++++++++++++++++++

R: No. Okay. Has, ahhh, folks in your family, have they given you any special advice about life as a black person in America?

TYRONE: Aaaammm, I think well, my sister always tells me like, aamm, like just to stay out, stay away from the law. She says once I am, get involved in the system that when I apply for a job, they gonna, that's the first thing they gonna be looking at, personally being a black male, that's what they gonna look at. My..???

R: And, how old is your sister again?

TYRONE: Oh, she's 38, I think.

Apparently, even for the black juvenile males in America guarding oneself against the criminal justice system is an important part of daily life. Often suspect merely because of race, they speak of things like a need to always carry identification and being law enforcement prey as if their existence is in a police state. Yet, these young men seemed unaware of how the larger social structure had conspired in increasing the likelihood of their conflicts with the criminal justice system in spite of police profiling.

++++++++++++++++++

R: You do raps, all right. Aaammm has your family, anybody in your family or so given you any special advice about being a black person in America?

ROSHAUD: No.

For the non-delinquents, the responses were very similar:

R: No okay. Has your family told you anything special? Any special advice ahh, ahhh as a Black person in America?

BUGSY: Well, my mother told me it's very good to get an education especially for a black person.

R: Ummhuh an education...an education is especially important, ok. Does anyone in your family have a major sickness?

++++++++++++++++++++++

R: Once in a while. Has your family told you anything special about being a black person in America? Any special words of advice to you as a black person in America?

MIKE: Something to do? Always carry ID with you.

These interviews were conducted after there had been a series of cases were New York police officers had killed or seriously maimed innocent black and Hispanic males. In some of the incidents the police were not found criminally liable. Most prominent at the time were the Abner Louima[2] incident and the Amadou Diallo case. Not too long after these interviews there was the fatal Dorismond[3] shooting.

++++++++++++++++++++++

R: Aaammm has your mother or anybody else in your family ever told you anything special about life as a black person in America?

ANTHONY: Yeah but, I really.... my brother did. He told me something about that but I really wasn't listening to him at the time.

R: Like what sort of things? Do you remember anything?

ANTHONY: Like there's a lot to being a black man, got to be strong throughout the years no matter what happens, you know.

+++++++++++++++++++

R: Has your family told you anything about being a black person in America?

BOBBY: No.

R: They don't talk about that?

BOBBY: They only say that aammm black person can't get a job as a white person.

R: So, they do say that?

BOBBY: Yes.

R: So what advice have they given you?

BOBBY: That I can't do what a white person can do?

R: They said that?

BOBBY: Not in those words, but that's what it comes out to me as.

+++++++++++++++++++

R: No. Aaammm, has your family, perhaps mostly your mother, maybe father given you any advice about being a black person in America?

EVAN: She's given me advice, she's just basically you know, not really "being like a black person" but being a person successful at whatever you do.

R: Ok, like, give me an example of one word of advice that you've gotten.

EVAN: She just said, aammm like, this study, she was talking about this study about...???

++++++++++++++++++++

R: That's poetry. Aamm has your family told you anything special about being a black person in America - life as a black person in America?

BARRY: Special?

R: Ummhuh. Any advice they give you for anything ..??

BARRY: Advice? They tell me what I shouldn't do as a black person in America.

R: Like what are some examples?

BARRY: Like say...how to act around the cops as a black person, aahhh just how white people feel about us as black people and the way we should conduct ourselves to make us, to make them think we're not like that.

R: Give me an example - like what exactly?

BARRY: Like they expect us to act like out of tone 'cause we black. But we should speak in the correct ways and stuff around them so that we can show. Like there's a time and place for everything. Like when you're around your friends you can speak like you wanna speak but when you're around certain people you have to speak that...to show that hey, black people, some black people do have good sense.

+++++++++++++++++++++

R: No, has your family given you any special advice as a black person in America?

ROSS: Yeah.

R: Like, give me an example.

ROSS: Stay in school.

R: Stay in school. Anything else?

ROSS: Yeah, but I don't wanna get into that.

Sheree Marshall (1995) found that ethnic socialization was correlated with low grades for middle class African-American students. Margaret Beale Spencer's "double talk" and Macleod's findings about how African-American parents attempt to protect their children from disappointments may explain the negative ethnic socialization effect.

Risk: When Parents Engage in "Double Talk"

Margaret Beale Spencer alluded to a concept that she called "double talk" in the early 1990s. Others Jay Macleod (1987) and John Ogbu (1990) discussed similar concepts. Using national data, Dembo & Hughes (1989) found that African-Americans received positive messages from relatives and friends regarding their life prospects but negative messages from members of institutions who embraced the larger society's devalued perception of African-American culture. Yet, the concept of familial "double talk" may be even more damning to the African-American child's future that the negativity of institutions.

"Double talk" refers to a situation where parents, for example may encourage a child to aspire to a high academic standard and a profession. Nevertheless, that same parent may then sabotage his or her words on the matter by exclamations in the presence of the child that black people will not get ahead for various reasons. The person may do this by complaining about his or her own encounters with racism in school and/ or work. Presently with such reports the African-American child may then lower his or her aspirations as the individual self-concept is more likely tarnished by reports from significant others. While important, capturing this concept in detail was beyond the scope of this study. Nonetheless, where possible, the researcher attempted to identify the source of certain juvenile beliefs about their futures. It appeared that most of the parents told their children that without education their lives were heading nowhere. However, for the "truly at -risk" someone had turned many of them off from educational pursuits. For example, the delinquents, Malcolm and Vinny despised the notion of taking out a college loan. Coupled with this was an ignorance of grants or fellowships. These same juveniles lived in high crime areas and had close relatives who had been convicted of crimes. What might their futures be? In Vinny's case, the aspirations came from the 23 year old brother who was raising him. Yet, another brother had been involved in property crime.

Why Some Parents Avoid School

To many impoverished individuals the middle class aura of schools is intimidating (Alexander et al., 1994). An impoverished teen mother does not necessarily care less about her child than a more mature mother but she may be uncomfortable going to a teacher in a middle class institution for advice about her child's progress (Berliner 1989). The school is partly responsible for maintaining an intimidating aura by often limiting its communication with parents to negative matters – such as student behavioral problems. In other cases grossly ineffective means of communicating with parents exist. For example at the comprehensive school herein, teacher-parent communications largely involved asking student to take letters home to parents. Often, these did not arrive.

The most effective teachers in reaching parents at the comprehensive school made it a point to call them during, and after regular business hours. At the alternative school parents had to provide information on their access both during school hours and non-schools hours. Transportation to parent-teacher conferences could be made available (for example, school bus pick ups). Meetings were held from 7:00 – 8:00 p.m. on Wednesdays and parents could stop by at other times if that hour was inconvenient - indeed, many of them did. For more active parental involvement, some parents were offered a stipend of a few hundred dollars for serving on the parent-teachers board.

Many parents of "truly at-risk" students are so unfamiliar with the inner dynamics of schools that they do not recognize the importance of their involvement in their child's schooling. Many of the juveniles stated that their parents would attend school meetings except for the fact that they worked long hours. Instead, these parents would call the teachers themselves if, they had cause for concern. These parents may also be so unfamiliar with effective schools that they may even rate a failing school as providing satisfactory services. Hence, cycle of the social isolation, devoid of sufficient cultural and social capital for upward mobility continues.

Regarding parental assistance with academics, this was a rare occurrence for these high-schoolers. Many claimed that if they asked for help, their parents would try to assist. However, many would avoid asking.

Despite the academic deficits of some parents they can still be effective socializers towards a pursuit of academic excellence. They are powerful primary socializers to the idea that achievement is more a function of effort than innateness, thus, fostering a strong self-efficacy. Of course, such notions are also influenced by the larger culture (for example, the media). Note, on television, the intelligent child is often the nerd or scorned outcast (Steinberg 1996). With the necessary cultural and social capital parents may model, reinforce and instruct effectively (Hoover-Depsey & Sandler 1995). For example, parents could facilitate their child's learning by practicing active learning with them since students do better with active as opposed to passive learning. Parents could also emphasize responsibility and self-respect since these are associated with more positive school outcomes (behavioral and academic). Yet, parents cannot pass on what they themselves do not have. The policy implication here includes parental education and training on a schedule that fits the busy working parent.

Religiosity and Achievement

Another concept of this study is religiosity (largely, the extent of a person's religious involvement). Traditionally black churches have been central institutions in the lives of African-American families, (Harrison et al., 1990). These churches have not only been about spiritual upliftment but the political and social as well. As such they have been important in shaping how African-Americans see themselves and how they cope in the larger society. Thus, religion is an important part of the psychological well-being of African-Americans, (Hughes & Demo, 1989).

Consider the "Protestant work ethic" a termed coined by Max Weber (1930). The term refers to exercising self-reliance and independence towards accumulating material success. In this ethnicity and religion interact. Nevertheless, Rosen (1959) noted that desire for status and upward mobility varies by ethnicity as orientation to achievement also varies. The fact is that certain ethnic groups (such as blacks) have made different uses of religion given the oppressive life social structures that they have had to endure. Protestants see education as a tool to careers and status; Jews see education as a tool to prestige, authority and a better marriage situation. Many African-Americans however, do not find large educational aspirations to be realistic (Cooper and Tom 1984).

The black church was the only legitimate gathering allowed for blacks in the United States for decades. Though still strong, the influence of the black church has wavered substantially in recent years for a number of reasons, one of which being the departure of better educated blacks from inner city congregations (Gibbs 1988). Witty's (1992) ethnographic study of single mother households in the rural south indicated that African-American parents stressed issues of religion more than ethnicity. Blau (1981) found that the more religious some African-Americans are, the lower their academic competence. More recently Brody and colleagues (1996) looked at religion (Southern Baptists) as one of the variables in a model predictive of academic competence. He examined 90 intact southern families where the children (African-Americans) were between 9-12 years of age. Religiosity was measured on a 7-point Likert for the question: "How often do you attend church?" and a 3-point scale for "How important is church to you?" They found that greater religiosity led to less parental conflict and more cohesive families. This in turn predicted positive self-regulation (such as a reduction in problem externalization), which then positively affected academic competence. The effect between religiosity and academic competence was thus, an indirect one.

The present study involves an adaptation of Brody and colleagues' (1996), religiosity measure. This study also went further in examining this variable. The researcher added two nominal items to indicate the type of church that the subjects attended. Since the instrument was administered in New York City - a place where there is a greater variety of black churches beyond Southern Baptist, churches were classified as "traditional" or "non-traditional."

One thing that might explain the conflicting findings on religiosity and achievement is a difference in the type of black church. Over the past two decades, a new type of black church has evolved. These churches are sometimes called "non-denominationals" or "faith churches." For the most part these churches adopt an adaptively resilient posture emphasizing academic achievement and material prosperity as part of God's will for His people.

The members in these churches appear to be more educated than the average with at least a middle-class income (that is, at least $30,000/year for northerners, a bit less for southerners). The present study categorized these churches as "nontraditional." Southern Baptists were classified as "traditional." There was also a section marked "other" for religious institutions outside of this classification. The researcher compared traditional black church members with nontraditional church members to see if this appeared related to academic achievement. It was expected that the extent of religious involvement would not indicate academic achievement, nor behavior, but that the type of religious institution might.

However, the present findings indicated that few juveniles and their families were active in religious institutions. The more religious subjects were also just as delinquent as their non-religious peers. The religious included Jerome, a chronic offender (largely fighting), Trevor who continued to run with a bad crowd (robbers and vandals); and Roger (a fighter, who also dealt drugs). Perhaps the person exemplifying the most positive religious effects was Player, a Catholic who went to mass daily. He claimed he had been falsely accused of threatening a girl with a knife. Many of the subjects had been Protestant (largely Baptist) or Jehovah's Witnesses while younger. Most claimed that religion was important - but going to church nowadays was infrequent or not at all because it was too much of a hassle. The subjects' religious behaviors reflected those of their parents. Indeed, those who attended church seemed largely externally motivated to do so and thus, held few deep religious convictions. Apparently, peer ideals took precedence over religious ideals.

Household Harmony

Although most of the juveniles indicated living in largely harmonious homes for some of the more at-risk students (delinquent and non) such was not the case. Most perturbed was Steven (whose charge was gun possession in a school). He described barely enduring an intense daily source of stress – a grandmother who often belittled him.

> R: How often do you talk to your parents about problems school?
>
> STEVEN: Never.
>
> R: Do you talk to them about your plans for the future?
>
> STEVEN: No. I tell my mother, not to my grandmother. Because my grandmother will put me down - "No you can't do that."

He had run away a few times from her charge. For him, missing school was not an option for it was sweet relief being away from "gran" – away in an environment where he was presented with the possibilities for a promising future. Although a dark-skinned fellow, he often referred to having mixed roots which seemed an effort at emphasizing "difference" in order to boost what was perhaps a severely bruised self-esteem.

Malcolm also experienced household chaos. Staffers described Malcolm's household as anything but calm given his recent conflicts with his mother over the return of an ex-convict father to their lives. Plus, he perceived his mother favored his sister over him. Other conflicts seemed largely routine teen ones such as differences over performing chores, curfews and shopping desires. Malcolm's present charge was "stabbing a kid" which he denied doing. His priors included auto theft.

Parental Aspirations and Expectations for the Child

Another concept of the present study is parents' educational aspirations for their children. A parent's educational aspirations for a child are predictive of that child's aspirations, (Bickley et al., 1995; Marjoribanks, 1984). Laosa examined parents' educational aspirations for their children in his 1982 study of school, occupation, culture and family on the parent-child relationship for Chicanos and non-Hispanic whites. He considered the influence of parent behavior on a child's thinking and learning. He attempted to predict parents' academic aspirations for their child with parental schooling and occupational status. Parental schooling proved the stronger predictor. Mothers with more education expected more. Interestingly, both groups had higher educational aspirations for their daughters than for their sons. There may have been a general assumption that educated or not, boys would be strong enough to survive, but girls (the "weaker", yet often more pliable to teaching gender) would need the extra preparation to do likewise.

Marjoribanks (1984) later used the Laosa's (1982) model in an Australian study. However, he found that children's aspirations were only moderately related to their parents' aspirations. On the other hand, Alexander and Entwistle (1988) found that African-American parental expectations were positively related to the children's self-expectations and academic achievement in first grade. However, this influence declines thereafter (Stevenson et al., 1990; Taylor, 1991) - possibly due to the greater significance of peers as children grow older.

More recently Stevenson and colleagues (1990) compared close to 3,000 white, black and Hispanic public and private elementary school children, in Chicago, on beliefs and achievement. The subjects were in different grades. Their family structures and family income varied. The researchers constructed curriculum-based tests for achievement in math and reading. They also interviewed over 900 mothers from the sample.

Black students had the lowest scores. For third and fifth grade math scores, family income and mother's education was more predictive than ethnicity. Black mothers' emphasized the importance of getting a good grade more than whites or Hispanics. Sixty-three percent of the black parents thought their children would go to college versus,

71 percent of whites and 43 percent of Hispanics. It appeared that although African-American parents had high expectations, they lacked the knowledge of how to effectively assist their children in attaining those aspirations.

Solorzano (1992) looked at race, class and gender effects on student and parent educational aspirations for a sample of over 20,000 eighth graders in the National Educational Longitudinal Survey of 1988. The measures were - for children: "As things stand now, how far do you think you will get? For parents: How far in school do you expect your child to go?"

He found that on controlling for parents' education and income, black students had higher aspirations than whites. As the socioeconomic status increased, so did aspirations. Fifty-four percent of black females and 38.9 percent of black males expected to have a professional job, versus 58.1 percent for white females and 42.8 percent for white males. Pertaining to obtaining a college education, there were gender differences: 79.2 percent of black parents expected their daughters to attend college while 76.5 percent expected sons to do so. Bickley and colleagues (1995) re-analyzed the same data set and rendered similar findings.

Additionally, African-American females have been more successful than African-American males at bridging the gap between their high aspirations and attainment, (Walker & Sutherland, 1993). African-American females have a lower dropout rate (Walker & Sutherland, 1993); stronger beliefs in the rewards of school, (Ford, 1992); and, perform better in school and are more likely to complete a college degree (Reed, 1988). Thus, the present study also noted gender differences in the classroom interactions. For the most part at both the comprehensive and alternative school girls seemed largely disinterested in academics and more interested in social matters and family responsibilities. Most were fairly quiet in class. They held rather humble expectations for themselves. One alternative school teacher lamented that although a female student might be capable of establishing a distinguished career, the social environment might be so thick a trap that it prevents this - alluding to pitfalls like teenage pregnancy.

For African-American males the view that education has a lower pay-off for them than for others may not be a misperception (Walker & Sutherland, 1993). Of course, such thinking is counter to holding high academic aspirations for one-self. According to

Bureau of Labor Statistics, in 1988, 17.5 percent of black females held managerial or professional jobs compared to 13.3 percent of black males (Walker & Sutherland, 1993). Amongst these individuals underachievement is related to a belief that they have minimal or no control over ever attaining what they attempt to achieve (Ford & Harris, 1994).

What might account for the gender difference? The literature (Coates, 1987) suggests that parental socialization contributes to the gender effect. As McLoyd (1990) uses the adage, African-American mothers "love their sons, but they raise their daughters." African-American females are more likely to talk to an adult figure to discuss their concerns, (Coates, 1987). However, African-American males usually turn to other male peers when they have problems (Coates, 1987).

Macleod (1995) found that many black parents held modest expectations of their children. Doubtful of the ability of blacks to make it in this white man's world many parents keep their actual expectations modest not wanting the child to be disappointed, perhaps as they had been. Thus, for many parents merely passing grades were expected. Indeed, many of the juveniles in the present study noted that all their parents required was that they "do your best" - whatever that was. However, if these vague goals were not met, most parents merely said "do better" in what the juveniles perceived to be a nonchalant response. This is not unique to black parents. It is a part of America's overall "anti-education" culture. For blacks however, it is a strategy to avoid disappointment.

> R: Ok. What's the lowest grade that you can bring home without her getting upset?
>
> RUSSELL: 75.
>
> R: 75. Ok and what does she do?
>
> RUSSELL: On my report card it shows you.
>
> R: Ok, what would she say if you brought home less than 75? What would she say?

RUSSELL: She'd get mad.

R: She would get mad and say like what?

RUSSELL: You're not getting enough.

R: Not getting enough. And she sticks to that?

RUSSELL: Yeah.

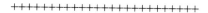

R: They were good? Alright. Aamm how do your parents expect you to do in school? Or what's the lowest grade that you could bring home without your mother being upset?

ROGER: 65.

R: 65, nothing lower than that?

ROGER: She'll say...she won't get upset...she'll get upset but she'll be like - you could do better than this. I know you could.

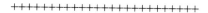

R: Ummhuh, ok, aamm all right, what's the lowest grade that you can take home without...who is it that you live with, your mother?

VINNY: My brother.

R: What's the lowest grade that you can bring home without your brother getting upset?

VINNY: 65. No, a 70. A 65 is...., he won't....he'll accept it, but ....

R: Ummhuh.

VINNY:....he know I can do better that that and I know I can do better than that.

Vinny lived with a 23 year-old brother. Although he said quite a bit during the interview his demeanor seemed somewhat evasive and his choice of words guarded - possibly to present the most positive image of his young guardian lest they be separated.

++++++++++++++++++++++++++++++

R: Ok. Aaammm ahh your parents or maybe I should say your mother and your grandmother, how do they expect you to do in school? Or what's the lowest grade that you can bring home without them getting upset?

STEVEN: If I fail, they just all "look at Steven," "look at Steven," my grandmother she like "look at Steven," "Steven stupid." "Steven..." but my mother she's like "Steven you can do better" know what I'm saying.

R: Ok. All right, Aaammm what does you mom want you to become when you grow up?

STEVEN: She's don't really...

R: Has she said?

STEVEN: She don't care what I want. She just don't want me to be like my father.

++++++++++++++++++++++++++

R: 10th grade, ok. Do you like? Oh, I asked you that? What's the lowest grade you could bring home without your, your, aahhh...who do you live with?

LUNCH: Mother.

R: Without her getting upset?

LUNCH: Like wha...my failing grade or passing grade?

R: Like what's the lowest you could bring...?

LUNCH: In the house?

R: Where she wouldn't say anything.

LUNCH: Man, say I get a 65, she'll still...a 70 she, she'll be glad that I passed the class, but she'll want me to get higher grades than those.

R: Umhuh.

LUNCH: I be telling her, I passed those and stuff.

R: You live with your mother, ok. So what's the lowest grade that you can bring home without her getting upset?

TREVOR: 65.

++++++++++++++++++++++++++

R: How do your parents expect you to do in school? Or, to phrase it another way: What's the lowest grade that you can bring home without them getting upset?

PETER: It depends on how I was doing academic-wise. If I was trying and I got a 65 they'd say "okay, you tried. But, if you need help just come to me and

I'll help you get your grade up higher." But, if I wasn't trying and I got an 80 they would accept the 80- but they'd be mad at me because I didn't try. If I tried I'd a did better.

+++++++++++++++++++++

R: Ok, aaammm....maybe I asked you this before, but what's the lowest grade that you can bring home without your mother getting upset? What's the lowest thing that she'll accept?

PLAYER: A 75.

+++++++++++++++++++++

R: What sort of grades does she expect you to bring home? Or let me put it this way - what's the lowest grade that you can bring home and she won't say anything?

JAOQUAN: Ahhh, probably a, 70, 75.

R: Seventy, 75, and what sort of letter grade is 70, 75 here? Is that a C?

JAOQUAN: I think it's a C.

R: Ammm.

JAOQUAN: She's really satisfied as long as I pass, but she wants me to bring it up higher.

+++++++++++++++++++++

R: Aaaammm what's the lowest grade that you can bring home without your mom getting upset?

RODERICK: A 70.

R: 70 and in the event that you brought home less than that, what would she say? How'd she take it?

RODERICK: She'd tell me I need to do better. She'd cut back on some of the things she let me do.

R: They would. Okay. Forgive me if I asked this before.....what's the lowest grade that you could get without them getting upset?

MARTY: Without them getting upset? 75.

R: Seventy-five. And, if you brought home less than that what would they say?

MARTY: You wasting talent, you're wasting talent, you're wasting your talents.

R: Ok, what's the lowest grade that you can bring home without her getting upset?

JEROME: Without her getting upset? She don't really get upset. She just say "you can do better" I...??? over 65, that's passing just passing and that's in gym, so, she don't really get, mad, mad, but she'll make me see it though. I'll be like "Ma let me get $5.oo." She'll be like "when you change that 65, you'll get money" and stuff.

R: Aaammm, where am I? What's the lowest grade that you could bring home without your parents getting upset, your mother getting upset?
[*Actually, Tyrone lives with his grandmother*].

TYRONE: My parents, they don't get upset when I bring home a low grade. It's like, they know I could do better so, I just tell them, "well Ma, I'm sorry for this and I know I'll do better next time."

R: So, what would she consider a low grade?

TYRONE: A failing grade, like 55.

++++++++++++++++++++++

R: Alright. So that's a "yes." What's the lowest grade that you can bring home without your mom getting upset?

ROSHAUD: What's the lowest grade?

R: Umhuh. How does she react to your grades?

ROSHAUD: When it's low she just say "do better."

For the non-delinquents, parental expectations were as follows:

R: Aaam how do you think your parents expect you to do in school?

BUGSY: Do well.

R: They expect you to do well. What's the lowest grade that you could bring home without your mother getting upset?

BUGSY: 55.

R: Fifty-five, and what's 55 in terms of letters? Is 55 passing?

BUGSY: It's failing?

R: It's failing but they want passing. They want us to do better, want me to do better.

++++++++++++++++++++

R: Getting money too, ok. How do your parents expect you to do in school? First, tell me about your father and then your mother.

MIKE: Father...I don't know. He says he wants me to do good though.

R: What about your mom?

MIKE: She wants me to do good.

....

R: What's the lowest grade that you can bring home without your father getting upset?

MIKE: We don't have none. He's not strict like that. If I get .....he'll be mad regardless.

R: So with your last report card was he upset?

MIKE: No, he was happy because he thought I was doing worse.

++++++++++++++++++++++

R: Aaammm how do you think your mother expects you to doing school?

ANTHONY: She expects me to do really well.

R: Okay, what's the lowest grade that you can bring home without her getting upset?

ANTHONY: She doesn't want any failing marks. No failing.

R: So anything above passing?

ANTHONY: Is good enough for her.

+++++++++++++++++++

R: How do your parents, your mother, how does she, both parents, you said both of them, how do your parents expect you to do in school?

BOBBY: Fine. They want me to pass my classes, graduate.

R: Pass your classes and graduate.

BOBBY: Ummhuh.

R: What's the lowest letter grade that you can bring home without them getting upset?

BOBBY: They only give three letters: E, G, S, and U - four letters.

R: Okay, don't they do A,.Bs ...no they don't do A, B and C?

BOBBY: No.

R: Okay, aaahhh so if they were to do A B and C what would be the least?

BOBBY: A "D."

R: A "D" would be the least?

BOBBY: No, "C."

++++++++++++++++++++++

R: Good experience. How do your parents expect you to do in school?

EVAN: They expect me to do good, well.

R: Aammm have they said what they would like you to become? When you grow up?

EVAN: They, they basically, they want me to become successful.

R: But they did not specify any particular job that they would like you to have.

(Indicates "no').

EVAN: Ok, What's the lowest grade that you could bring home without your parents getting upset?

R: Lowest grade...aaammm...lowest is like 55.

R: Aaammm what sort of grades do you think your parents expect you to get?

BARRY: Like 85 or better.

R: 85 or better, what's the lowest grade that you can bring home without your parents getting upset?

BARRY: I think anything under a 65, they off the roof.

[NonHH : 767 - 770]

She does, ok, all right. How important is it to your parents that you work hard in school?

It's very important.

R: You like all of them. Aaammm your parents how do they expect you to do in school?

ROSS: Good.

R: Good?

ROSS: Nothing but the best.

R: So what's the lowest grade that you can bring home without them getting upset?

ROSS: Don't get upset.

R: They don't get upset?

(Indicates "no").

R: Have they ever mentioned what they'd like you to do when you're older? What career? Hummm...did he? No.

ROSS: No..???

R: They ask me what I want to be.

For high goals to become a reality requires a plan of action which includes a willingness to persist through difficulties and a sense that success is within one's reach, (Johnson & Johnson, 1985). It also involves knowing how to alter one's circumstances (Alexander et al, 1994). This may require that parents teach their children skills for resisting the behavior patterns of their low-achieving peers for, in some cases it could lead to the ethnically treasonous peer-label of "acting white" (Fordham & Ogbu, 1986). Nevertheless, the present study found no evidence of concerns about being labeled "white" if academically successful. At the alternative school in particular, the students really wanted to learn - they were serious about catching up. It was most evident that they had been weary of ignorance much like those James Coleman studied in the 1960s. They spoke of large class sizes, teachers who were too busy and/ or unapproachable as the norm of their old schools. Thus, the traditional schools had been of little benefit beyond providing a social life. The desire for knowledge may be partly a New York phenomenon given the fact that the city surrounds almost anyone with images of wealth. Indeed, on a city subway, a child from the projects might be sitting next to a 24-year old corporate attorney, broker or physician representing America's top ten percent of wealth. Additionally, New York as a media hub, places images of the young and wealthy all over town and such people came in various shades and colors. Indeed, given the right course, it would appear success was accessible.

Mother's Education

> Educate a man and you educate an individual; educate a woman and you educate a nation.
>
> - Johnetta Cole
> President Emeritius, Spellman University

Marjoribanks (1984) found that a mother's education level was predictive of a child's academic achievement while the father's education level produced no significant effects amongst parents of the same class. Marjoribanks' study did not include African-Americans and many African-American males are growing up in female-headed homes under the charge of young under-educated females. This may explain part of the lag in African-American youth's education. Yet, for African-American girls the situation is slightly better than for African-American boys (Regoli & Hewitt 1998). In terms of educational aspirations and attainment the literature suggests that this difference is a function of a demonstration of effort. In single-headed homes the girls can see their female role model (mom) making an effort to provide and improve their lot. Boys with no constant father figure are bereft of such a male model.

Alas, the vicious cycle of a young mother with little education and social capital to pass on to her children. Thus, the cycle of the young having young goes on as mothers pass on the ways that they do know. For the present study, the researcher observed the parents (largely mothers) of the alternative school students when they visited the school for various reasons). Except for two parents, it seemed most of the mothers had given birth in their teen years.

All of the mothers had working class jobs except one who was disabled. Amongst the delinquents, little more than a third of the mothers had some college, but none had a bachelor degree at the time of the interviews. Amongst the non-delinquents, three out of eight mothers had some college - but also no bachelor degree. Not too surprising then, there was a lack of social capital to pass on to the children.

The mother's education level affects the child's day-to-day life as far as teachers are concerned. Jenkins (1997) found that higher educated parents were more likely to discuss the advantages of higher education with their teachers. They were also less intimidated about working with teachers on their child's behalf. Thus the higher a mother's education, the greater the child's bond to the school and the less likely the child is to be labeled delinquent. Herein, the juveniles described their mothers as largely interested in their education, but busy - busy with other children and working often late into the evenings - thus, missing school meetings. Some juveniles mentioned that parents corresponded with school personnel if there was some problem. This lends credence to the educational psychology literature speculation that based on teacher patterns some parents come to assume that contact with school personnel is only necessary when there is a problem.

The fathers' educational level were similar to that of the mothers. A few had some college and all of those who were employed had working class jobs. Thus, there was a dearth of professional relatives whom the juveniles might emulate.

Education Press

"Education press" is a term from the educational psychology literature. It refers to parents emphasizing aspects of the social capital necessary for success to their children. Such includes correcting a child's grammar, encouraging the use of Standard English and encouraging the academically constructive use of spare time with tasks such as reading. Most of the subjects stated that some such activities had occurred in their upbringing - but not much. A noted exception was Player whose mother enforced a daily ritual of no television, or acts of leisure unless her children could produce proof of at least two-hours of solid academic effort at home. Overall, per juvenile reports most of the parents and guardians tried to pass on what little academic know-how that they could.

Parental Involvement in School

Although many educators would disagree, parental involvement in school activities seems less important than quality student-teacher relationships. With such relationships in place, academics, cultural and social capital may be imparted. As such, the juveniles may then take part in more legitimate routes to success. The social capital includes social skills that would also lead to more positive choices in handling conflicts besides violence.

Parental involvement then, only becomes necessary in terms of parents acting as advocates within the school system on their child's behalf. This would be to secure the best of the school's scarce resources for their child. The problem is that many of these working class parents lack the social capital to navigate the school system – hence, a need for a parent education effort. The other problem is a scarcity of parent time given the long work hours of many secondary labor market positions.[4] Given the harsh nature of life in New York, for the masses, missing work is often not an option for these parents. Schools can and must be flexible in their efforts to include parents in education.

Yet, increased parental involvement alone will not do. A clearly broken public school system must be fixed. Teacher quality issues must be addressed. Take the issue of reduced class sizes. Studies collected by the United States Board of Education (1998-2000) indicate that even when class sizes are reduced, quality instruction does not necessarily improve in poor schools. The caliber of the teachers and what they actually do (despite their best intentions) make a difference.

General Parental Monitoring

In response to the statement "my parents often ask what I am doing in school" all of the subjects either agreed or strongly agreed. Additionally, all of the delinquents stated that their parents trusted them. In response to questions about a duty to report to their parents on their whereabouts most of the subjects stated that their parents insisted on being informed. However, an oversight of the study is that the subjects were not asked how often parents actually knew of their doings regardless of what the parents desired to know. However, the boys suggested that they were largely cooperative except for routine curfew violations. For the most part, the parents knew only some of the juveniles' friends and liked and disliked various friends.

So, how much do the parents really know? The responses suggest that some parents would rather not know too much about their children's doings. In various ways they even communicated this to their children by not prying too much. For example, the delinquents were far more likely to have a girlfriend than the non-delinquents. Of the delinquents with girlfriends (11 of them) five parents did not know these girls. The boys had managed to keep someone as close as a girlfriend at bay from their parents. A striking point on this came from Jaoquan who stated that not bringing his girl home to meet his mother was an act of respect towards mother.

A Look at Resilient Families

Resilient families are more likely religious, emotionally warm and characteristic of consistent parental monitoring. It is also a family with goals. Goals involve the active implementation of a plan towards fulfilling the aspirations thus, they differ from say - a mere wish to win the lottery. Only one non-delinquent (Devon) stated that his family had a long-term goal - acquiring a big house with walk-in closets. Amongst the delinquents only seven (Russell, Roger, Vinny, Steven, Lunch, Peter and Mutt) mentioned that their families had goals. These included things like owning a house in the suburbs, owning a car and seeing the children graduate from college. The delinquent Marty (the only one from what may have been a middle class background) stated that his folks had already accomplished their residential goals.

Resilient families are also characterized by strong family beliefs. Besides a belief in God for the few religious delinquents, the juveniles had little to say. Among the non-delinquents the beliefs included "stay straight and narrow" (Anthony); and families should stick together (Bobby and Devon). For the delinquent Peter's family the theme was "be your own person" and for Marty "no bums in the family" allowed.

Table 9: Parental Monitoring

DELINQ.	My parents want to know who I am / With when I am out with others	My parents want me to tell / Where I am if I don't come home right after school	In general what do your / Parents or guardians think of peers	In gerneal what do your parents / Gaudains think of your girlfrined / Boyfriend?	Pparents / Trust me
Russell	Strongly Agree	Agree	Approves of some	Approves	Agree
Roger	Neutral	Agree	Approves	Lots of girls - she approves	Agree
Vinny	Strongly Disagree – "the trust me"	Strongly Agree	Approve	Approves	S. Agree
Steven	Strongly Agree	Strongly Disagree	Disapprove	Seen, but doesn't know her	Disagree
Malcolm	Neutral	Strongly Agree	Don't know	No girlfriend	S. Agree
Lunch	Agree	Agree	Approves	Approves	Nneutral
Trevor	Agree	Strongly Agree	Approves of some	Does not know her	Agree
Peter	Strongly Agree	Strongly Agree	Doesn't know them all; would Disap.	Approves	S. Agree
Player	Strongly Agree	Strongly Agree	Appro.	Doesn't know her – to avoid sex talk	S. Agree
Jaoquan	Agree	Strongly Agree	Disapproves of their smoking	Doesn't know her - out of respect	S. Agree
Roderick	Strongly Agree	Strongly Agree	Approves	No girlfriend	S. Agree
Marty	Disagree – "none of their business"	Disagree – only if after dark	Disapproves of some	No girlfriend	Agree
Jerome	Strongly Agree	Strongly Agree	Dislike one	No girlfriend	Agree
Tyrone	Agree	Strongly Agree	Approve of some	Strongly approve	Agree
Roshaud	Agree	Agree	Approve of those known	No girlfriend	Disagree
Mutt	Agree	Strongly Agree	Neutral	Don't know her	Neutral
NON-DELQ.					
Bugsy	Strongly Agree	Strongly Agree	Approve	No girlfriend	Agree
Mike	Strongly Agree	Disagree	Strongly approve of this they know	No girlfriend	Agree
Anthony	Agree	Strongly Agree	Approve	Strongly approves	Agree
Bobby	Agree	Disagree	-	No girlfriend	Agree
Evan	Agree	Neutral	Neutral – she trust my judgement	No girlfriend	Agree
Barry	Strongly Agree	Strongly Agree	Strongly Approve	No girlfriend	S. Agree
Ross	Agree	Agree	Neutral	No girlfriend	S. Agree
					Agree
Devon	Strongly Agree	Strongly Agree	Approve	Haven't met her, but would approve	Agree

Table 10: Resilient Families

DELINQ.	Ethnic Socialization	Extended Family Support	Unity, e.g. Family Gatherings	Family Beliefs
Russell	Education	Yes – e.g. grandmother's death	Yes – fun	None
Roger	Don't recall	-	Yes	-
Vinny	3 strikes e.g. skin color	Yes – from brother or friends	Yes	-
Steven	Education, life is	Yes – from aunt and uncle	No	None
Malcolm	No	Yes	Only baby showers	Don't know
Lunch	They want us in jail	Yes – e.g. death, sickness	Yes	None
Trevor	Education	Yes – e.g. lived with aunt before	Yes	God
Peter	Work harder because clack	Yes – close family	Yes	Be your own person
Player	No	Yes – Mom's female friend	Yes	
Jaoquan	Not really – go to school	Yes – e.g. paid rent in the past	Yearly reunions	
Roderick	Do the right thing (being black)	Yes	Yes	No
Marty	Hard being black in America	Yes – e.g. paid rent in the past	Yes	Success-not just matr.
Jerome	Avoid stereotype– black pride	Yes – from grandm. And cousins	Yes	God and Church
Tyrone	Stay away from the law	Yes – e.g. when uncle in hospital	Yes	God
Roshaud	No	-	Yes – not particularly fun	
Mutt	Lead, not follow	-	Yes-fun, but family	
NON-DELQ.				
Bugsy	Education	No	Yes	Believe in self, God
Mike	Carry ID		Yes	Nothing
Anthony	Be strong			Straight & narrow
Bobby	Can't do as whites	No	No	Family together
Evan	De success		Yes	Nothing
Barry	Don't	No		Nothing
Ross	Stay in school	Yes – by the grace of God	Yes	Curfew
Devon				

Table 10: Resilient Families (continued)

DELINQ.	Family	Parental	Not meeting parent	Parent wish
	Goals	Affection	Expectations	I were different
Russell	Trip south	S. Agree	Disagree	S. Disagree
Roger	Church, Florida	S. Agree	Neutral	Disagree
Vinny	Grad. College	S. Agree	S. Disagree	S. Disagree
Steven	Car, big house	Disagree	Agree	Agree
Malcolm	None	Neutral	Agree	S. Disagree
Lunch	Make money	S. Agree	Agree	Disagree
Trevor		Agree	Agree	Neutral
Peter	College, move to Jersey	S. Agree	S. Disagree	S. Disagree
Player	-	S. Agree	Agree	Disagree
Jaoquan	?	S. Agree	Agree	Disagree
Roderick	?	Agree	Neutral	Disagree
Marty	Already achieved it	S. Agree	Agree	Disagree
Jerome	-	S. Agree	Disagree (?)	Disagree
Tyrone	None	S. Agree	Neutral	Disagree
Roshaud	None	S. Agree	Neutral	Disagree
Mutt	Home in Queens	Agree	Agree	Disagree
NON-DELQ.				
Bugsy	No	S. Agree	Disagree	Disagree
Mike	Keep family together	Disagree		S. Disagree
Anthony	Grow up, live healthy	S. Agree	Agree	Disagree
Bobby	No	Agree	Agree	S. Disagree
Evan	No	S. Agree	Neutral	Disagree
Barry	Self & sis. Grad. College	S. Agree	Neutral	
Ross	Own house	Agree	Agree	
Devon		S. Agree		

Another trait of resilient families is the availability of significant external support often from extended family members. For the most part, the delinquents had this (13 out of 16 of them). Help came largely from grandparents, aunts, uncles, older siblings and family friends. However, among the non-delinquents, only two (Ross, Devon), indicated the presence of wider family support.

Formal and Informal Support Systems

Formal support systems refer to those for whom offering support is a structured role requirement such as for counselors and tutors. Informal support systems refer to relatives and friends who voluntarily offer various forms of support - materially and emotionally. Support systems from various life pressures. Galbo and Demetrulias (1996) found that for African-Americans, teachers and coaches are significant supportive non-related adults. For the comprehensive school students this could hardly have been the case where their teachers were concerned, because though they met with their teachers five days per week, the classes were large (about twenty-five students when most were in attendance), the sessions hurried (forty minutes per period) - so few teachers got to know their students. In 1996, the comprehensive school had a single homeroom.[5] From walking the halls during these periods the researcher noted that the teachers said very little to the students and vice-versa. By 1999, this homeroom period was no more. Overall, many of the teachers had divided loyalties such as a second job. Most claimed they were grossly underpaid in the schools. Thus, they had no extra time for student support. For others, the curriculum was restrictive - they had to cover it and so claimed they had little if any time for anything else. Most indeed lacked basics such as an office in which to meet with students. No wonder these teachers projected a dim future to their students - a reflection perhaps of their own sense of helplessness in what many of them described as a dead-end post. Some teachers admitted that they would never send their children to this school.

At the alternative school things were very different. The support role, though largely a required one went beyond that of a job. These teachers while paid slightly more than regular teachers worked longer hours, through the summers, and had full lives of their own (for example, some were taking graduate classes at night). Yet, they cared for their students like their own children and managed to communicate that to them. As such spending their own funds on meals or activities for the students was not uncommon. Indeed, the effort at bonding worked as evidenced by the students confiding in their teachers and staffers about the intimate details of their lives. These teachers had been interested in knowing their students. At the comprehensive school, whatever the reasons, the opposite was largely the case.

The Resilient Juvenile

Cause Orientation

Where there is no vision, the people perish.

- Proverbs 29:18.

Cause orientation is a resiliency trait. It refers to having and actively pursuing goals. Thus, if individuals are focused on certain accomplishments, they are more likely to move towards those attainments. In this regard pursuit of cause is more than a mere wish - for wishes need not involve any actions at all. Most of the juveniles appeared more willing to pursue prospects in sports than in academics. This is not terribly surprising since the most common images of successful African-American males is in sports. This interest has an inverse relationship with belief in academic self-concept and the legitimate opportunity structure as many ethnic minorities feel disenfranchised. As a result they often focus on living for the present.

The Value of Materialistic Pursuits

The literature holds mixed reports on the effects of materialistic pursuits on deviance. Some report that a desire for materialism motivates many juveniles to offend. Others say that that same desire keeps some juveniles away from illicit activities. Herein, most of the juveniles - delinquent and non, stated that having a lot of money was important. Yet, in describing their reasons for stating this, it became clear that "a lot of money" to them meant simply having enough money to take care of needs and modest wants - like a house with a yard (as opposed to an apartment) and a family car. Despite America's emphasis on materialism, some of the juveniles made it a point to say that "money isn't everything."

Where West Indian blacks are concerned the materialistic orientation is more closely tied to what Weber called the conservative "Protestant work ethic." This belief that persistent and honest hard work will eventually lead to plenty is what separates many African-Americans from black immigrants. Many African-Americans have lost faith in the belief that the legitimate "opportunity structure" exists for them too. Historically, with racism, effort had not always brought a strong return.

Context from which the Students Hail

In our increasingly global and technologically advanced society it is important that minorities become full participants in an educated and competent work force, (Englert, 1997; Jacullo-Noto, 1991). Yet, even as these demographic shifts occur many an urban classroom serves as a funnel that sucks in and spews out graduates doomed to be little if any better than their parents before them. This continuing cycle diminishes the local communities' prospect for economic growth. This in itself breeds its own abundance of other social ills. A large part of the teacher ineffectiveness problem is the social distance between many urban teachers and their students (Gay 1993). This manifests in a cultural discontinuity in the classroom.

Most teachers come from isolated ethnic groups, and from a professional preparation that usually excludes direct interaction with different cultures (Cannella & Reiff, 1994: citing: Banks, 1994; 1991; Fereshteh, 1995; Gay, 1993; Gollnick & Chin, 1986 Russo & Talbert-Johnson, 1997). The same is true for many education professors (Parker & Hood, 1995 citing: Zimpher & Ashburn, 1992). With "the blind leading the blind" in an isolated cultural existence, the resulting teachers are ones who push for "the others" conformity (Payne, 1980). Significant? Yes! For less than 35 percent of the pre-service teachers of the next five years will be minority. Currently about 76 percent of pre-service teachers are female and about 91 percent are white. Most do not speak a second language and most would rather teach in a rural or suburban setting. Indeed, before actually teaching there is often a grave expectation that dealing with culturally different students would be a larger problem than it eventually proves, (Aaronsohn et al., 1995; Grottkau & Nickolai-Mays, 1989; Haberman & Richards, 1990; Narang 1984; Rashid, 1990).

Many teachers are unaware of the cultural discontinuity between themselves and their students beyond admitting that they would never send their own children "to this school." To many the only difference is "the inferior" versus "the superior" culture, and not mere difference. Such were the thoughts of many a teacher at the comprehensive school. Despite the greater formal hours of training required of teachers an alarming number are still frustrated at their incompetence in achieving academic success with their urban students. This is not to say that administrative and larger social factors play no role in the low achievements of many urban minority students.

Table 11: Cause Orientation

DELINQ.	5 –year	10 year goals	Sense of control over one's life
Russell	College, basketball	NBA, stock investments	Yes – plan & day-by-say
Roger	Alive	Engineering, basketball	No-things just happen
Vinny	Maybe work way through college	College – engineering (if scholarship)	No-hoping school will change me; live day by day
Steven	Maybe work way through college	Bachelor, lawyer, playing sports	No-the court does; wanted to say what happened
Malcolm	Successful own business	No money - no college; girl, not wife	No-things just happen; live day-by-day
Lunch	NFL, transit, then college - radiology		Yes – control
Trevor	College – psychology	On a beach, mansion, wife, kids	Yes-plan life
Peter	Law school, married, apartment	Taking the bar	
Player	College-economics	Children, them possible marriage	Yes-control, but also live day-to-day
Jaoquan	College-business	Basketball, working, own business	Yes-control
Roderick	Later college-accounting, stocks	Own business – selling computers	Yes-control, but also live day-by-day
Marty	Later college-accounting, stocks	Wall St., own home, girl, not wife	No-probation
Jerome	John Jay College – DEA agent	DEA, 2kids, house, no wife	Make rough plans, but live day-by-day
Tyrone			
Roshaud	Construction, married, housed, car, no kids	College, NBA, stocks	Maybe achieve goals
Mutt	Businesswoman, apartment, engaged,	Married, one kid	Yes
	Pro-wrestling, football		
NON-DEL			
Bugsy	Trade school for mechanics; live in Jersey	Own business	-
Mike	No Ides, finishing college in business adm.	Bro.-in-law an accountant in mentor	-
Anthony	-	-	Will achieve goals; live on day at a time
Bobby	Basketball	C.P.A.	Will get to NBA; I have control, e
Evan	College – business, communications, computing; prefer the NBA		-
Barry	Design sneakers, still	Have a lot of money	I have control – plan some, but live day to day
Ross	College for computer	Job career on track	Live one day at a time
Devon	Finishing college: own mechanic business	Own business	-

While many teachers continue to speak of their profession as a calling, (Grant, 1989; Ooka Pang, 1994) they quit for the same reasons that the students do - a sense of failure from poor student-teacher interactions and ineffective teaching strategies (Weiner, 1993). Thus, early on many teachers begin to plot their escape to suburbia or to non-teaching jobs (Gallegos, 1995). Paradoxically, many urban teachers leave after about three to five years which is about the length of time that it takes to become competent in the urban classrooms (Haberman & Rickards 1990). Clearly, retaining good people is as important as finding them. These were strengths of the alternative school. Partly responsible for the retention was a sense of power that teachers enjoyed in that their perspectives mattered in the operation of the school and such input was solicited daily. At the comprehensive school most teachers indicated having no such influence. Also at the alternative school how teachers were treated also indicated that they were important people. For example each teacher had a classroom that also served as an office. Therein, they had access to a telephone. At the comprehensive school the norm was that teachers had no office space and those who did were sometimes sharing with three other teachers. They had a payphone for their use in the school basement. The message to the teachers was clearly not one that they were valued much, if at all.

In short, "discrimination drains everyone" (Lessard, 1994). Discrimination is not limited to color, but extends to class, culture, nationality, and gender, among other things. The literature is clear that such background differences between teacher and student often factors into differential treatment," (Rios, 1993: citing Good 1981; Jackson & Cosca, 1974; Morine-Dershimer, 1985).   Such treatments include: delivering knowledge in very different content tracks, disparities in discipline and the establishment of "caste systems" in schools based on things such as race or ethnicity (England et al., 1988 citing: Ogbu, 1978).

For the most part, many critics believe multicultural pre-service education efforts to be either too radical or too conservative. A common conservative argument is that an emphasis on diversity is too divisive. For example, they often point to the ill-effects of such consciousness in places like Czechoslovakia and Yugoslavia (Sleeter, 1995). Others argue that multiculturalism detracts from intellectual rigor - substituting psychotherapy for academic prowess. Others state that building self-esteem via multiculturalism does not build success. However, a focus on effort would. Such views also posit that a different way of achieving is an inferior way of achieving (Montecinos, 1994). Such thinking is erroneous. True, there should to be a greater emphasis on effort in achieving, but African Americans have high self-esteem. Multiculturalism is thus not as important for building self-esteem, but for eliminating the social marginalization of classrooms wherein African-Americans come to believe that school is not for them.

Although responding to cultural diversity remains a formal objective in pre-service teacher training, substantively, the implementation efforts have been lackadaisical (Garcia and Pugh, 1992). As concrete evidence of its failure - the academic scores of blacks and Hispanics are still dismally poorer than whites, and the dropout rates are higher than whites (Scott 1995 citing: the National Assessment of Educational Progress report, 1992). More recently, Gunzenhauser and colleagues (1996) concluded that the negative reactions of several pre-service teachers to affirmative action indicated a lack of historical perspective and a lack of appreciation for cultural diversity. The conclusion? The past three decades of multicultural programming has failed (Cannella & Reiff, 1994). True or not, this does not mean "quit" multiculturalism, but it means "improve" it.

Christine Sleeter (1995) studied the recent criticisms of multicultural education. According to Sleeter (1995), multiculturalism's most popular critics include Bloom (1989), D'Souza (1991), Ravitch (1990; 1991; 1992), Schlesinger (1991; 1992) and Smoler (1992). Sleeter's (1995) response to the critics was that their negative arguments flew in the face of research. Schools are an important arena for democratizing competition by balancing the distribution of opportunities to acquire the skills and knowledge necessary for material success, (Barrett, 1993; Weiner, 1993). Undeniably, teachers play an important role in shaping "students career aspirations, academic goals, personal expectations, and life chances," (McMahon et al., 1995 citing: Garibaldi, 1992). Moreover, multicultural ignorance is responsible for the disproportionate placement of African-Americans (especially males) in special education (32 percent). This is especially true in urban areas where 57 percent of all African-Americans who are below the poverty level reside (Russo & Talbert-Johnson, 1997).

Sheets (1996) also found that interpersonal conflicts had more dire consequences for students of color. "Once a bad reputation was established, teachers and peers alike expected and even encouraged misconduct," (Sheets, 1996). Some teachers who differ from their students in class and race are not only frustrated but feel demeaned by their association with their students (Sheets 1996 citing: Brantlinger 1993; Metz, 1990). On the other hand, the students will complain about a lack of respect from teachers as license to respond to them with hostility. Not surprisingly, a common way of addressing these interpersonal problems on the part of both teachers and students is avoidance (being absent whenever they can) (Sheets, 1996).

So where does one go from here? The recent literature (1990-2001) on the direction of multicultural pre-service training indicates three directions: 1) ensuring cultural knowledge of different groups; 2) addressing the beliefs and attitudes of pre-service teachers and, 3) training in culturally relevant pedagogical skills.

Passing on Cultural Knowledge

"A lack of knowledge and understanding can lead to stereotypes in which culturally different students are seen as intellectually inferior..." (James, 1980). Often the problem is a lack of sufficient information about "the other" to make worthwhile comparisons (Clark et al., 1996 citing: Rome, 1995). Silence on such societal issues discredits the value of learning, (Singer, 1994). Yet, in many pre-service education programs there is still considerably little said about race. Thus, educators are ignoring race-related issues of power dynamics, (Jervis, 1996). There is an assumption that pre-service urban teachers will somehow acquire the "knowledge, skills and attitudes" that they will need (Grant, 1989). Still, in spite of large knowledge gaps, teacher educators will sometimes implement programs that have intuitive appeal but not the controlled evaluation data to back them up, (Frisby & Tucker, 1993; Nieto et al., 1994).

The effect of culturally educating teachers should go a long way if the teachers bring their lessons back to the classroom. For the most part the educational curriculum and the required texts in New York's public schools also exclude the students in diverse classrooms. Such was the case with both of the schools in this study. However, at both schools the effective teachers of at-risk students took it upon themselves to teach students their histories and those of others in the city.

Addressing Teacher Beliefs and Attitudes

Pre-teachers need to learn how to analyze their beliefs and attitudes on cultural differences, (Clark et al., 1996; Gunzenhauser et al., 1996; Scott, 1995). Through guided introspection pre-service teachers may "reconcile differing versions of reality" - thus, going beyond a surface understanding to an effective understanding of culture (Richards, 1993).

Failing on this particular point has been the problem of traditional multicultural education programs, (Weiner 1993). Often pre-service multicultural training focuses on disseminating cultural knowledge, but ignores negative cultural attitudes and beliefs, (Lipman, 1996). Not surprisingly therefore, many pre-service teachers are not internalizing multiculturalism principles, (Garcia & Pugh, 1992).

This matters because a teacher's cultural beliefs will affect his/ her interpretation of events and, thus, the response to those events, (Rios, 1993). While some pre-service teachers will express a desire to work with urban students - they are often unaware of their own beliefs of white cultural superiority (Grant, 1989). This applies whether or not the teacher is white.

Walters (1994) in a study of pre-service teachers found that a third of his respondents considered fluency in Standard English to be an indicator of intelligence. Most of these same individuals spoke only English themselves. These results indicate a narrow vision of largely Anglo-Saxon norms as universal and a view that "different" means "inferior."

Additionally, teachers often attribute the success of white students to internal factors such as motivation. However, they tend to attribute black children's performance to external factors like the family (Winfield, 1986). The research is consistent that teacher expectations influence student achievement (Winfield, 1986). High expectations often mean high achievement, while the low expectations often mean low achievement. Also, teachers often criticize their low achievers frequently when they fail, and rarely praise them when they manage to excel (Winfield, 1986).

Training Teachers to Teach in the City

No amount of cultural awareness can make up for a shortage in good teaching skills (Frisby & Tucker, 1993; Marshall, 1996). Pre-service teachers must learn proper classroom management and instruction techniques (Sheets, 1996). Multiculturalism involves cocooning these skills with sincere caring. Instead of communicating "survive in the system" education professors should be communicating - "create a system celebratory of diversity" (Cannella & Reiff, 1994; Russo & Talbert-Johnson, 1997) - a system which empowers students to perform academically (Clark et al., 1996 citing: Cummins 1990).

Students are empowered when they believe that they are a part of the information (Asante, 1992) - when they believe that they exist emotionally or spiritually to others (Henry, 1994). It takes special skills to make the classroom a safe place psychologically for "the other's" language, (Nieto et al., 1994). When a child perceives him or herself to be different it can cause anxiety and obstruct learning, (Weiner 1993 citing: Vivian Paley White). Thus, effective teachers make their lesson content applicable to the cultural background of their students. The result of such efforts is student engagement. On the other hand, ignoring cultural differences can provoke student resistance, (Wlodkowski & Ginsberg, 1995).

Peterson and colleagues (1991) did an ethnographic study of teachers who were successful with at-risk students. They found that these teachers knew how to create a sense of belonging and identity. Apparently, when teachers lack the relevant skills to relate to students from other cultures they choose to ignore the powers of ethnic dynamics in the classroom (Jervis, 1996). This silence contributes to rendering the students who differ invisible. Then, teachers become mere "custodians" of those in their charge. Effective teachers placed demands on their students in tasks at which they knew their students could achieve (Peterson et al., 1991). Winfield (1986) spoke of such teachers as individuals who respond to failure as a challenge. They would require their students to re-do poor work rather than "write-them-off" by referring them to remedial classes.

Lipman (1996) in a study of successful inner-city teachers had similar findings. Her successful teachers had the following traits: They saw strengths in students where others saw only deficits; they communicated well with both students and parents; they facilitated the students' sense of belonging in the school environment; they took care of their classrooms like it was their own space; they showed students respect while holding high expectations of them; they demonstrated a seriousness towards academia; they engaged in "personal and socially meaningful learning" (linking academic tasks with the students daily experiences). Additionally, being an effective urban teacher often means being skilled at negotiating with authority rather than passive compliance (Haberman, 1995). The effective teachers at both the alternative and the comprehensive schools possessed all of the above traits.

Holding high standards for all students is also important to producing positive results (Lipman, 1996). However, when teacher expectations are low teachers tend to teach down to their students (Hilliard, 1992). Of course, this is counterproductive to empowering African-American and Hispanic students to overcome their debased status in American society. The empowerment process must begin early. While success in the early grades does not guarantee success throughout the school years and beyond, failure in the early grades virtually guarantees failure in later schooling, (Slavin et al., 1992; 1993).

Additionally, behind many school difficulties for cultural minority students is the conflict between behaviors valued in the home and community versus those valued by the school, (Bowman, 1994). The differences involve "cultural values, patterns of communication and cognitive processing, task performance, work habits, self-presentation styles, and problem-solving" (Gay, 1993). Thus, the literature indicates a need for reconstructionist teaching which connects home and school life (Russo & Talbert-Johnson, 1997).

All of this training however, may be stifled by a principal who does not support teachers. At the comprehensive school many of the teachers who had the potential to make a significant impact considered themselves left to "sink or swim." Indeed one of the comprehensive schoolteachers reported that those teachers who dared to give failing grades to students with very poor attendance could be subject to departmental sanctions for doing so. Alas, the politics of keeping up appearances.

Tenure and the difficulties in firing inept teachers is also a problem. Why sacrifice students on the altar of teacher incompetence when few corporations would do the same? According to social reproduction theorists like Bourdieu and Willis - to keep present winners as winners and current losers as losers. After all, who willingly surrenders power? Hence, the recent affirmative action backlash. Yes, high school graduation rates have increased significantly over the past three decades but how many African-American males with a high school diploma read beyond a fourth grade level?

The Larger Context in which the Schools Exist

Blacks and latinos are over-represented in school districts with the least amount of physical and intellectual resources. In New York City this has been at crisis proportions with collapsing and overcrowded schools and a shortage of thousands of licensed teachers.

At both the alternative and the comprehensive schools the teachers complained about a lack of resources. The comprehensive school was in much worse shape than the alternative school. The former lacked books. Those that existed were dated paperbacks which were severely dog-eared and often coverless. The teachers did not encourage the students to take these scarce materials home. Instead they resorted to writing homework on the board or handing out photocopied assignments. But, how do students learn without taking books home for study? Should the public be surprised that many of these students are ignorant of how to study? Is this the student's fault? The availability of computers at the comprehensive school was also grossly deficient. There were less than 40 terminals available for this school of thousands and the models were older than IBM 486s. So most of the students wound up in regular typing classes instead.

On the other hand, as is typical of much in American society it appears that more dollars go to secondary prevention instead of primary prevention for the alternative school had new books in excellent condition. Those students were permitted to take textbooks home for homework and study. The alternative school also had enough state-of-the-art computers with Windows 95, Adobe Photoshop et cetera to accommodate all of its students.

The School Locale

The locations of both the comprehensive and the alternative schools were less than ideal. At both schools sounds from off-campus were quite noticeable. The comprehensive school locale was rundown and on the way to the campus students passed throngs of unemployed persons awaiting assistance.

The alternative school locations were not much better. One site was near a trucking yard frequented by prostitutes. For the most part the only other people in the area were mental health patients taking a break from a nearby facility. The exterior of the school building looked extremely dilapidated much like the classic image of a crack den, so much so that on my first visit, I passed the site a few times thinking that I must have had the wrong address. To enter the school, students walked through a metal detector and within this eye sore building was a whole new world - clean, neat and warm.

The other alternative school building was beautiful. From the outside, it looked like a modern church building. However, it had a barbed wire on top of a part of its walls suggesting that something sinister moved within. Interestingly, the barbed wire was an effort to keep ill-intended former associates out rather than keeping in the attending students. This alternative school building was in the heart of the projects - albeit an attractive housing project with neat brick buildings and amicable culturally diverse people going to and fro. Law enforcement regularly patrolled the area. While I observed no violence in the area, teachers and students claimed that in the evenings melees were common. Sometimes even the alternative school students were targets of this violence. Overall, the images that both the comprehensive and alternative school environments offered were not the best.

A potential positive for the comprehensive school was that its students could easily have been exposed to university life had someone taken the initiative to see to it for there were university campuses about. Nonetheless, since many of the comprehensive teachers had concluded that college was not in their students' futures that did not happen.

The Money and the Politics of Special Education

Special education, while necessary for some, seems more of a political enterprise to secure funding for school coffers. Special education costs more than $32 billion per year (Reynolds and Wolfe 1999). As such it subtracts substantial resources from regular education programs. In 1993 special education served 4.7 million public school students or more than 10 percent of the public school population (Reynolds and Wolfe 1999). Of these there was a major increase in those labeled "learning disabled" from less than a third in 1980 to close to a half of those in special education (Reynolds and Wolfe 1999).

Reynolds and Wolfe (1999) examined the on-going Chicago Longitudinal Study data for 1,234 students in a panel group that graduated from kindergarten in 1986. Over 90 percent of the original sample was African-American and most were also eligible for school lunches (indication of poverty). They found that special education students achieved significantly lower than their age peers. Additionally, special education effects seemed compounded by grade retention (except for the first grade). Yet, Reynolds and Wolfe (1999) made no argument for social promotion. Instead they emphasized the importance of school readiness when a child begins school. Studies continue to support the view that greater investments into early childhood education and fostering parent-teacher partnerships are very effective in preventing deviance (Reynolds and Wolfe 1999).

For a child to receive special education services parent consent is required. In the present study, some of the alternative school teachers believed that they had students in need of special educational services. Some of these students expressed a strong desire to be interviewed for the present study. Nonetheless, their parents would not permit it. It was in later discussions with the teachers that I understood why. The parents feared having their children tested lest they be (mis)labeled "special ed." Such action also indicates a distrust that some black parents hold for the educational system - a system that should be serving their children. No wonder - since black children are only over-represented in disabilities that are subjectively diagnosed like attention deficit hyperactivity disorder (ADHD) (Staff, *Caribbean Life* 2000).

CHAPTER 5
THE SCHOOL PLAYERS

The Teachers

Where teacher quality was concerned, age seemed irrelevant. Nonetheless, at the alternative school, most of the teachers were young (mid-20s to early 40s). A noted exception was the popular and energetic physical education teacher - a white male near retirement. At both schools, most of the teachers wore semi-formal or neat casual attire. At the alternative school many of the male teachers wore a single earring stud suggesting some popular culture endorsement. Most of the comprehensive school teachers wore no such stud. A more conservative lot, most of them wore semi-formal attire.

One of the teachers whom I followed closely at the comprehensive school, Ms. Rogerstein was emblematic of most of her peers. She felt called to her profession, cared about her students' progress, but felt largely helpless to assist them. Like many of her colleagues she described being severely curtailed (by the administration) in her efforts to make a difference. However, unlike many of her peers she was one of a few with office space because she had volunteered to be a student counselor.

Ms. Rogerstein was indeed caring and she taught diligently while also working hard to limit student disengagement. Her demeanor was very approachable. Yet, in failing to share of herself (largely life experiences), her students likewise did not share of themselves. There was a subtle silencing taking place. Indeed, the most disengaged students in Ms. Rogerstein's class were West Indian females who either talked during class or had their heads on the desk. When they produced work, it was after copying from their peers. Ms. Rogerstein believed their problem to be profound illiteracy. Yet, she knew little of these students' lives or culture. She made valiant attempts to otherwise build relationships with her students. However, her connections with them were weak. The comparative data with her more successful peers and the alternative school teachers indicate that Ms. Rogerstein's weakness involved a low "realness rating" (discussed later). In short "being real" involves an exchange of meaningful information (relevant personal experiences, and advice towards building rapport and cultural and social capital) for both teacher and student.

Teachers That Money Can't Buy

Below are what the delinquents had to say about the teachers whom they preferred over the years. The descriptions offer insight into the students' academic past. It is worth nothing that some of the students spoke of their "favorite teachers" while others spoke of their "best teachers." Of course, a "favorite teacher" is not necessarily the most effective in terms of ultimate academic and behavioral outcomes. For example, one of the most effective teachers per my observations at the alternative school was Mr. Michaels, the English teacher. He got a lot of work out of his students, kept the class focused, and created a safe environment for students to be vulnerable enough to seek help with the basics. The students mentioned that Mr. Michaels seemed anxious about their well-being. Yet, he was scarcely mentioned as a favorite because as one adolescent put it - he worked them too much.

Here are what the delinquent students had to say about their preferred teachers:

R: Aaammmm....Tell me about the best teachers in this school.

RUSSELL: This school?

R: Ummhuh.

RUSSELL: Mr. *(teacher's name).*

R: What's good about him?

RUSSELL: He's cool. Like he could relate to the children.

R: Alright.

RUSSELL: On our level. You can really talk to him about things.

R: Alright.

RUSSELL: And he will understand.

R: Is this a Hispanic male? White male?

RUSSELL: No, he's a black male.

R: Black male. Ok What does he teach?

RUSSELL: He teach Global History.

R: Global History, ok. What about at your other school - you have a favorite teacher there?

RUSSELL: Other school.......mummmm...no.

R: Alright what about your school history before coming here - who was your favorite teacher?

RUSSELL: Well, when I was younger, yeah ...???? favorite teachers...I had a crush on one of my teachers.

R: Ok, when you were about how old?

RUSSELL: I was like, I would say I was like 10....10, 11 *(he laughs)*.

R: Ok, what about the teachers that you don't like?

RUSSELL: Where, in here?

R: Here or anywhere.

RUSSELL: I don't have no problems with no teachers in here.

++++++++++++

R: Ok, like who are your favorite teachers here?

ROGER: Ms. Rochon., but I don't have her no more.

R: Ummhuh.

ROGER: Mr. Vincent and Ms. Black.

R: What is it about them that...?

ROGER: They care about us.

R: They care? How do you know?

ROGER: They talk to us with respect.

R: They talk to you with respect.

ROGER: Yeah. A lot of times they look out for us.

R: Ok, like how?

ROGER: Like Ms.Rochon, when aamm Mr. *(name of staffer)* was treating us wrong on ...., she stepped out for us and told Mr *(name of administrator)* how they was treating us and all that stuff.

R: Ok, like what was *(name of staffer)* doing?

ROGER: Mr. *(name of staffer)*, he'd tell us....he'll curse at us. He hit me before.

R: He...oh.

ROGER: Yeah, he hit me before and I never hit him back but he hit me before....??? and Mr. (*another school staff member*) was "oh, I didn't see nothing" and he seen it.

Ms. Rochon was quite caring. She was a black female (of possible Hispanic descent) about early forties. She managed to build a strong rapport with her students through demonstrating her caring in various ways, for example - giving each of her students some individual attention for a few minutes each week. She maintained high expectations of them and infused popular culture into her teaching methods (for example, showing movies to illustrate points). Indeed, she was amongst the "realest" of them all. She built this realness largely with her friendly demeanor and sharing of her own life with the students. For example she brought in several of her daughter's wedding pictures to share with them as if they had been extended family members. The students really appreciated this bonding. In turn, they took an interest in her well-being. All students may not need such interest for they get it elsewhere, but at-risk students certainly do.

++++++++++++++

VINNY: I like social studies a lot. That's really it. That's the only really class that I like.

R: And who's social studies with? Is that Ms. Black?

VINNY: Ms. Black.

R: Ms. Black. What is it about that class that you like so much? Is it the topic? The teacher? Both?

VINNY: It's just the whole subject. I always liked social studies; that's like the easiest class, class for you to pass.

R: Ummhuh.

VINNY: Like, I know most of the stuff so it was easy for me to learn it.

R: Ok, who are your favorite teachers here?

VINNY: Ummm Moxley, Vincent, Roland really, I like all the teachers here.

R: Ok, what is it that you like about them? Some of the traits?

VINNY: Like Moxley, Vincent, Roland they fun and (*name of staffer*), they fun, they play with us, they laugh with us. They know how to have fun. And like some teachers they just here, just to be here for you....

R: Ummhuh.

VINNY: Like certain teachers that ain't fun but you can just go and talk to them with a problem...

R: Ummhuh.

VINNY: Some teachers that's too fun you can't really talk to them 'cause they always like to joke around with you....

R: Ummhuh.

VINNY: Stuff like that, so...

Ms. Black was the alternative students' all around favorite teacher. She was in her mid- 20s, a white female, the descendant of European immigrants. She was caring, smart, real, innovative in her teaching methods and she ran a most orderly classroom. Her colleagues often commented on how much she knew about life given her tender years. This was actually her first teaching position.

In the fall of 1999, Ms. Black had an epiphany regarding her students. Early that fall semester Ms. Black had noted poignantly that her ancestors came to the United States destitute, yet they had risen above their circumstances. In comparison she wondered why the families of her minority students had not done the same. As she spoke back then, her ignorance on the complexities of racism, poverty and the marginalization of people of color in America was evident. However, by the end of the semester she had far more sympathetic views. Why? She had not engaged in silencing. Thus, both in and outside of her classroom she had come to understand that her lot and those of her students could scarcely be compared. She had come to realize that the obstacles that her students faced were far more complex and sinister than mere poverty alone. She had merely been poor, but her students – faced emotional deprivation from absent or otherwise unavailable relatives who sometimes did them harm. Additionally, despite years of hard work African-Americans continued to be held back from the "American dream" because of racial prejudice.

+++++++++++++

R: Ok, aammm who are your favorite teachers here?

STEVEN: Ms. Black aaaamm Mr. Sellers.

R: Ok. And why do you like them?

STEVEN: Ms. Black, she, she, she not strict but she want you to do your work. She don't bug you about it like "do your work, do your work, do your work." She just tell you "do you work and I respect her."

R: Ok.

STEVEN: (*sneeeze, sneeze*) and Mr. Sellers, Mr. Sellers he just ....???.

R: Umhuh, alright. Who are the worst, who don't you like?

STEVEN: Let me see, Mr. aaamm Mr. Moxley. I like Mr Moxley. He cool but he get on my nerves. Mr. Michaels he cool too, but he get on my nerves. I don't dislike none of the teachers. They just get on my nerves.

R: Ok., what do they do that gets on your nerves?

STEVEN: They bothering about do this, do that, do this, do that.

R: Ok, so you'd rather they didn't?

STEVEN: Yeah, I got, I tell them, I know how to do it. I'm doing it. Stop bothering me about doing this. They just keep....

R: And in all the classes you do the work?

STEVEN: Yeah.

R: Do you get help?

STEVEN: Unless when I'm mad.

R: Except when you're mad?

STEVEN: Yeah.

Note the ambivalence of Steven above regarding his favorite teachers. Indeed, the most common perspective was that the teachers need not be nice. They need only be real, caring and academically competent to teach. Indeed, the students disliked even friendly teachers who fostered their ignorance. Each of them thirsted for knowledge.

+++++++++++++++

R: Ok, all right aammm. Tell me about the best teachers that you've ever had at this school and other places.

MALCOLM: Naaw, I think, I think, I was in like kindergarten first, second grade I had a teacher....

R: Ummhuh.

MALCOLM: She treated me nice.

R: And what does that mean?

MALCOLM: Matter of fact. it was, it was elementary school. Third and fourth grade I had the same teacher. I used to do good. She used to take me out to lunch; buy me MacDonalds, Chinese food....

R: Ahhh.

MALCOLM: She used to do all that. She helped me. She helped me with my spelling real good. All that,. I appreciate that too.

R: Ok.

MALCOLM: Who's your favorite teacher here?

R: (*Hisses teeth*) I ain't got no favorite teachers here.

Feeling ignorant is apparently worse than feeling uncared for. Thus, stern teachers who were academically effective were common favorites.

++++++++++++++++++

R: Alright, aaahh who were the best teachers?

LUNCH: In here?

R: Could be here and before. Well, start with here. Who are the best teachers here?

LUNCH: I got Ms. .....Mr...... and Ms.......(*names of teachers*). She nice too.

R: Alright what's good about them?

LUNCH: They, they teaching me.

R: Anything else about them that make them good?

LUNCH: Huh?

R: Anything else about them that makes them good?

LUNCH: They challenge your mind.

R: Ok, what about the teachers before coming here? Who were the best ones?

LUNCH: *(He pauses)* See I don't really know dem teachers. Let me see, the best teacher I had?

R: Umhuh.

LUNCH: Yeah, I liked him, but he wasn't...Mr *(teacher's name)*. This guy, he was a math teacher.

R: What was good about him?

LUNCH: 'Cause, 'cause, he was.... 'cause, that's when I really started getting into math right there, 'cause he show me how to do algebra and stuff like that.

R: OK, so he took time to show you?

LUNCH: Yeah, that's when I was really started like getting into math but now I try, now have passed that class, now I'm in math three no math B, it's B and that's hard with diameters and stuff, equations. Can't mess with that.

A common response from the students was that they really wanted to learn. Thus they truly appreciated those teachers who had taken the time to help them catch up.

++++++++++++

R: Ok, who are your favorite teachers here?

TREVOR: My favorite teacher - Ms. T., Mr Somers, Mr. Moxley, Mr. Vincent, Ms. Rochon, Mr. Michaels.

R: What does Ms. T. teach?

TREVOR: She, she's aamm she teaches Global Studies.

R: Ok, and what are some of the things about them that you like?

TREVOR: How they teach. Aaaammm, I guess, I guess, how they teach.

(Later in the interview)

R: It did. Aaammm so what is it that you enjoy about this school? What are some of the things that you like about this school - besides it being small classes? Anything else?

TREVOR: The teachers.

R: Teachers? What about the teachers?

TREVOR: They like, they nice and they help you and stuff.

R: What about the teachers at the school where you were before? Were they like this or, or not?

TREVOR: No.

R: What were they like?

TREVOR: They just didn't care about you.

(Trevor went on to describe effective junior high teachers)

TREVOR: They was nice; they, they told me if I needed anything or something don't be scared, come to them and ask them questions and stuff - anything about home work - anything.

+++++++++++++++

R: Best teachers? Who are the best teachers that you've come across? Why are they the best teachers?

PETER: My math teacher because she knew I was good in math so she kept pushing it on me, and pushing it on me instead of just "oh well, if you wanna waste it, now waste it." She just kept pushing it on. And, Mr *(teacher's name)* you know, because, he's cool you know.

R: Uhhhuh. What does he teach?

PETER: He doesn't teach. He's like a, aaammm counselor.

R: Okay, okay and he's just cool?

PETER: Like "what are you doing. Why you not going to school? Why you miss yesterday?" You know. "I'm gonna tell your mother."

R: Okay.

PETER: Like that.

As noted in the literature successful teachers encouraged their at-risk students to persist in manageable tasks. They also forged successful alliances with parents on the student's behalf.

+++++++++++++++++++

R: Aaammm who are the best teachers here?

PLAYER: I would say Mr. *(teacher's name)* and Ms. *(teacher's name)* and *(subject)*, Mr. *(teacher's name)*.

R: What makes them good?

PLAYER: Because they here and they know how it is and when all these new teachers come in here they try to change up things and the way they handle their things in a good way.

R: Try to clarify that.

PLAYER: Like Mr. *(teacher's name)* the kids that he likes, he'll like you enough to get you in trouble when you do something bad, like call your mother or send you home. But the kids that he don't like, he don't care what they do as long as they don't get in his way or mess up anything that he's doing or mess with the kids that he like. He let them do what they would do and the principal.....???? Like I don't like that principal as much as I liked the old principal, Mr *(principal's name)*. Oh yeah, one more teacher is Mr. *(teacher's name)*, because he's a .... I like and it's just that the way they work, that's it.

R: What's good about Mr. *(teacher's name)*?

PLAYER: Mr. *(teacher's name)* he teaches **real**. He tells you what he wants done and if you don't do it, you gonna fail. But if you do it and ask him for help, if you don't understand, he'll help you and everything but some people take that for granted and....

+++++++++++++++

R: No. Ok. Ammm Who would you say are the best teachers here?

JAOQUAN: Here?

R: Yeah.

JOAQUAN: I don't really know. But I'd say Ms. Black and Ms. Rochon.

R: Alright, what do you like about them?

JOAQUAN: Like Ms. Black, she has like more control of her class.

R: Ummhuh.

JOAQUAN: So it's easier there to learn.

R: Ummhuh. And Ms. Rochon?

JOAQUAN: She's cool. She has her class in control too.

R: Ummhuh.

JOAQUAN: So, everybody listens and stuff.

R: Ok. Ahh, how come they have their classes in control and the others don't?

JOAQUAN: The others do too but...

R: They just have more control. I don't really know.

++++++++++++++++

R: Aaahhh, who would you say has been your best teacher, not necessarily at this school, but overall? Is there a teacher that you really like?

RODERICK: Mr. Somers and Ms. Rochon.

R: Ok. What is it about them that makes them best?

RODERICK: They talk to me. They just be **real**. They don't hide nothing. They just tell it how it is.

R: Ok, ah, give me an example, one example of something that they would talk about that you would say makes them **real**?

RODERICK: They would tell me like how it was when they was growing and try to make me see that we been living easier than when they was growing up. Try to influence me to do the right things.

Mr. Somers was a very candid, yet caring white male guidance counselor, possibly in his early forties.

+++++++++++++++++

JEROME: Yeah. I like it, but I want to get out too.

R: Alright, but what, what are some of the best things about high school?

JEROME: They got some teachers that care about you that wanna see you learn.

R: Unhuh.

JEROME: You get to meet new people every day. That's basically it. some of them... The work be fun sometimes too; and you get to go on trips. Especially here, like, they take us to like Riker's Island and stuff...??? a Scared Straight Program.

R: Unhuh.

JEROME: So you can see what it's like. and stuff........

R: You said that there are some teachers who care about you. What are those teachers like? Describe the teachers who care about you.

JEROME: Alright, first there's Ms. *(teacher's name)*. She'll....like..alright, she'll make us learn the hard way. Like, if we don't listen in class, she'll give us an essay that night Like if you don't want to listen, you have the essay that night and you know, if you don't bring it in, it's 10 points off, every day it's late. So, she gets our attention a lot when she does that.

R: Ok. Anybody else?

JEROME: Mr. *(teacher's name)*, he's cool; Ms. *(teacher's name)*, Mr. *(teacher's name)* .... the two teachers that was in there.

R: Yeah.

JEROME: They funny, but at the same time, when they say work, you gotta work.

R: Ok, what about your teachers back in the other high school? How do they compare?

JEROME: They compare a lot. There was always some teachers that but...??? elementary school, yeah, there was a lot of teachers like up in here and the first junior high school I went to which was *(number of school)* I didn't really get to know them. I was only three for three months. Then I went to *(number of school)*. And, that was about it......Like, I say, if it's cold, I don't want to come...??? so, I just think about oh, my people's coming to school today and all that and I think about some of the teachers, like Ms. *(teacher's name)* she's cool you know. Her class is cool. That's English.

R: What does she teach - English?.

JEROME: Yeah that's cool. She's gives us books, like books I never heard of in my life and then once I see the book I don't want to read it, but then once I start reading it, I ...it's cool, like she gave us this one book Night by Elliot Weasel (sp.?) and tells us how he lived through a concentration camp, he was a Jew. And, that's cool.

R: Aaaammm, tell me something about Ms. *(teacher's name)*, what sort of things make Ms. *(teacher's name)* cool?

JEROME: For one she's young, so she knows where we're coming from most a the time.

R: Unhuh. Is she black or Hispanic?

JEROME: She black.

R: Oh she's black.

JEROME: She aamm, you know, she's just like, she comes, she comes at us the same where we, you know she just knows what we looking for, so she just tells us straight up, you know you don't wanna learn, you have to do essays every night.

R: Umm.

JEROME: So, that just scares 'em, like alright we come here and do our work.

R: O, oh yeah, you mentioned Ms. *(teacher's name)*. Forgive me, forgive me, it's early. How do your parents expect you to do in school? In other words...?

JEROME: My mother likes the way I'm doing, but then again she gets mad because I get in a lot of trouble. So she said "your report card don't mean nothing if you're always in trouble."

R: Ummm..

JEROME: She always says "what good is this report card, if you're always in trouble?" 'Cause she likes my report card. So, but, getting and and out of trouble.

Again, these students really wanted to learn. They wanted to learn of worlds beyond their communities. Now they had quality access to the social and cultural capital for which they yearned. This was not about endorsing the wider world, but merely learning how to utilize it to their advantage.

++++++++++

R: Who are your best teachers here?

TYRONE: I like all the teachers.

R: You like all the teachers?

TYRONE: Everybody in here treats me well. They respect students.So, I think I like all of them?

R: Ahhh what about the high school before coming here, who were the best teachers there?

TYRONE: I'd say the...., well, the ones I had, I'd say the, probably the gym teacher, the English teacher. Those were the only two I liked.

R: What made them good?

TYRONE: 'Cause they took time to work with you.

R: Okay and the other teachers didn't? A lot of the other teachers didn't?

TYRONE: Wasn't a big deal. I don't think they had time, 'cause they had other students about like forty students in the classroom. So, I don't know if they could a got to me.

R: But, that would make a difference between this school and the other school wouldn't it? If that's the case, because you don't have forty students.

TYRONE: Yeah, you're right.

R: Okay. Aaammm what kinds of grades are you getting?

TYRONE: Well, my average is like a 81 last report card.

R: Okay, at the other high school what were your grades like?

TYRONE: Aaammmmm they were a little lower probably like 70.

R: What makes the difference in terms of the grades that you get? What's behind the grades that you get?

TYRONE: Aaaammm I think a lot of studying. I started studying a little bit more.

R: Okay. What sort of grades do you think your teachers expect from you?

TYRONE: Aaamm probably 80s and better.

As Tyrone indicated above, the most effective teachers were approachable and afforded him the opportunity to catch up in learning the material.

+++++++++++++++

R: What's the difference? (*pause*). Who's your favorite teacher here?

ROSHAUD: In this school? Nobody. *[the response is indicative of a call for help]*.

R: Did you say Ms. (*teacher's name*) at one point?

ROSHAUD: She was but not no more. 'Cause they trying to snap on people; they trying to get off somebody.

R: What do you enjoy most about school?

ROSHAUD: Ummmm...free time.

R: Anything else?

ROSHAUD: Gym.

Below are the reports of non-delinquents describing the teachers whom they preferred:

R: So who would you say are the best teachers at this school?

BUGSY: Aaammm, the best teacher I have is Ms. *(teacher's name)* in English, teacher from sophomore year.

R: Ok, and what was it that made this person the best?

BUGSY: Well, she like, she didn't talk like student-teacher; she talk like, like one of, of, a friend.

R: Ok, was this a younger person?

BUGSY: Yeah.

R: Ok, so give me some examples of things that she might say or do...?

BUGSY: I don't know...well...explain different problems in our lives, you know, how peer pressure we gotta get through.

R: So not just the school material, but personal things.

BUGSY: Personal things that we gotta go through, like the teen years.

R: *(requesting clarification).*

BUGSY: Teen years.

R: How does she compare to Ms. McKenskie, because Ms. McKenski does that?

BUGSY: Yeah. she, Ms. McKenski is okay. I like Ms. McKenski.

R: But, she's older?

BUGSY: No, it's not that (*pause*). They like both the same to me.

+++++++++++++++

R: Aaammm the best teachers....who are the best teachers?

MIKE: Miss (*teacher's name*).

R: Miss (*teacher's name*), She teaches?

MIKE: English.

R: English.

MIKE: Miss (*teacher's name*) that's the lady that works in the science department.

R: Ummhuh.

MIKE: Aaammm..hummm I don't know.

R: With those teachers, what makes them good?

MIKE: They, they are nice but they always try to push you to do your best and it's gonna help you out in the long run.

R: Ok, ok so they push the students?

MIKE: Ahhh and they not mean even though they do scream sometimes.

R: They do scream, but it's not mean?

MIKE: Ummhuh.

R: So, you get the sense that they care about you?

MIKE: Ummmhuh.

The data herein support the literature that effective teachers hold high expectations for students and push them in manageable tasks. The data also indicate that teachers need not be amicable as long as they effectively pass on the academic knowledge while also convincing their students that they care. Communicating caring is more of a function of actions than words. By being approachable and available to students caring gets communicated.

+++++++++++++++

R: Okay aaammm tell me about the best teachers at this school. Who are the best teachers?

ANTHONY: They are not here anymore.

R: They're not here anymore?

ANTHONY: Unnuh.

R: Aaahhh, who were they?

ANTHONY: Well my favorite was Mr. *(teacher's name)* my business teacher I had for sophomore year. He taught me a lot. Besides school, he really taught me a lot.

R: Ummhuh, aahhh, what to do you mean? Like what sort of things besides school?

ANTHONY: How to grow up, be a man and showed me the ropes.

R: Showed you the ropes. He spoke to you in class or in class and out of class? Or? He was available outside of class?

ANTHONY: Out of class, yeah, he was always available.

R: Okay. Anybody else?

ANTHONY: Pretty much no.

I had had the opportunity to interview and observe the above mentioned teacher back in 1996. He was a twenty-something African-American male teacher who had been raised by a single mother. His classes often included practical exercises like mastering job interviews. In utilizing such applicable life exercises his classes were more interesting than most. Taking the time to be flexible in his instruction suggested that the teacher had a personal interest in his students. This teacher was also one of the few on campus with office space albeit shared space. Indubitably, this increased his ability to be available to his students outside of class time and possibly, it facilitated his ability to build relationships with his students. He was caring, real and available to students.

+++++++++++++++++

R: And, tell me about the good teachers, who are they?

BOBBY: They help you with your work and they don't criticize you and they are fun to be around.
...
(Later in the interview with Bobby)

R: Aaammm. Who would you say are the best teachers in this school?

BOBBY: Mr. *(teacher's name)*, Ms. *(teacher's name)*.

R: What does *(male teacher's name)* teach?

BOBBY: Math.

R: And *(female teacher's name)* teaches?

BOBBY: Science.

R: Ok, and what is it that's good about them?

BOBBY: 'Cause they, they help us, teach us more.

++++++++++++++++

R: Aaammm who are the best teachers at this school?

EVAN: I really can't say but from my standpoint, from the best teachers I have, I have aaammm my Eng., my English teacher.

R: What's the name?

EVAN: Ms. *(teacher's name)* and Ms. *(teacher's name)* an old English teacher I had in this school and Ms. *(teacher's name) * [a Jamaican-born teacher]* history.

R: History, aaahhh and what is it that makes the teachers good?

EVAN: They care about their student passing and they make sure that we care about ourselves, so that...some students say "well, this, this...I failed" or "she failed me" and they, they, they try to make us understand that nobody fails us.

R: Ummmhuh.

EVAN: ...... that we fail ourselves or something like that, or we pass ourselves and fail ourselves. So, they really push us to do work...they make us want to work.

R: Ok, aahhh can you tell me something that one of the teachers may have said that...aaammm, you know, inspired you to work?

EVAN: Aaammm, I really can't think of one right now, but basically they're teaching methods. They, they take their jobs seriously and you know.

R: Unnhuh. What? Describe the teaching method for me.

EVAN: Alright well. Some teachers may just write on the board and that's what the teaching method is, write on the board. some of the...they'll like talk out they lessons and some will just, they'll explain they lesson, they'll ask if you have any problems and then that's how the lesson go.

R: Ok, so you prefer which? What kind of teacher?

EVAN: I prefer more open like you explain what you write and stuff like that.

R: So when they write as they explain it?

EVAN: Explain it and then ask if we have questions and stuff like that.

R: Alright, who are the worst teachers that you've had?

EVAN: I really, I don't have a worst teachers at aaamm...all my teachers was good.

The best teachers did not use curriculum restraints as an explanation for not interacting effectively with their students. These at-risk students needed to be afforded the opportunity to ask questions about the lesson while in class - lest the teachers make erroneous assumptions about what the students already knew. Successful teachers also empowered their students by encouraging them to exert effort so that they might experience some academic victories. Herein, the data supported the literature in that experiences of academic success after an investment of effort empowers students to succeed via building their self-concept.

++++++++++++++++

BARRY: I passed three classes, but I failed four.

R: ..??? Oh, what was going on? how come you passed three?

BARRY: Well, I think the three teach...the three classes I passed, the teachers are really good and they really push you to do your work.

R: Ummhuh.

BARRY: Like the four, the other four classes they like do work, but some of them don't do work at all, don't teach at all but like they don't really motivate you to work.

R: Ok. The teachers who teach, what is it that they're doing? They teach meaning what?

BARRY: I mean they make learning fun. They like check home work every day, so you gotta have it. It's like no way you can slip up without having it because they checking it every day.

R: Ummhuh.

BARRY: And basically, they just make learning fun.

R: Ok.

BARRY: They make it interesting.

R: Ok, just the way they teach?

BARRY: Yes.

R: Give me some examples.

BARRY: Like umm, my teacher in English, *(teacher's name)*, she's a very good teacher.

R: Ummhuh.

BARRY: She's having us do, like a project, where we have to create our own talk show and just to discuss topics that's going on in today's society. Like I'm doing police brutality against teenagers, we're like a group of students.

R: Ummhuh.

BARRY: It's just more interesting than basically doing like your uuummm regular work and going home and doing the project by yourself. You're allowed to pick students that you would like to work with and it's more interesting that way.
...
(Later in the interview)

R: Aaammm...how would you say you get along with the teachers? Do you have a... talk to them..???

BARRY: Yeah, I talk to them. I think I get along pretty well with them except for Mr. *(teacher's name)*.
...
(Later in the interview).

R: Aaaammm how do you think your teachers expect you to do?

BARRY: My teachers?

R: Ummhuh. What do they expect from you?

BARRY: I think they expect a lot.

Since the lives of many at-risk students outside of school may have been more interesting than life at school, it is not terribly surprising that the most effective teachers infused aspects of the popular culture into their lessons (such as the talk show exercise above). Failing to do this makes school unattractive and adds to a subtle marginalization from this prescribed avenue to material success.

+++++++++++++++++

R: Ok. Aammm who are the best teachers that you've had...meaning "good" - who would you call a good teacher?

ROSS: Ah math teachers

R: Math teachers. Who are they? You can mention the names.

ROSS: Ms. (*teacher's name*), Mr. (*teacher's name*), no, Mr. (*teacher's name*), Ms. (*teacher's name*), Mr. (*teacher's name*), and...???

R: And they all teach math?

ROSS: Math.

R: What is it that makes them good? What do you like about them?

ROSS: I just like math period.

R: Ummhuh

ROSS: ...??? with the extra help if you search...??? for it. Same thing with the Global teachers too.

Many teachers at the comprehensive school considered mathematics to be one of the school's renegade departments because those teachers were effective in teaching. They broke the school norms by maintaining high expectations of their students. I had observed a number of math teachers in action in 1996. They were very "real" with their students. Their classes were always large (at least 30 students). Yet, they got to know their students by name, evidenced caring, and demonstrated academic expertise. The mathematics department included only one African-American female, one Asian female, two white females and the rest were largely white males. It was not uncommon to find African-American males sitting front and center in the mathematics classes (unlike other classes where the tendency was to sit towards the back of the room). These teachers had managed to make their classrooms and the subject matter appealing.

At the alternative school many of the teachers, as effective as they were, were not licensed. One particularly effective teacher (whose students did very well on state standardized tests) had failed the licensure exam more than once. All held a bachelors degree in the subject matter they taught. Few had studied education at the undergraduate level. Such leaves one to wonder about the merits of studying education at the tertiary level or the usefulness of teacher licensure exams. Indeed, many education critics have argued that subject matter training is better than a predominance of general education credits. Nevertheless, many of the alternative school teachers were pursuing masters degrees in education (paid by the state). Often, these unlicensed teachers taught more specialized subject matter like technology, natural sciences and foreign languages.

Similarly, at the comprehensive school, one of the most effective teachers was unlicensed – a business-woman whom after many years decided to teach. She had made a comfortable sum in business, so the relative paucity of a teacher's salary was not much of a bother. Perhaps a past laden with discrimination per her now open, alternative sexual orientation had made her respectful of differences and a good listener. She described feeling obligated to stay in teaching to offer support to gay students.

Identifying the Effective Teachers of At-Risk Students

The literature (Peterson et al., 1991; Aspy et al, 1972, citing: Prescott, 1957) states that effective teachers of at-risk students engage in the following:

- high expectations of students
- sincere caring
- unconditional positive regard for students (maintaining a belief that students can and will learn)
- quick responses to student problems
- listening to individuals
- flexible instruction
- coaching students on matters of interpersonal relations and social skills
- pushing students at tasks in which they can succeed
- encouraging persistence

- closely monitors student progress
- communicates with parents/ guardian about student progress and school programs

The present study strongly supports the above findings. Additionally, the data illuminate and adds the following:

1. At both schools effective teachers knew the names of students who attended regularly. While the comprehensive schoolteachers addressed their students by their first names, the alternative school teachers used either first or last names, but more often, the latter preceeded by "Miss" or "Mister." This effort was one of instilling a respect of person. The students appreciated receiving such signs of respect (*see quotations above*). In response the students often referred to the female teachers as "Miss" followed by the names. With the male teachers they often used the last name, absent the word "Mister." Knowing students names seemed to suggest to the students that as individuals they mattered.

2. Effective teachers were so interested in their students that they did not permit them to "do time" in class or otherwise disengage. If students had their heads on the desk, they had to be also working. Those who insisted on doing nothing were not permitted to disturb the others. The options - sit quietly or leave.

3. Effective teachers gave few compliments to the students. Some of the worse teachers frequently complimented their students (rendering at least one every five to ten minutes) with vague words like "good." The effect? The compliments came across as largely shallow and habitual and the students appeared to take them either very lightly or with contempt. More effective teachers gave more descriptive heartfelt compliments such as when an alternative school English teacher described at length the great artistic ability of one of his students before the entire class.

4. More effective teachers (even in the 40 minute classes of the comprehensive school) gave each student individual attention on a regular basis while finding time to lecture and put work on the board. Thus, they were overall, better at utilizing their class time. One way of doing this was photocopying assignments and handing them to the students as opposed to loosing time putting the work on the board. Others, whenever possible got to their classrooms a few minutes earlier to write materials on the board. This reduced the likelihood that students would be talking notes while the teacher lectured. Indeed, some comprehensive students complained that they often misunderstood the lessons when they had to both listen and write at the same time.

5. Effective teachers were willing to confront students about non-productive behavior. For example, here is what one of delinquents had to say about a teacher who was an all around favorite at one of the alternative school sites:

> JEROME: She aamm, you know, she's just like, she comes, she comes at us the same where we, you know she just knows what we looking for, so she just tells us straight up, you know you don't wanna learn, you have to do essays every night.
>
> R: Umm.
>
> JEROME: So, that just scares 'me, like all right we come here and do our work.

6. Effective teachers were flexible in their teaching techniques. They utilized different means of communicating information including incorporating aspects the popular culture. For example, one of the most effective teachers at the comprehensive school, Ms. Sweeney knew the names of all of the Spice Girls (a pop music group). Another effective alternative school teacher, Mr. Vincent, had pictures of Bob Marley prominently displayed in his classroom. This was a significant ground on which to connect with his students for many of them claimed some affiliation or admiration of reggae music. A number of the male teachers at the alternative school wore a single earring stud. Like many of their male students - a possible sign of a defiant male fierceness with which the students (many of whom also wore studs), could identify.

7. Effective teachers had a personable demeanor. As such they were not only easy to talk to, but trustworthy with personal information. This does not mean that teachers did not share information amongst themselves but only in the best interest of the student.

8. Effective teachers made parent alliance references part of their efforts to secure student conformity. Of course, these teachers could do this because unlike their less effective peers they had succeeded in building a relationship with parents and guardians. From observing parent-teacher conferences at the alternative school, the teachers were surprisingly very candid with the parents about their children.

Least candid of all was the dean of discipline. This Hispanic male was very charming with the mothers who attended the teacher conferences. He tried to be as positive as possible about each student. Then, the next day, he made it a point to tell the students that he had met their parent or guardian the night before. For having given the parent a glowing report about the student – he gained leverage. It was understood, the students owed him the favor of cooperative behavior in return.

9. Most revealing from this study was that the most effective teachers of at-risk students were, in the students' words "real." (*To be discussed at length later*). Real teachers were masters at building rapport with their students. They were the "down to earth" ones. They told the students "just how it is." In so doing they shared realities on how to overcome obstacles to upward mobility. The knowledge included the social and cultural capital for success.

10. Effective teachers were successful at communicating that they cared to their students. They did this by stating that they cared and/ or by encouraging persistence. These teachers were not always amicable in communicating with their students, at times using harsh tones. Yet, such rarely seemed to matter, for the students apparently, understood that no matter what the tone, the teacher had their best interests at heart. Some teachers even guarded their students fiercely.

Identifying the Less Successful Teachers of At-Risk Students

Below are the delinquents' responses to questions about their worst teachers:

RUSSELL: Before. Yeah, junior high school I had a teacher I didn't like. He was a history teacher.

R: Ummhuh. What didn't you like about him?

RUSSELL: Aaamm I think, I think he was prejudiced.

R: Alright. This was a white male?

RUSSELL: Yeah.

R: Like what did he do or say that was...????

RUSSELL: Like to the white kids he was more friendlier, but when it come to like the black kids more meaner, give us more work.

Note: Student references to the teachers' race were rare.

++++++++++++++++

R: Okay (*slight chuckle*) worst teachers that you can think of?

PETER: Teachers at my other school.

R: What was so bad about them? What do you think of?

PETER: Going to class, ready to work and being kicked all over the place, (kids) throwing stuff acting stupid and teachers be the ones picking at everybody. When somebody goes "Peter" and I turn around "huh?" Then, "you was talking." You know. "You have to get out." He would pick me out of everybody else too to set an example of. And I don't appreciate that.

1. Ineffective teachers were perceived as being unfair. Many of the delinquent students displayed a marked acuity in spotting instances of unfairness. This may have been a result of an accumulation of such experiences. Additionally, Jankowski (1991) noted that such attitudes may be the result of the competitiveness and survivalism over scarce resources which poverty breeds. These resources include attention. The alternative school teachers were very aware of this focus on fairness and thus, were very careful not to engage in acts of favoritism.

+++++++++++++

R: Ok, aamm so, the worst teachers then would be who?

ROGER: Moxley. That's it.

(Later in the interview he continued).

R: Ok, aammm has anybody ever said anything to you that sticks out in your mind - something that they shouldn't have said? Anything at all?

ROGER: Moxley...

R: Ok.

ROGER: ...when he told me when I was arguing with him he said "you can't do this. You can't even...who do you think you are - make it to the NBA?!" 'Cause I wanna go to the NBA.

    R: Ummhuh.

ROGER: *(Quoting Moxley)* "You think you goin' make it in the NBA? Yeah. Shoot. The ball goin' fall right on the floor and that's just where you're going - the floor."

R: Mummm, how did you feel when he said that?

ROGER: I felt bad. I thought he was a teacher; I thought he'd look out for me. I thought he was the one supposed to help us with our dreams. Tell us we could do this.

2. Ineffective teachers did not inspire students as the students may have expected. Roger's words about what he expected from his teacher indicated his script on how teacher-student interactions should proceed - teachers were expected to inspire. Regardless of what triggered the harsh exchange, the teacher's words were uncharacteristic of the alternative school teachers. Nonetheless, the teacher seemed merely candid about the illusiveness of the NBA. But, was this confrontation the best way to proceed? Roger was from a highly dysfunctional family. His father was a crack addict and there were other signs of problems in Roger's home life. Though not amongst the best basketball players at the school, he clung to his NBA aspirations like a key to escape from his present context and life.

+++++++++++++++++

R: Muummm ok, any teachers here that you're not too fond of or you like them all?

VINNY: Naaaw, I like 'em all.

Vinny was one of the "truly disadvantaged." Bounced around, he was being raised by his 23 year-old brother. Part of the survivalist code of streets involves not squealing (Jankowski 1991). Thus, Vinny might scarcely be expected to "squeal" on his teachers unless, he had been severely harmed. Of course, it was possible that he truly liked all of his alternative school teachers.

+++++++++++++

R: Alright, ahhh tell me about the worse teachers that you've had. What have they been like?

MALCOLM: Worse? I used to get hit with a ruler from my teacher *(he laughs)*.

R: When was that - in elementary?

MALCOLM: What grade? I think I was in, like kindergarten.

R: Kindergarten?

MALCOLM: Naaw, it wasn't really my teacher. She lived around my, my neighborhood. so, every time I did bad she used to hit me with a ruler.

R: Ok, but she wasn't in the school?

MALCOLM: Yes.

R: Yes, but she wasn't your teacher?

MALCOLM: Naaaw, but....

R: What was she? Was she from the Caribbean or something? Why'd she hit you with the ruler? I know Caribbean teachers do that?

MALCOLM: She like, I think she like Jamaican or something?

R: Yeah, that's what I figured. Caribbean teachers do that....

MALCOLM: She used to always hit me with a ruler on my hand......???

R: Yeah, alright, any other teachers....?

MALCOLM: Naaaw... that ain't my worst teacher. I'm saying....*(he pauses)*

R: That you just didn't like that....

MALCOLM: Yeah.

+++++++++++

R: Ok, who are the worst teachers that you've had in your school career? School life?

LUNCH: I can't say there was no worse teachers.

+++++++++++++++++

TREVOR: They just didn't care about you.

R: How do you know that? What did they do that would lead you to believe that they didn't care?

TREVOR: How they was talking to me - they be talking nasty to me and stuff.

R: Give me an example.

TREVOR: Like, ammm I say "can I use the bathroom?" or something and they be like "you can't use the bathroom. Finish the work." Then I'll be like "I'm, I'm going to the bathroom." I'll just walk out and stuff. They like mark me for something stupid.

(Later in the interview)

R: Ok. And your worst teachers what were they like?

TREVOR: Worst teachers? Screaming on me.

R: Screaming for like what sort of thing?

TREVOR: Like, if I don't understand something and they show me and I still don't understand...

R: Ummhuh.

TREVOR: ....they be like aammm "you're not paying attention" and I'm... I be paying attention but I still don't understand so you gotta show me like a couple of times make me get it through so I can know it.

R: Ok, so they just didn't spend enough time on that stuff. Alright aamm has anybody, ever said anything to you - this could be anybody at all - that you wish they hadn't said? Is there anything that stands out in your mind? Anybody?

TREVOR: *(Indicates "no").*

3. Ineffective teachers provided little individual attention to students. Trevor described a strong desire to learn. Yet, he faced increasing frustrations from having fallen behind. Given large class sizes, curriculum restraints, and inadequate resources - it is no wonder that many comprehensive schoolteachers have little time for individualized attention.

++++++++++++++++

PLAYER: My worst teacher was here - Mr *(teacher's name).* He's not here no more but he didn't teach the class right. He based the whole class on tests. If you failed the tests you failed the marking period. So, say you missed something in test review or something like that he wouldn't go it over. You basically failed the test. But....

+++++++++++++

R:....Ok. Who are the worst ones?

JAOQUAN: The worst? It's not really no worst ones. You know, basically the same when they... just don't...they misunderstand you and they get an attitude with you.

The above statement from Jaoquan suggested a gross lack of introspection on his part - for there was hardly a soul more moody than he. The alternative school teachers described him as immature.

+++++++++++++

R: Alright, aaahhh worst teachers - can you think of who your worst teachers were? And, what made them the worst?

RODERICK: Old math teacher. He didn't care nothing else, but about the work. He just wanted the work done.

R: Ok.

RODERICK: Nothing else.

R: So when you say "he didn't care," what do you wish he had done? You wish he had said...

RODERICK: He'd put problems on the the board and tell you to do it and hand it in.

R: And that was it?

RODERICK: And that was it.

R: Did he explain things? Was he helpful or just...?

RODERICK: Sometimes, but he'd just explain it; put it on the board; you do it and hand it in.

+++++++++++++

MARTY: They don't care about me. Know what I'm saying. They don't want me to..., they don't want to see me succeed. All they care about is giving me a grade and that's it. Know what I'm saying. It's like. I had a couple of teachers who really didn't like me, who really tried to fail me. You know what I'm saying.

R: Uuummhuh.

MARTY: It's like that.

R: Where was this high school? Junior high?

MARTY: High school.

R: Okay. Tell me a bit more about them. I'm interested in finding out about what the bad teachers are like.

MARTY: Bad teachers are like....huh (*sarcastic chuckle*) bad teachers like...

R: Like what do they say that let's you know that they're not good?

MARTY: What do they say? It's like what they do, not what they say.

R: Okay. Tell me more about what they do.

MARTY: Like, you can't really pin-point it, but it's like.. you can tell with a bad teacher, you know what I'm saying. The bad from the good. A good teacher will see you do your thing. A bad teacher don't really care. ...paid for it - pass or fail.

R: Okay. Who are the best teachers here?

MARTY: The best teachers? I can't really call that. All the teachers in here is alright.

R: All the teachers here are all right? Before coming here can you think of some best teachers? Teachers who were good?

MARTY: I wasn't cool with them.

R: Was that always the case?

MARTY: No. Not really.

R: When did you start to encounter these bad teachers? Elementary? Junior high?

MARTY: Junior high school really.

R: Junior high school. Okay. What do you think? What happened? How come junior high teachers were different? Teachers were different? Did you change?

MARTY: In the elementary school you stay with one teacher throughout the whole day. You get a close relationship with that teacher. In junior high school you switch from teacher to teacher to teacher. 'Til they don't really look at you like this is my class, this is my student. It's just another student I gotta pass or fail. You know what I'm saying?

R: Okay, and this school is another place where you really get to know the teachers too.

4. Ineffective teachers appeared to their students to be uncaring about students. Marty's comments above are particularly significant. There has been a longstanding suspicion that something happens to students as they go through the middle school phase - something beyond the complexities of puberty. Many of the comprehensive schoolteachers thought that middle schools in the area failed to prepare students for high school. These teachers also spoke of junior high school teaching as an experience to dread. On the other hand, a common complaint of at-risk students amongst both the New Jersey pilot group and the New York subjects was that too many teachers "had attitudes." Such of course is not good customer service. Do teachers see their students as customers?

5. Ineffective teachers, often, not always – lacked "realness." Another primary significance of Marty's comments is its support for "realness" - that exchange of information whereby teachers may build rapport with at-risk students. It is worth deeper investigation regarding whether the breakdown of a solid relationship with a conventional teacher from elementary to junior high school contributes to the willingness to deviate. Possible implications include a need for smaller classes sizes to foster relationships and having students interact with a certain class or teacher on a long term basis in order to build more lasting positive relations which enhance achievement motivations.

++++++++++++

R: Oh work, oh okay...What do you find particularly frustrating about school life? Not necessarily here but - just school life in general you said sometimes the day can be too long, anything else...you don't like about school?

ROSHAUD: I don't like grouchy teachers.

R: Muummm. Have you met a lot of grouchy teachers? Or?

ROSHAUD: I have mean teachers...??? schools.

R: Ah, anything else? Tell me a bit about the mean teachers...???

ROSHAUD: Even if you do something wrong they don't communicate with you they just start yelling at you.

Below are what the non-delinquents had to say about the worst teachers that they had encountered.

R: Ahhhh who're the worst teachers?

BUGSY: My worst teacher is Mr. (*teacher's name*) in Spanish class *[same person thus described back in 1996]*.

R: Ok, what makes him bad?

BUGSY: He don't know what he's talking about?

R: What do you mean? The subject material? Or...?

BUGSY: Sometimes like other Spanish kids tell him how you say this word, you know what I'm saying.

R: Oh, he doesn't know the Spanish?

BUGSY: Yeah.

6. Ineffective teachers did not know their subject matter well enough to garner the respect of their students. Several students (and a few teachers) mentioned the incompetence of the teacher noted above - both in 1996 and in 1999. The bureaucratic difficulties involved in removing inept teachers from the classroom are cause for concern. Would this sort of thing be tolerated anywhere else?

(Later in the interview)

R: Only him, okay, so he doesn't know the material. How do the students respond to him?

BUGSY: Respond?

R: Do they behave in the class?

BUGSY: No, not really; they like talk a lot or screaming at the teacher if something goes wrong. It's like they don't understand so they angry.

++++++++++++++

MIKE: Yeah, but some of the teachers I don't like.

R: Some...??? you don't like. Who are the teachers you don't like and why?

MIKE: Mr. *(teacher's name)* who teaches chemistry...oh, 'cause he just doesn't like me *[said with passion]*.

R: He doesn't. Why do you think he doesn't like you?

MIKE: 'Cause he aammm, he was like all the people that wanna pass sit up in the front and he gave me a seat like towards the back.

R: He gave you the seat towards the back?

MIKE: Ummhuh.

R: So, he seats people.

MIKE: Ummhuh, but towards the end people just started taking different seats that they wanted to.

R: Ok, so what kind of people did he seat at the front? What did you think was his criteria for putting some people in the front?

MIKE: I don't know, I guess some people, they was quiet or they didn't say nothing like they didn't speak their opinions towards him.

R: Ummhuh. Ok, but you're not quiet?

MIKE: Well, I speak my opinions towards him.

R: Ok, give me an example.

MIKE: Like when he, when he made that statement about people, I'd say how come the people in the back didn't pass or something like that. There's no difference between us?

R: Ummhuh. But he didn't answer it.

MIKE: When you challenge him, he just be quiet. He doesn't say nothing and when you finish talking he'll just continue on with his lesson.

R: Ok, so like what has he said to you? Give me an example of something he said.

MIKE: Like that, just right there.

R: Ok, you mean you just asked him, he just didn't respond. Ok, other teachers what are the other teachers like?

MIKE: Mr (*names same bad Spanish teacher from '96*).

R: Who teaches what?

MIKE: Spanish....aaammm that's probably it. There's more, but I can't remember. Oh, Mr. *(names teacher)*. He teaches *(subject)* and he's dean.

R: What's the problem with *(name of Spanish teacher)*?

MIKE: He doesn't know how to teach. He comes into class and he writes down the page of the book and he expects you to do it and to just know the work.

R: Ummhuh.

MIKE: And then, when he teaches and stuff he goes over real quick so you don't get no time to understand it and anything....

R: Ummmm....

MIKE: So, you can't possibly do the work.

R: And the other one, what's his problem?

MIKE: Oh, *(last name of teacher w/out the "Mr." before it)*, *(hisses teeth)*, he just harass me all the time.
R: Ok, like what's going on? How come he harasses you?

MIKE: Alright, alright, when I'm in the hallway....

R: Ummhuh.

MIKE: I'll walk and like the bell might just ring, and since he knows my whole name and ID number and all that he'll go like "*(name of subject)* come here" and the whole hallway could be crowded - he'll call me and be like "let me get your program and ID." I don't give it to him.

R: Ummmhuh, ok, so you think he, do you think he cares about you at all or he's just bad?

MIKE: A little bit of both.

The last description above represents a healthy ambivalence towards well-meaning teachers. It would be worth exploring elsewhere the extent to which a student's appearance influences his or her interactions with both teachers and peers. Mike was a huge fellow for his age and very dark skinned – an American stereotype for some of "the dangerous classes."

+++++++++++++++++

ANTHONY: I don't know why they's here.

R: Who are some of the examples of worst teachers?

(Later in the interview).

ANTHONY: Worst teachers gives home work every day. Gives homework everyday, doesn't give you a break during class [*he chuckles*]....and, pretty much has coffee breath.

+++++++++++++++++

BOBBY: Racing to finish to get through the lesson. They don't take time to teach us.

R: Ummhuh. so the other teachers lecture more, they talk more, explain it. But the other, the ones who aren't....ok, you said they just race through the lesson. All right, the worst teachers in this school in your opinion?

BOBBY: Mr (*teacher's name*).

R: What does he teach?

BOBBY: Science.

R: And what's his problem?

BOBBY: He's nasty, he' s mean, he's grumpy. He's just a mean old man.

R: Mean old man, like what sort of...give me an example.

BOBBY: He never, he never, he teaches science lab too and he don't go over the lab, he just eats and eats and eats and that's it.

R: In class? Doesn't go over the lab? So, what do you do when you're in that class?

BOBBY: I don't do the labs....??? Everybody fails his class except for one girl.

R: So, how come that girl didn't fail? She did what?

BOBBY: She understands the labs.

R: She understood it before coming in or..?

BOBBY: Yeah. Before coming in.

...

[Later in the interview]

R: Ok. Aaammm Let's see aammm, the past couple of years at your other school did you get along with the teachers there?

BOBBY: Off and on.

R: Off and on, okay, regarding your teachers here, what would you change about them?

BOBBY: More patient.

R: Ummhuh

BOBBY: More reliable, more sensitive.

R: What do you mean by reliable?

BOBBY: Aaammm sometimes they not here on time. And then when they come, they rush you to do what you not supposed to do so fast.

R: Ummhuh. Ok, and sensitive?

BOBBY: They don't got no sense of humor, they always getting angry at the least little thing you do.

R: Oh, so, they're worse than teachers in Jamaica or what?

BOBBY: Well teachers in Jamaica hit you, these ones can't hit you, so, I think they even.

...

[Later in the interview]

R: Aaaamm, have you ever been suspended from school?

BOBBY: Not in this school do.

R: No. What about before?

BOBBY: Yeah.

R: Junior high?

BOBBY: Fifth grade.

R: Fifth grade? Why was that?

BOBBY: Because the teacher said that I was going to hit her.

R: Is that? That incident? That was the only time?

BOBBY: Yeah.

R: How did you take that?

BOBBY: I didn't really care. 'Cause I know she was lying.

R: Why do you think she was lying?

BOBBY: Huh?

R: Why do you think that happened?

BOBBY: I don't know. She just didn't want me there.
...
[Later in the interview]

R: Sometimes, ok. Tell me about your relationship with your teachers.

BOBBY: Some a dem I like; some a dem I dislike.

R: Ok, but you talk to them?

BOBBY: Yeah.

+++++++++++++++

R: Ahhh, is there a problem with the class? Or is it you? Is the teacher helpful?

EVAN: Aaammm, I not gonna like be the one to point fingers. I mean, first, I gotta start off with myself.

R: Ummhuh.

EVAN: You know. But the teacher she's, she's a great teacher but seems like she has favoritism towards students.

R: Ummhuh.

EVAN: So, it's like that, that breaks my concentration, So, I really can't...??? like that.

R: ...Ah, what's the teacher's name? (*Noise*). What's the teacher's name?

EVAN: Ah, Ms. (*name of teacher*).

R: And, she shows favoritism like who does she favor?

EVAN: It seems like...alright, there's a group of students in the class in her class, in the front of the room. They are good students you...

R: Ummhuh.

EVAN: ...know. They are good people. Not saying they're bad but she'll act different towards them and towards me she'll act a certain way.

R: Ok, why is it that she does that? What do you think?

EVAN: I don't know. Maybe she thinks I...like, I like, I come in class I do the work, aaammm but they understand it like better than I do. So, I guess she, she aaammm takes consideration into that you know.

+++++++++++++

R: Ok, so you said some of the teachers just don't teach. What do they do?

BARRY: I mean they put work on the board but they don't explain it very well.

R: Ok, they just put work, come in.. .and then...

BARRY: We just copy it down, stuff like that.

...

[Later in the interview]

R: Who's the worst?

BARRY: Mr. (*name of teacher*) by far.

B: What does he teach?

BARRY: Chemistry.

B: And what's so horrible?

BARRY: He doesn't know how to teach it very well. He knows the work, but he just doesn't know how to explain it to students.

B: Ok, so what does he do?

BARRY: Basically he just makes you write, he just makes you write on notes on, from off the board, copy 'em.

R: Ummm..

BARRY: He doesn't explain it at all.

R: Umm...

BARRY: And then he gives you a test on it. And like, hardly nobody in the whole class knows the work. Only like two people pass the whole test.

R: ...???He asks the stuff that's on the board or what?

BARRY: Yeah he asks us the stuff that's on the board.

R: Ok.

BARRY: But if you, you copy it and you go home and study it, you still don't understand it.

R: Ummm. So, that makes the test a problem?

BARRY: Yes.

+++++++++++++++++++++

R: Ahhh, which are the teachers that you don't like?

ROSS: I like everybody but you just ask me for the best.

R: Ummhuh, but now who are the ones you don't like?

ROSS: I like all my teachers.

7. Ineffective teachers were poor instructors. A striking finding from the above interview data and classroom observations is that being a caring teacher in itself was not enough for the students. Amicable or not (as long as the person was basically respectful), teachers had to be able to teach. If the person also cared and evidenced realness, then students were all the more satisfied. Indeed, amongst the truly at-risk there were many who actually wanted to learn something despite their occasional disruptive behavior.

Letting Teachers Know How Little We Value Them

At the comprehensive high school, the teachers' lounge was a tiny dingy room with mismatched, torn furniture that looked like a shelter's reject items. The teacher's cafeteria while very neat and clean was somewhat bare - (nothing on the walls) except for a payphone. It was in the school's basement down around the corner from the student cafeteria. The cafeteria payphone was popular as few teachers had direct access to a telephone otherwise. Cell phones were also rare. I never saw one on campus. Besides the cafeteria and the lounge each department had a dinette-sized table for all of its teachers in lieu of offices. Thus, privacy was extremely scarce for the teachers. For those who took on extra roles such as advisers or program coordinators there were offices available - but these were hardly private - often shared by two to four persons. Overcrowded as this school was, it was clear that the administration did not hold its teachers in the highest esteem.

Additionally, at the comprehensive school, teachers complained that the principal:

- talked down to them as if they were children.
- did not support their disciplinarian efforts
- had their assistant principals harass them over giving students deserved failing grades
- supported only those teachers who were a part of an administrative inner circle (this extra support included financial perks)
- was not doing enough to secure adequate resources for academic needs
- was unknown to most of the students (there daily, but rarely leaving the principal's office).

As an example of possible administrative rifts, one department assistant principal told me that he would not speak with me without an appointment. Then, almost two weeks passed before I would be seen. He inquired about who had granted me access to the school - then promptly told me that he would not permit me to do the study with his teachers. This was in spite of teacher enthusiasm to participate. He seemed bent on being oppositionally defiant to anything the principal had endorsed (the present research project included). His teachers, apparently unaware of the true differences between their assistant principal and the principal seemed sincerely surprised by his response to my proposed study.

While rejection can be hard, I had decided not to take any such things personally. Indeed, as I went about my research and passed him on occasion there was civility with vague gestures of "hello." Later, I learnt a bit more about this particular assistant principal from a teacher outside of his department. According to the teacher, assistant principals were expected to lean on their teachers to pass as many students as possible, by rendering the students repeated opportunities to make up work - whether the students attended classes or not. However, there were at least two renegade departments and this particular department was one of them. Hence, a possible reason for the earlier hostility and desired secrecy.

The alternative school was also short on space. There the teachers' lounge was also the faculty kitchen and an extra supply room. However, the room was very neat, always brightly lit and thus, it had a very homely feel. The teachers' had a sense of possession and care about the premises and they fostered this in the students as well. The teachers had a tidy kitchen in which to cook their meals. They also cleaned up meticulously on a daily basis with the assistance of students.

At the alternative school the administration had made a concerted effort to maintain a family atmosphere at the school - thus cultivating attachments and involvement. Bonding students and teachers to the institution and to each other was exactly the point. From the bonding, respect, caring, order and learning emerged. These were the very things for which the comprehensive school-teachers longed.

Nonetheless, at both schools more than a half of the teachers interviewed complained about not having ready access to their principals. Their perception was that the principals accepted the words of students over their words. They resented that.

Another element important for teacher satisfaction and effectiveness is having space - one's own space. At the alternative school, the teachers' classrooms served as such a space. Each teacher had a designated classroom which they adorned to their liking. Into these rooms students would come and go for classes. Nevertheless, free periods were built into the day for the teachers. Each room had a telephone, though its use was restricted. At the comprehensive school most teachers had no individual offices. So how might they spend that extra time bonding with at-risk students?

American society indicates value by how much it pays people. It is common knowledge that most public school city teachers make $30,000 - $40,000 per annum. In New York City's high cost of living this is "little." Not hollowed in the wider society, many teachers feel unappreciated. They promptly take second jobs or responsibilities to make up the lack in prestige and fiscal power. Thus, these teachers have little time to linger and to get to know their students. Regardless, it is worth remembering that - happy and productive teachers mean happy and productive students.

The Principals

Principals play many roles. One of their most important seems to be that of guardian of "the numbers" for indeed, it is by "the numbers" that funding is secured. Unfortunately, many principals tout proud graduation figures, but have little to say about what their students know when they graduate or where they go. It is also common to omit from "the numbers" those who began the journey of "high school," but who did not complete it.

The literature indicates that a school's success largely depends on the principal and what he or she does. The present study strongly supports this premise. Both principals in this study were minorities - the same gender and about the same age. However, they ran their respective schools very differently. While both were physically distant from most of their staff - at the comprehensive school this was by the principal's design. Physically in the school building, this principal elected to stay in the principal's office virtually every day, all day. After almost two semesters at this school, I saw this person once and that was by appointment in the office. This principal did not walk the halls nor interact regularly with students, nor staff. Instead, most school activities were handled directly by the assistant principals.

At the alternative school the principal's distance from staff and students was beyond the principal's control as campus sites were in different locations. Despite the distance, this principal was well-known to both students and teachers. Nevertheless, while accessible, this principal made it clear that site directors could act on the principal's behalf and with substantial independence. Given the satellite spread of the alternative school, this principal delegated much of the daily operations to site coordinators. But at the primary alternative school site for this study the teachers described their site coordinator as a sort of out-of-touch "middle manager." The heart of the problem however, seemed to have been one of basic philosophical differences on how the students were to be treated and taught. Nonetheless, at both schools the teachers believed that their principal should be a highly visible force - regularly walking the halls. In both cases teachers described this absence of "their leader" as being without adequate support and thus, isolated to either "sink or swim." This feeling was much greater at the comprehensive school where most teachers believed that their input, or suggestions about the school were totally unwelcome. The alternative school teachers were more empowered. Their input was even solicited each day at the after-school wrap-up meeting amongst faculty, staff and administration. Thus, their frustration seemed more rooted in the fact that their ideas were often not even heard much less adopted. However, the administration had a certain program philosophy and methodology to which they wanted to stick as closely as possible.

In a few of the departments at the comprehensive school, the dissatisfaction was much less than elsewhere as staffers seemed pleased with the under-leadership from their department's assistant principal. These were the departments where the under-leadership acted as advocates for their teachers. This worked where that assistant principal was sufficiently close to the principal to secure office space or other perks for the department.

At both schools the principals sometimes spoke to the teachers as if they were unruly children. At the comprehensive school the teachers complained about this bitterly. The alternative school teachers did not complain about this, but I observed this firsthand. It was prior to the beginning of the fall 1999 semester during teacher orientation. The principal reprimanded the teachers for their tardiness claiming to be aware when it happened even though the principal was not on site to witness it directly. The principal further noted that they were expected to be in place at a certain time - not parking or running into the school building at that hour. The principal's scolding tone about the matter – suggests perhaps that the issue had come up before but had gone unheeded.

The Counselors

It is unclear how effective the counseling at the comprehensive school was. However, what was clear was that they were severely understaffed (over a hundred students per counselor). This being the case there were teachers who had volunteered to assist with counseling students. At the alternative school the counselors were trained at the masters (social worker) and doctoral (psychologist) levels. There were two such therapists in addition to the guidance counselor. Counselors had a manageable caseload of approximately 30 regular school attendees at about two school sites. The consensus at the alternative school was that the counselors did an excellent job and were indeed effective. The sole complaint from teachers was that they met with students during class time. Of course, for counseling to have a sustained positive impact, family members and other school personnel must support the counseling effort. This did not seem to be happening at the comprehensive school, but it was at the alternative school as parents, counselors and teachers communicated with each other.

Teacher Relations Amongst Themselves: The Comprehensive Versus the Alternative School Settings

At the comprehensive school the teachers were predominantly females and over 80 percent white. The assistant principals were also predominantly white. The teachers socialized largely within their own departments. Nonetheless, in the less effective departments, even within departmental socialization was weak. Therein, was an air of mistrust of colleagues and a dissatisfaction with leadership. Apparently, the assistant principal for each department had a lot to do with determining the departmental atmosphere via how much they supported their teachers. Some of the teachers seemed too busy to socialize and others seemed like anything but "people persons" wearing extremely cold demeanors. Overall, the teachers did not appear terribly interested in socializing with other departments nor other schools. A satellite teacher improvement conference during fall 1999 drew only three teachers. For the most part cross-departmental mixing occurred in the cafeteria. Significantly, a few of the teachers who were more involved in their profession spoke of having teaching friends at other schools. Not surprisingly, the more effective comprehensive schoolteachers were the ones who made it a point to socialize with the more successful teachers in other departments.

The literature indicates that in small schools there is more amicability and teacher collegiality. This was true of the alternative school. The teachers were as diverse (age, ethnicity and gender) as a group of teachers could be. The site coordinators were white males. As one site coordinator put it, the teachers had to be bonded to each other because they were all that each other had (only seven teachers on site). In the mornings the teachers all sat in the kitchen over breakfast or coffee engaging in lively discussions about a wide range of topics such as the latest news, politics, sports, biology, religion, philosophy, health, their own lives (such as their past, marriage, children or finances) various students, dissatisfaction with various administrative doings and their ideas on improving things. The discussions were always spirited and engrossing. These teachers were interesting characters who had lived interesting lives. They took pride in their work and thus, most wanted to be the best at their jobs.

Teachers and Parental Involvement

According to Grolnick and colleagues (1997) parental involvement is multidimensional involving "behavior, cognitive-intellectual and personal" relations. "Behaviors" would include attending parent-teacher conferences and meetings, assisting children with homework and inquiring about school. Cognitive-intellectual involvement would include going to the library with the student, and discussing current events with them. Personal involvement includes being aware of the happenings at school. Factors affecting involvement levels include: i) the parent-child relationship; ii) thoughts patterns that limit or foster parent involvement; iii) the parents' sense of personal efficacy to help the children with academics, and iv) the child's traits (for example, if the child's behavior is particularly difficult parents may be less involved.

Parent involvement affects school success (Grolnick et al., 1997). Students do better when their parents are able to advocate and otherwise form alliances with teachers on their behalf. For example, if there is one outstanding fourth grade math teacher - Ms. Smith to whom students are assigned "randomly" an active parent in school matters may be able to get his or her child into Ms Smith's class somehow. Low-income, less educated, single parents are less involved than their higher income, more educated married counterparts (Grolnick et al., 1997 discussing Hoover-Dempsey et al., 1987; Lareau 1989; Epstein 1990). Thus, the former would be less informed about the subtle unwritten rules of school advocacy on behalf of their child. Parental involvement measures include help with homework (Walberg 1984) and "attendance at school events," (Stevenson & Baker 1987). Herein, parent involvement was measured by the questions indicated below. Parents were also observed as they visited and interacted with teachers.

Grolnick et al., (1997) found that stress affected parental involvement especially in the case of mothers with sons. Overall, mothers seemed to view their sons as more independent than girls and were thus less involved. Teacher traits also affected this dynamic. For example, if the teacher was such that female students had a stronger relationship with him or her, then, that student is more likely to communicate school happenings to their parents than might boys with a weaker student-teacher relationship (Grolnick et al., 1997). Nevertheless, all of the non-delinquents indicated that their parents frequently inquired about how they were doing in school.

However, this did not mean that parents got these facts. As one student Ross stated - his parents only knew what he told them. In the case of Bobby, he pretended to be his mother one day on the telephone when a teacher called the home about him.

Table 12: Parents and their Children's Schooling

DELINQ.	Education	Lowest grade	Help with Home	Know how doing	Attend teacher	Would watch you
	Press	Acceptable	Work if asked	In school	Meetings	In Sports, etc.
Russell	YES	75	Yes	Of course	Sometimes	
Roger	YES	65	Yeah	Agree	Sometimes	
Vinny	YES	65		Strongly Agree	When brother can make ie	
Steven	NO	A PASS		Agree	-	
Malcolm	YES	65		Strongly Agree	Yes	
Lunch	YES	65	Yes – I wouldn't	Agree	Yes	No time to do so
Trevor	YES	65		Agree – daily	Always	
Peter	YES	DEFENDS		Strongly Agree	No – she works	
Player	YES	75	Yes	Agree-assigns wk.	Never – works until 6:30 p.m.	
Jaoquan	N- REALLY	70 to 75		Strongly Agree	No – she works	
Roderick	YES	70		Agree	Yes	
Marty	YES	75	If I ask	Agree	"When it's necessary"	
Jerome	YES	NONE	Yes	Strongly Agree	Once in awhile – works until 7 or 8 p.m.	
Tyrone	YES	NONE	Yes – I wouldn't	Strongly Agree	Sister comes instead of grandmother	
Roshaud	NO	NONE	Yeah	Agree	No – lots to do, plus it's too far from Bk	
Mutt	?	65		-	-	
NON-DELQ.						
Bugsy	YES – some			S. Agree (often checks)	No-works nights, but calls counselor	No too busy
Mike	NO		Yes – if around	S. Agree	Been to two	He does
Anthony				Agree	Can't health problems, calls counselor	Can't – health
Bobby	YES			Agree	If called to come	Yeah
Evan	YES			S. Agree	No, no time	Yes
Barry	YES		Helps w/ H.W.	Agree	Yes	-
Ross	YES		Yes – if asked	Agree	Yeah	Yeah
Devn	YES	65	Mother & Bro. Do	S. Agree	When called in.	?

Table 13 Parent-Child Communication

DELINQ.	Discuss Problems at School	Discuss Plans for the Future
Russell	If there is one	Once in awhile
Roger	No	Sometimes
Vinny	Yes-first one I call (his bro.)	Yes – both thinking college
Steven	Never	Grandmother will say "No, you can't do that"
Malcolm	When there's one	No
Lunch	Don't have problems now	Yes – once or twice / week
Trevor	Yes – but don't like to	No
Peter	Yes	Yes
Player	Sometimes	Yes
Jaoquan	No a lot	Not a lot (bro. Says little of college life)
Roderick	No	Sometimes
Marty	When there is one	Yeah
Jerome	Everyday	Not much
Tyrone	Yeah	Yes, but
Roshaud	No	?
Mutt	-	-
NON-Delinq.		
Bugsy	If ther were – mother & bro.	Once in awhile
Mike	Nom, not often	-
Anthony	Yes	Yes – often
Bobby	-	Almost daily my father asks
Evan	Once in awhile	-
Barry	A lot	Yeah – more often than once in awhile
Ross	Not all – teachers tell them	Hardly
Devon	Would, if there was one	Not often

Additionally, many of the comprehensive schoolteachers complained that students were responsible for hand delivering their report cards. They suspected that many of these reports never got to the parents and some expressed being at a loss about why these parents sometimes let many months go by without inquiring about a missing report card. Their most common conclusion was that "these people" simply did not care. Nonetheless, there were several indicators that many of these working class parents cared, but were perhaps intimated by the middle class aura of the teachers. They simply lacked the social capital necessary for effectively monitoring their students' academic activities.

Note, at the alternative school where parent contact was required - very busy parents were involved - albeit, merely by phone at times given their work schedules. The difference between the two schools was that the latter exerted the extra effort to secure and maintain parent-contact. They also taught the parents what to do and how to do it in terms of involvement. This can be done, if school personnel care enough to do it. It requires teacher flexibility.

It appeared that many of the less effective teachers believed that parents should come to them. Reaching out to parents beyond sending a letter was beyond their call of duty. Fact is that many minority communities expect that personal interest from teachers. Thus, at the comprehensive school the Jewish female teacher, and a few other white colleagues, plus some of the black and latino teachers were far more effective with their students after having established an alliance with parents.

On The Receiving End: The Students From Two New York City Public High Schools In The Bronx

At the comprehensive high school, many African-American males were reluctant to participate in the study. This reflected a passivity not uncommon in comprehensive schools. According to the environmental psychology literature, in such large schools, extracurriculars are so limited that students learn to be passive watchers, not active participants – a trait they may well take with them throughout life. Indeed, many of the students noted that they were interested in basketball and football. However, this was available almost exclusively to seniors who made the teams. In this regard, small schools are to be preferred. Therein, extra-curricular opportunities are often more available and engaging. The few students therein learn to "wear many hats," in the name of uplifting student life. This in turn increases the students' bond to a conventional institution (the school). With such a bond the likelihood of offending decreases.

Nevertheless, the comprehensive school in this study had extracurricular activities with slots available for students. However, these activities were in fine arts and tennis - areas in which many African-American males had no interest being yet unaware of any need for cultural capital of this sort. The dominant interests were basketball and football. Thus, only two of the subjects were actively involved in extracurriculars. These students had made their school teams in these sports. And no, the students were not permitted to organize their own activities at the school, after classes. Thus, after school, a barrage of school security officers (sometimes assisted by police personnel) would promptly shoo the students from the school grounds and surrounding areas. There was a clear concern that if the students were left unsupervised "incidents" might occur drawing unwelcome publicity. Plus, many of the teachers had a second job and thus, would scurry off promptly at the end of the day. So what did the students do? Many had been instructed by their parents to head straight home and stay there. Others congregated in various places like neighborhood basketball courts, parks, video arcades, or MacDonalds for amusement themselves. A few went to work.

The problem here is a failure on the school's part to provide activities and encourage student participation thus fostering school attachment, involvement and achievement. There is also a failure on society's part to adequately regard and provide for its teachers, thus, encouraging many of them to hold second jobs. Like others in an America which worship the symbols of wealth, these teachers cap at approximately $70,000 per annum. Many of the teachers at this, one of the more failing schools are not near this maximum. Thus, like the students they teach in New York City (a place where the images of wealth abound), teachers want more. Thus, on both sides - the bonding of the students and the bonding of the teachers to the school were weak.

So, how did I get students to participate? I targeted some of the more popular or respected students. I thought that if they volunteered, others might follow. It worked. Thereafter, others approached me who were especially interested in securing some cash.

The alternative school students were on at least a one-year Board of Education Superintendent suspension for committing a delinquent act at, or near a public school. For the most part these were for weapons possession or assaults on teachers, staff, or students. Their time out of regular school had a minimum, but no maximum. Students were expected to earn a total of 150 behavior points during their stay at the alternative school in order to return to a regular school setting.

Table 14: School Risks and Protection

DELINQ.	EXTERNAL PROTECTIVE FACTORS		BEST	FRIENDS		
	Mother's Education	Religion	Family Pride	Household (Dis)Harmony	Coping Skills	Approval Expressed
Russell	High School	Used to – Kingdom Hall	YES	Once in awhile	-	Mother – basketball
Roger	High School	Every week (CLC)	YES	Once/week	Can't do anything, against Mom	Parents, friends – test, classes, basketball
Vinny	Bro. some college	No	YES	Never – similar		Brother – classes, karate
Steven	9 or 10th grade	Only crusades	YES	Daily stress	Argue	Mother – report card
Malcolm	Forgot	Used to – Baptist	?	Twice/ month	Go to room, play music	Mother – school, etc.
Lunch	2 yrs. College	Used to – Kingdom Hall	YES	Not much	Walk away	Coach – football
Trevor	High School	Yes – at least weekly	YES	On weekends	Walk away or we sit and talk	Mother, teachers – grades
Peter	Some college	Used to – Baptist	YES	Yes+w/litt.sis.	We still talk	Parents, teachers – school
Player	Some college	Daily – Catholic	YES	Yes w/ sibling	Keep to myself	-
Jaoquan	Don't know	Once in awhile – Baptist	YES	Once in awhile	Keep mouth shut	Mother – grades, bkball., staying off streets
Roderick	Finishing college	Twice per month	YES	Once in awhile	Go to room, or sit and talk	? – report card
Marty	In college	Once in awhile	YES	Once in awhile	-	Parents – achieving
Jerome	High School	Twice per week + Lutheran	Of course	Once in awhile	Argue with everything she says	Mother, grandmother – report card
Tyrone	Can't recall	Every Sunday – Baptist	M. Definitely	We get along	-	-
Roshaud	?	Used to	YES	1 in blue moon	Leave the house	No
Mutt	Two years college	Once in awhile – Baptist	?	-	-	Parents, 4th grade teacher

Bugsy	High School	Every Sat; mother too		-	-	Mother – attending plays and church
Mike	Don't know	Used to – now working		Often, when in	We still talk and I stay by myself	Parents and gran.- behavior & school
Anthony	Junior yr. high sch.	No, and rarely in the past		Once in awhile	Stop talking	Mother and grandmother
Bobby	High School	Almost weekly – Baptist		Never	Not talk	Parents and teachers for grades and pass
Evan	Don't recall	No – can't say it's important		Hardly	We still talk	Going to school
Barry	Some college	Not in 3 or 4 years		Less than wkly	We still talk	
Ross	College graduate	No-but it's important		Hardly	I throw stuff	Boss & parents for job performance
Devon		Twice/month – Baptist		Not often	I always talk to them	

Students earned points by merely doing what they were supposed to do, all day. Students lost points or rather failed to earn any when they misbehaved. Apparently, a single report of non-cooperation could make this happen. For outright rebellion, the student could be returned to juvenile court and from there, the next stop would be - Spafford Juvenile Detention.

The alternative school was examined in two locations. Although students were interviewed at both of the sites, the observations and interviews were done largely at one location. At both of the alternative school sites about 50 students were on roll. However, between 33 to 37 students attended each site on a regular basis. Yet, how ironic it is for the truly at-risk students of New York City. It takes committing an offense to get a first rate education.

Of course, there are a few public schools which offer the "regular" student an excellent education. However accessing this illustrates a subtle difference between the "truly at-risk" and the "at-risk" student. The "truly at-risk" are those who lack the guidance of parents, guardians or even teachers who might inform them or otherwise lead them to the few public schools in the city offering a quality education. Thus, what separates the "at-risk" from the "truly at-risk" is that often the former, though impoverished, has some information (social capital) to help move themselves into mainstream society if given the chance. On the other hand, the truly at-risk simply have no clue about how to be upwardly mobile - legitimately.

Para-Professionals

At the comprehensive school para-professionals ("paras") rendered no instruction, but merely custodial maintenance when the regular teachers were out. Usually, the regular teacher would leave an assignment and the paras would administer it. Some were distant in this role, others fondly engaged in small talk with the students. The paras were more likely to come from the same living conditions as their students. This, facilitated the small talk.

At the alternative school paras and other teacher assistants were extremely active and attentive. They prepared meals, drove the school bus; assisted the teachers with lab activities; assisted security when it was necessary to re move students from specific areas; visited students' homes and counseled with parents about student behaviors.

After all, they were able to observe students both on and off campus. Thus, unlike the paras at the comprehensive school who were relegated to providing custodial maintenance, at the alternative school paras were a very active extension of both teachers and counselors.

School Security Personnel

At the comprehensive high school, the security guards were aloof enforcers. There were a few exceptions - largely Hispanic officers who at times would chit-chat with some of the Hispanic students. Overall, the students were not particularly fond of them. They considered the guards lax at their jobs (for example, they said the guards were inattentive at the security scanning station), but too particular about what the students deemed minor matters - like dress code violations. These guards were also less meticulous in maintaining their sign-in procedures than the guards at the alternative school. Granted, the latter had more at stake. At both schools visitors had to show identification and sign-in before entering the premises. After awhile at the comprehensive school this procedure was suspended for me, but not so at the alternative school.

At the alternative high school, "security" meant two New York City police officers (a Hispanic male and a black female). On a few occasions various unfamiliar officers would cover for one of these. Nevertheless, the two regular officers behaved largely like stern but affectionate older siblings towards the students. They were meticulous in performing their duties and maintained this throughout the semester. They were never observed losing their tempers. The Hispanic male guard would at times engage in banter akin to a crude case of "the dozens" with the juveniles. The female guard was popular for her knowledge of the latest and hottest electronic toys on the market. Both guards were a part of the familial atmosphere of the school. Their caring nature was evident. They cared enough, not to bend the rules and thus, were a source of consistent discipline for the students. One of the teachers mentioned that initially, the Hispanic guard had been somewhat aloof, but he had come around.

At both schools the guards were posted at key points, largely building entrances and they patrolled the halls between classes. So, should there even have been police officers in the schools? It depends. The alternative school was an example of police presence that seemed to work because the guards were personable. While consistent in enforcing the rules and the law, the officers were firm, but "cool" relations.

General Security Procedures

At the comprehensive school, students had to walk through metal detectors before entering the building. However, students mentioned that the security guards often paid little attention when the metal detector went off. Also, there were many opportunities during the day when students went outside of the building and then re-entered unchecked (for example, for physical education and when the fire alarm went off - which it did often during the spring of 1999). At the alternative school security was more strictly enforced. Thus, students were consistently scanned before entering their school building.

At both schools classroom doors were also to be locked during classes. Some teachers strictly kept the doors locked, others were more lax about doing so. While the comprehensive schoolteachers locked the doors to keep students in, the alternative school teachers locked the rooms to keep students out. In the former case students sometimes wanted to flee the tedious class setting; in the latter case students frequently attempted to enter other classrooms to playfully pick on the students and / or teachers.

Additionally, the restrooms at the alternative school were supposed to have been locked at all times. Nonetheless, at one of the alternative school sites, the annoyance of securing the key led some people to deliberately leave the door unlocked on occasion. Indeed, at least in the case of the female restrooms, the place was used as a private meeting space by female students. Yet, just like a family, the space was common in that staff, students and teachers all used the same restrooms. At the comprehensive school the restrooms for teachers and students were different. Teacher restrooms were kept locked, but student restrooms were unsecured.

Another part of bonding students to their schools was the provision of student lockers at the alternative school. Such provisions also reduced the likelihood of a loss of personal belongings. The comprehensive school did not provide personal locker space.

Lockers existed, but for the most part teachers used them to store books and other class materials. For whatever reasons - it seemed the teachers had decided that the students would not need their textbooks at home (exception being the ragged paperbacks used in the English literature classes).

At the comprehensive school, teachers took turns in joining security guards as they monitored the cafeteria during the different lunch periods. Teachers also shared in the vigilance of hall activities during classes. At the alternative school, the security personnel also patrolled the halls during classes. They promptly responded to the calls of teachers to student disturbances. If the student calmed down quickly without incident the student was often allowed to remain in the classroom but if they persisted in being disagreeable, security removed them. More often however, to avoid loosing points, students would calm down.

Indiscipline is a common precursor to violence and vandalism (Toby 1995). At the comprehensive school, teachers felt largely unsupported by the administration in their efforts to create an orderly school setting. The teachers stated that their instructions were to leave disciplinary issues to the security officers. With this the teachers intensely disagreed. To a large extent they perceived that the message to the students was that students could do whatever they pleased when guards were out of sight. Between 1996 and 1999 this situation improved slightly. The novel City Chancellor Rudy Crew had called for greater discipline in the schools - such as the proper address of school staff, and a banishment of walkmans and hats in schools. Notably, the attire of female students improved significantly between 1996 to 1999 (largely, there were longer skirts being worn).

The discipline was sharper and more consistent at the alternative school. The administration, staff, teachers and security maintained a uniform stance on discipline. Minor offenses like chewing gum in class were often allowed to pass, but rarely anything else. No hats, meant no hats. Everything in a room would stop until that one offending student complied or was removed. A significant example of this unity at the alternative school occurred the day a Hispanic female came to school wearing a revealing tube top. Various teachers approached her reminding her of the school rules and letting her know that she would not be allowed to attend class in her attire. One female teacher even found the student a t-shirt with which to cover herself. Initially, the girl vehemently refused to change but a unified staff that would not budge on the issue was no match for her. She eventually assented. Of course, these teachers had administrative backing in such disciplinary steps.

The incident may have also had a general deterrent effect because the showdown happened while other students were about (though it began as a private matter, the student's resistance drew attention). It was clear that these teachers had acted not only to maintain order but because they cared about the student's welfare.

Beyond administrative support it takes caring to take a stance for order. In the comprehensive school, the effective teachers were persistent in their efforts to enforce the few rules that they had been called upon to enforce - like, no hats in the classroom. Other teachers, those who perceived themselves to be helpless seemed all too willing to relinquish their role of disciplinarian for their state of helplessness. This was as if they had decided "that is the way 'those people' behave anyway - so why jeopardize me and mine?"

In short, the contexts from which students, teachers, and school school-personnel come determines the quality of the interactions therein. In this, money matters - for with more funds better quality teachers may be hired, or the present ones re-trained, or otherwise paid enough to be more available and involved with their students.

CHAPTER 6

THE STUDENT-TEACHER INTERACTIONS

Field Notes: A Typical School Day: Comprehensive High

A typical school day for most students at the comprehensive school began at approximately 8:24 a.m. which was the third period of the day. The first period was at 6:59 a.m., with few students present and apparently, little expected to happen at that hour. The final period began at 1:57 p.m., ending 40 minutes later. For the most part students would arrive at about 8:30 a.m. They would then go through a security scanner (with further searches as necessary). Girls with clothing that was too revealing were sent to change into either clothing available at the school or back at their homes. More cunning and covert females waited until after clearing security check-in to change into their revealing attire. Otherwise, students claimed that when they arrived at school after third period was in progress they were instructed to stay in the assembly hall instead of interrupting their classes. Thus, many students did poorly in their first class of the day (third period). During this third period, classes would be interrupted anyway with school announcements over an intercom speaker in each classroom (often about extra-curricular activities). Also during this first session a staff member would go to various classes checking the day's attendance.

Each class was approximately 40 minutes long. Each class occurred on weekdays at the same time most days (exception - staff meeting days and examination weeks). At different times during the day (depending on class schedules) students had a period free for lunch. Students were not expected to roam the halls during classes. If not in a class, students were expected to be in a designated area, for example, in counseling, in their schoolhouse room, in the lunchroom area or in the library. Any other movements required a pass from faculty or staff. Between classes, students had three minutes to transition. Each student took about seven subjects. At the end of the day (minus fire alarms or bomb threats requiring early evacuation), most students were promptly ushered from the premises by security as few stayed behind for extra-curricular activities.

A Typical School Day: Alternative High

At the primary alternative school site under examination a typical school day began at about 8:00 a.m. with teachers and para-professionals preparing breakfast for themselves and the students while security guards prepared to scan in students. Students were not permitted into the building until 8:30 a.m (even on the bitterest of winter mornings). One-by-one students and their bags were scanned with a hand held scanner. Any contraband (example, hand-held video games) was seized. For the most part the school bus, which picked up students as far away as Brooklyn was late almost every morning (often arriving close to 9:00 a.m.). The first class of the day began at 8:54 a.m. However, the school bus students could trickle into class as late as 9:30 a.m. after staffers served them a late breakfast. During the regular breakfast time the teachers took turns sitting with the students at the breakfast table. They were also joined by at least one para-professional.

For the most part all of the classes were double periods (approximately 124 minutes). For most of the juveniles interviewed for this study, the day began with English, then Biology, followed by (Gym on Monday Wednesdays and Thursdays) Computers, Lunch, Mathematics, Health (which looked a lot like a second Gym class) and Global Studies. Classes ended at 3:12 p.m. at which time the site coordinator met with all of the teachers and staff to discuss briefly the day's happenings (largely any significant changes in student behavior). The day ended with the close of this teacher and staff meeting by 3:30 p.m. except on Wednesdays when parent-teacher conferences were held at about 7: 00 p.m.

The Comprehensive School Experience

Many African-American males in comprehensive schools are disengaged from the pursuit of academic excellence. Possible explanations for this include a perception that school can be very dull compared to life outside of it - a life involving the responsibilities of care-taking, the joys of having income from employment, et cetera. Thus, school personnel need to concern themselves with the family life of students (Berliner 1989). Children exposed to responsibility, independence, and major decision-making outside of school will be at odds with school operations where a very subdued conformity is expected (Berliner 1989).

Another explanation for the disengagement places the responsibility on culture. Anthropology teaches that cultures differ in their value orientation for example, Anglos emphasize conquering nature; Hispanics are fatalistic (frequently the dialogue is a lamenting of hardships); Native Americans emphasize living in harmony with nature; Asians emphasize hierarchy. Indeed, many minorities tend to be hierarchical in orientation and thus rarely assert individual rights over yielding to the collective rights of the group (Gutierrez 1997). Hence, this contributes to the reluctance of African-American students to ask questions in large comprehensive classrooms. Yet, might the school itself be communicating to African-American males in particular that they are unwelcome?

The Alternative Experience

The alternative school offered seven subjects intensively to help their students "catch-up." This was exactly what most of the students needed and wanted. Most of the class sessions were double periods (approximately 124 minutes). The classes were Mathematics, English, Biology, Global Studies, Computers, Gym and Health. A full class had about 12 students. With such a small class and a double period teachers could offer individual assistance effectively. Nonetheless, what appeared most remarkable in the classroom was the sense that students had that they were all weak academically. Thus, unembarrassed they asked their teachers for help on the most basic academic points. This, was facilitated by the teachers' highly approachable demeanor and sincere interest in each student's progress. As one student put it - the question might be simple, but I bet someone else had the same question. This difference from the comprehensive school setting in help-seeking student behavior was most pronounced.

The data suggest that certain things must be in place first before truly at-risk students perform well. Many of the comprehensive schoolteachers thought that there must be order first. But what the alternative school situation demonstrated was that even before order, there must be relationship. Indeed, there is a naval adage: "rules without relationship leads to rebellion."

After the first series of observations and interviews at the comprehensive school in 1996 questions remained about what might change its situation of dismal academic failure. Despite America's torrid racial past, the largely white teaching staff expressed a sincere interest in the life outcomes of their minority students. However, many of these teachers seemed at a loss about what to do. Based on the success of the alternative school, the comprehensive school was missing a number of things:
- strong principal leadership
- activities to facilitate teacher bonding both to the institution and the students
- activities to facilitate teacher bonding with each other both within and without their departments
- basic resources such as quality books and computers
- air conditioning (which makes it difficult to accomplish much when class is conducted in the dark on 90+ degree Farenheit days)
- administrative support of teachers when they insist on discipline
- comfortable staff space and some privacy during the day (plus other gestures that might communicate to the teachers that they are of value to their employers)
- greater financial compensation for teachers
- incentives for stellar teacher performance
- and, most of all, instruction on effectively utilizing "realness" in relating to students from diverse backgrounds.

Realness

The most significant emic code emerging from the data herein is the importance of teacher "realness" to the academic and behavioral success of these truly at-risk students. When asked about their positive experiences with teachers either in the present or the past, a common word emerged - "real" - the good teachers were "real" the juveniles said. "Real?" I asked them to explain. Prior to hearing about "realness," I had made the following conclusions:

The effective New York City public school teacher was sincerely caring. Yet, the researcher had observed in the field that caring alone, although important, was not enough. There were caring teachers in the comprehensive school who appeared academically incompetent to teach. Those teachers lacked the students' respect. Teachers who could teach the academic material, but evidenced little personal interest in their students also lacked the students' respect. Thus, to be truly effective a teacher needed to be both competent in passing along academic information and caring. Hence, a stern remark or harsh look from a caring and competent teacher passed without even momentary malice by the student because somehow the student seemed to understand that such came from a place of caring and a sincere desire to see students accomplish. More often than not these two traits came from the minority teachers, but it was not exclusive to them. Signs of caring and competence fell across age, ethnic and gender lines.

Then emerged this word from the lips of the juveniles themselves. The good teachers are "real" they said. From their descriptions of "real" - meshed with the researcher's observations of commonalities amongst the "real" teachers, here is what "realness" entails:

RODERICK: They talk to me. They just be **real**. They don't hide nothing. They just tell it how it is.

R: Ok, ah, give me an example, one example of something that they would talk about that you would say makes them real?

RODERICK: They would tell me like how it was when they was growing and try to make me... that we been living easier than when they was growing up. Try to influence me to do the right things.

- **"real" teachers imparted social capital to their students.** Often students appeared fascinated when teachers shared pieces of information about life in general, but especially about upward mobility, such as how to make it through college. For example one alternative school teacher who was also in graduate school showed a student a copy of his (the teacher's) graded term paper that had been returned to him the night before. The student had been complaining about having to re-write an essay. "I have to do it too" - was the teacher's message. The student appeared struck that the teacher would share something so personal, but smirked with glee at all the red ink on the document. Now, in a family with no college graduates - if not a teacher, who would have shown this student a glimpse of the possibilities ahead?

- **"real" teachers did not engage in silencing.** Michelle Fine (1991) and others in psychology have written about the occurrence of silencing in public schools. Silencing involves avoiding discussions of certain specific topics related to the lives of people who are different (often racially and/or socio-economically) from the "other." Without this exchange of information a meaningful relationship between student and teacher fails to develop. Such a relationship may not be important for every student in order for them to learn, but to the truly-at-risk student who is emerging from a difficult social context it is important. Many of these marginalized and thus, truly at-risk students lack information about what and how to proceed in mainstream society. Often, they will raise questions in school about these facts of life in an effort to comprehend their position in the larger world. However, in the comprehensive school, such points appeared too sensitive for the "non-real" teachers to address. Thus, they would hastily dismiss issues of difference for the solace of "sticking to the curriculum." "Real" teachers at the very least acknowledged their students lives, experiences and questions as real, even if they did not have time to address the issues raised then and there in any great depth.

- **"real" teachers maintained order in their classrooms.** The delinquent boys considered a young twenty-something white female who was a master at running an orderly and interesting class to be one of their favorite teachers at the alternative school, and thus, she was a champion of realness. In her class there was relationship, thus, no rebellion.

- **"real" teachers would not allow students to disengage.** There were times when students at the alternative school had their heads on the desk. As long as they continued working, they were not hassled about this posture. At the comprehensive school, amidst "non-real" teachers, a student could put his or her head down on the desk (appearing oblivious to the classroom activity) for most of the class period without interruption. Cutting class was also common at the comprehensive school.

- **"real" teachers were sincerely interested in the lives of their students and evidenced some understanding and empathy for their struggles.** Consider the same young white female at the alternative school mentioned earlier. At the beginning of the fall 1999 semester she spoke of certain students as "having it good" and squandering their opportunities. She had been the descendant of poor immigrants whom she claimed had had life much worse than her students - yet, they overcame. Yet, how ignorantly she spoke for by the end of the fall semester, this teacher rescinded her statements. She had gotten to know more about the lives of the students she taught. She realized that indeed the lives of her ancestors those of her students were hardly comparable at all. The former endured poverty and some racism, but the latter also faced street violence, abuse and great instability. One student in particular had been very troubling. He had been born crack-addicted, then, he was bounced about in the foster care system. The teacher was both sorrowful and angry at the avoidable academic and life struggles that the student was facing because of his mother's bad choices. But how many teachers dare take the time to see and to understand their students who are different from them?

Relationships are two-way things. They require that both parties learn something of the other after having taken an interest in the other. The "real" teachers knew something of their students' personal lives and otherwise, they shared pieces of their lives with their students (for example family photographs), and details about how they handled various teenage situations when they were growing up).

- **"real" teachers responded to their students as they might their own children.** This involved insisting on decent attire, behavior and academic effort. On the other hand many of the comprehensive schoolteachers indicated that they would hardly consider ever sending a child of theirs to the comprehensive school.

- **"real" teachers were knowledgeable about popular culture and its effects.** They utilized that knowledge in both building rapport with the students and in making lessons more inviting to the students. Ms. Sweeney was a middle aged white woman; Mr. Vincent was a young

Caribbean immigrant, yet, they took the time to be familiar with pop icons of the day such the Spice Girls and the latter (who claimed that he did not watch much television) took the time to become familiar with the media images that often occupied his students' days.

Significant or not, the alternative school teachers were more likely to have been city residents for more than a couple of years at some point than their comprehensive school counterparts. Nonetheless, it seemed that being "real" was an embodiment of relationship building around an exchange of intimate information that is both interesting and useful to the hearer. The exchange of information flows both ways - student to teacher and teacher to student. At the comprehensive school the weakness involved teachers silencing this exchange of information. For example Ms. Rochon at the alternative school shared pictures of her daughter's wedding with both students and co-workers. Many teachers claimed that the administrative restraints and lack of resources to perform effectively (including time) hindered effective interactions with their students. Possibly true. But, then again, perhaps not.

Peer Effects

Delinquency is more common when with delinquent peers (Gove & Crutchfield 1982). Amongst peers, acceptance is influenced by "age, race, socioeconomic status as well as physical and personality characteristics," (Langlois & Stephan 1981). The individual's social behavior in the midst of peers is determined by the strength of the peer acceptance plus personal temperament and family background, (Dodge 1983; Hartup 1989). Thus, not surprisingly, the delinquents herein had delinquent peers, though they offended independently at times. A half of the non-delinquents also had delinquent peers who were involved in offenses such as attempted murder, drug dealing, and smoking marijuana. A common trait amongst both delinquents and non-delinquents was that friendships were esteemed above and regardless of actions - law-abiding or not.

Noteworthy however, the activity of peers need not affect a student unless the student holds that peer in high regard. Three quarts of the non-delinquents indicated that their closest friend got good grades (often, they defined this as "above passing"), were interested in school and attended classes regularly. A half of them indicated that their friends were serious about going to college (*see Table 6, pg. 70*).

For many of the delinquents the influence of peers was significant. Consider Vinny's comments below:

R: Ahhh, now you said you weren't passing anything at the other school. How come? What was going on?

VINNY: Like, I was too popular. Every time something happened they came and they got me and I was always getting into stuff. I wasn't going to school; stuff like that.

R: Ok, aaammm, so that was at the junior high, you were popular. Ahhh, when did that popularity thing start, were you, weren't you doing the work as much?

VINNY: It started like when I was in 5th grade 'cause when I was in 5th grade - these two 8th graders they tried to jump me.

R: Ummhuh.

VINNY:.....and I, I beat 'em up. I beat 'em up bad and after that everybody just started liking me.

R: Ummhuh.

VINNY: Everybody wanted to be my friend.

R: Ummm ok, aamm, so how do you like high school? So far, overall?

VINNY: I'm enjoying it.

R: Enjoying it, ok. So when you eventually go back to the other school - do you think you're gonna have that popularity problem again or...?

VINNY: Naaw, I'm, I'm hoping that this school will change me in some way though.

R: Ummhuh.

VINNY: So that when I get there, I'll know how to behave myself.

The Student-Teacher Relationship

Students know when teachers are being insincere with them. Regarding the insincerity of some teachers, the delinquent Russell made the following remarks in response to a statement about whites:

> R: Blacks should be suspicious of all white persons who try to be friendly.
>
> RUSSELL: Neutral.
>
> R: Ahhh why do you say that?
>
> RUSSELL: Because aammm some, some white teachers like, or, should I say like, some white people like sometimes like, they know they don't really care. They'll try to act like they care. So, I don't judge 'em all like that, but from what I be seeing...

Russell went on to render an example of one teacher's negativity towards her students which made the school context less appealing to him.

> RUSSELL: .....she had asked aaammm one of the kids, this was a math class, she had asked one of the kids a question that we wasn't even doing, we wasn't even doing that subject; she had asked him the question. We wasn't even up that that? And she know he didn't know it, so she asked him on purpose, 'cause he didn't.
>
> R: What did the student do?
>
> RUSSELL: Like he, he got mad - see it in his face that he got mad.

For Russell and others the lack of caring and interest came across in the way the teachers taught. Yet, despite curriculum limits, some teachers found the time and made the effort to be real. Others simply did not:

> RUSSELL: Is like, now I'm working harder and the teachers they, they, help me more. In my old school they don't help you at all. They just rush on the board. If you don't get it - oh well. Rush through it. Now here, they take their time. Like if I don't understand it, they'll explain it to me more so I understand it better.

In support of the literature, this study indicated that student behavior, teacher unconditional positive regard and home-school discontinuity all factor in to the quality of the student-teacher relationship.

Behavior

When concentration problems make academics challenging a behavioral restlessness often fills the void of progress. Farrington (1989) found "that teacher ratings of male children's concentration problems and restlessness – including difficulty sitting still, the tendency to fidget, and frequent talkativeness – predicted later violence. Indeed, "boys with restlessness and concentration difficulties were five times more likely to be arrested for violence than those without these traits," (Klintenberg et al. 1993). Herein, this was most true of the delinquent Roshaud, son of a crack-addicted mother, with severe attention deficit hyperactivity. He was the juvenile who threw a bottle at his teacher. Such behavior might not be expected to endear the average teacher to Roshaud-type characters.

Boredom (as sets in when schools repeat the same material year after year and the choice of instruction methods display no consciousness of the influence of popular culture) is another factor that students claim leads them into restlessness. These behaviors may manifest in deviant acting out, verbalizations or withdrawal from the context in mind or body (as when students put their heads on the desk and doze off. This was observed in many of the comprehensive classrooms and reported by the delinquents in reference to their comprehensive school experiences before their present alternative school placement.

An important part of the alternative school program was teaching students to think before acting. To this end the main alternative school site had a new gem on its main message board each day. This board was immediately visible when a person stepped into the building. However, after about the first third of the semester the gems ceased. Nonetheless, the adages posted throughout the building remained. These adages focused on thinking. For example: "If you loose your temper, you loose," "be all you can be," "you curse, you loose."

Unconditional Positive Regard

The ingredient for seeing past the negative behaviors of students is a trait called "unconditional positive regard." A teacher with this trait will not take the behaviors of students personally. This teacher will maintain a belief that all students have some positive traits and that all students can learn albeit differently. It is non-condemnatory caring where the object of care ideally feels free to be him or herself without concern about such honesty jeopardizing the relationship (Cohen & Cohen 1999). Such was the atmosphere in the alternative classrooms. It was most necessary and it worked.

Home-School Discontinuity

What hindered the flourishing of unconditional positive regard at the comprehensive school appeared to be a refusal on the part of most teachers to acknowledge that the differences in the students before them were of value. Many of the teachers were so intent on recreating the school environments with which they had been accustomed to the point that they verbally devalued the diversity before them.

The Euro-American culture emphasizes "individualism, materialism, a future time orientation, a single standard for views and behaviors based on the European experience...and an identity and mode of self-expression based primarily on...one's job, social status, and educational achievement," (Brookins 1996 discussing: Myers 1988; Siedman & Rapport 1986). African-American values include "communalistic values, spiritualism, an orientation to time that emphasizes experience over structure, greater acceptance of diversity...self-expression based on maximizing interpersonal harmony with others," (Brookins 1996 discussing: Myers 1988; Nobles 1973). A child coming from this cultural background would be at odds with the teachers' culture. If the student feels marginalized then learning is in jeopardy. Sharing information via meaningful interactions can get both parties away from impending differences. Students often begin educational endeavors willing to talk. Do teachers? Below are descriptions of teachers who have been successful at bridging the differences gap.

Field Notes: Alternative Education - The English Teacher

Mr. Michaels, the alternative school English teacher had been at the school only a few months. His students all agreed that he cared about them a great deal. Thus, they seemed to appreciate his demandingness although they often complained about the work. The students complained about the work periodically. He was a white male, maybe in his late thirties. He was a tall calm man with what one might call a priestly demeanor (humble, quiet and diligent). He was one of the best teachers at the site in the researcher's opinion. His academic expertise and an ability to communicate materials effectively, worked well with his non-judgmental demeanor to elicit effort and progress from his students. From student reports he was not the most interesting, (not that he did not try - on one occasion he did a brief jig before the class) but his caring transcended that. His "realness" largely involved imparting the academic capital (basic reading and writing) necessary for upward social mobility.

The following are the researcher's notes from her first day of observations of Mr. Michaels interactions with his students *(BM refers to a black male student)*:

> The sign on Mr. Michaels classroom door reads: "No food, gum, candy in classroom."

> As a BM enters, he says "what we doing?"

> Another student knocks loudly on the door saying "what the fuck?"

> Mr. Michaels responds "report to work."

Mr. Michaels to BM (L): "You're the workaholic, me I'm just the driver."

When the teacher asks one BM (Malcolm) to read and he refuses the teacher moves on to another who volunteers.

Students read pieces of their work largely voluntarily. Teacher says to BM (L) at one point: "I didn't hear you read one (L)."

BM (L) responds "You gonna start that stupid shit...."

BM (L) to teacher:" Michaels, if you don't take this book you won't see it again."

Teacher responds saying something about "......to babysit for you (L)."

Teacher calls to a student in the hall who is yelling - student responds "my fault."

Note amidst all of this the teacher is in control of the room.The students know their boundaries.

Students instructed to grade their work and make corrections as necessary.

As the class ends Mr. Michaels says "Nice work everyone." He continues:: "I see some good work - so this is very encouraging."

At points (L) quietly asks for help as if mildly embarrassed to ask more overtly, though the room was so tiny, everyone could hear him. The sense that "everyone" else was in the same proverbial boat no doubt facilitated his help-seeking behavior. The knowledge that this was a last stop before Spafford (Juvenile Detention) may have also garner student cooperation.

On the teacher's first day in this class the room became so crowded - the teacher gave up his seat. Nevertheless, some students still had to sit outside the classroom door. There were about fourteen students. In the days to follow this class was moved to a larger classroom.

Mr. Michaels teaches. He is not one of those teachers who simply places work on the board..

(L) to teacher: "Michaels., you ain't no help."

Later (L) continues "Michaels., you're a bad teacher man." Then in a hushed manner he protests to the teacher "this is boring." As he later complains about being tired the teacher responds "I know you're tired - big commute to school."

(L) is a student who is very large for his age, thick, muscular, with corn rowed hair. Yet, even this tough looking guy requests help with rather basic points. As the saying goes, looks can be deceiving and with this adolescent such could easily have been the case. This youth who looks like the large menacing black male of America is actually a young teenager bearing a number of emotional wounds and even physical scars.

When students ask to be excused, they are.

As the students work Mr. Michaels moves about the room. Like most of his colleagues he wears semi-formal attire. However, the students dress casually.

Field Notes: Alternative Education - The Second Class of the Day: Biology
(The following are the researcher's notes from her first day observing this class)

The teacher, Mr. Vincent was a tall slender black male in his late 20s. He was casually attired in jogging pants and a long sleeved casual shirt (clothing similar to that worn by his students). His demeanor and dress made him very approachable to his students. He was from the Caribbean - but had grown up in New York City project housing. He knew his subject matter very well and managed to break it down for the students by indicating with several examples how the textbook materials related to everyday life. His presentation manner was engrossing and his sincere caring for the students evident. Other teachers and the students noted his diligence and caring towards the students in interviews with the researcher.

Mr. Vincent was the sort who was observed treating the students to a delightful bacon breakfast prepared at his personal expense. This was a man with a deviant streak as well. He shared this with his students. Thus, he connected with them on a whole other level. This supports the findings of Jay Macleod (1995) in describing the type of teacher that such at-risk students favor. Mr. Vincent believed that he knew what was best for his students (a trait that most of the best teachers held). He had worked with adjudicated juveniles in a detention facility before joining the teaching staff of the alternative school. He addressed his students by either their first or last names - alternating between the two.

* In the notes *BM means "black male"; BF means "black female": HM means "Hispanic male":*

The room is very spacious and well lit - one wall lined with windows; the walls are blue and the desk top beige, both add to the brightness of the room. Pictures of reggae legend Bob Marley are prominently mounted on both sides of the blackboard (ahhhh embrace of culture other than the mainstream) - a powerful signal for anyone who walks into the room that "black culture" is okay here.

Class begins with students copying notes from the board, then they have an assignment to do.

Mr. Vincent to students: "Excuse me. The language.....Would you turn off the AC please."

BM (Vinny) responds in jest "next time you're not gonna ask so nicely."

When teacher later asks a student to adjust a window, Roderick responds "If I break it, niggers want me to pay for it." (indicating that students are held accountable for their actions - indeed driving home the connection between choices and their consequences).

To which teacher responds "what does that mean...'your peoples'?"

Roderick asks if "tongue kissing is profanity"

Mr. Vincent says "yes."

A group of guys go "Ohhhh...."

Teacher goes on about a need to move them to the religious school across the street.

Teacher: "it's easy not to say anything...should I escort you out for the day and give you a zero?"

The threat has teeth for students must accumulate 150 points while at the school before returning to a regular high school.

Roderick protests having gotten a zero the previous day.

Mr. Vincent responded that it was for doing nothing that day.

Teacher spots a student's bag on the floor. He asks: "Whose bag is this?"

A BM (Steven) indicates that the bag is his.

Mr. Vincent: "You throw your bag on the floor man? You know how many people walk on that floor." *[caring]*.

BM (Steven) responds: "That's what laundry is for man."

The teacher responds with a word about washing machines, and his family's laundry situation. This back and forth banter goes on as students copy their notes from the board.

*[Such was the case with most of these "**realness**" chats throughout the semester].*

In between note-taking the teacher would lecture on biology.

BM (Steven) goes to move some charts on the board.

Mr. Vincent says: "Steven, this is my classroom...anyone moves anything off this board it will be me. I don't want to get on anybody - but if I have to I will."

Teacher: "Mr. (Vinny's last name) spit the gum out please."

Several BMs jump on seeing a spider on the floor.

When it was pointed out that the researcher did not budge a BM defends himself "you gotta be afraid of something. She probably didn't see it.....we dissecting that nigga today." *[Incidentally, the researcher had seen it, but was unafraid, being from the country and thus, familiar with various types of spiders].*

Then, as is typical of boys, they became rather excited at the prospect of taking the spider apart.

BM (L) - the rather large fellow admits "scared the mess outta me."

Steven does something and the teacher calls him: "Steven, next time you do that - you get body slammed."

In response Steven asks teacher staff assistant a HM who is audiotaping the class: "You got that on tape?"

Mr. Vincent: "Hope you guys are talking about the work over there."

Steven responds "Yeah."

Jovial exchange between BM (L) and teacher about who can fight.

Roderick speaks of not liking being locked in a classroom "doing shit." He states that he would rather go to the gym because he is under pressure.

The teacher mockingly asks: "Do you wanna talk about it?"

Roderick does not respond.

(L) asks a question about the work - teacher tells him to ask someone else - (L) protests that he was writing notes and thus, he missed the information. *[scripted pact as (L) sees it]*.

BM (Vinny) to HM teacher assistant: "Why you crying (last name of teacher assistant)?"

BM (L) responds for HM teacher assistant: "The onions man."

Vinny later gives HM teacher assistant a playful tap of sympathy.

*Note: A HM teacher assistant comes in to assist from time to time. He tape records segments of the class. He mentioned later that he sometimes does this to present evidence of student language to parents who swear that their children would never use certain words.

As Mr. Vincent gives the answer to a question, the students groaned or cheered as if their thoughts on the matter had been either right or wrong.

A BF throws a piece of paper towards the dustbin. It misses, hits a BM and she says "I'm sorry a few times." The teacher picks up the paper and pretends to read it saying: "I'll meet you after school at 3:00 p.m." She laughs.

BM "Don't turn on that fucking A.C. man."

It is turned on and the teacher threatens to sanction the next person who curses.

A BM, apparently testing the situation says "Fuck."

BM (Vinny) accuses BM (Malcolm) of being on welfare.

Malcolm vigorously denies this and they argue about it.

Teacher removes Malcolm from the room.

Malcolm returns abruptly, seconds thereafter and the teacher walks rapidly behind him as he tries to get away. Teacher says "I'm not having it this year."

Roderick begins to open the petri dish holding the spider saying "If you were a spider would you want to be locked up like this?" *[introspective; many of these students are very witty - it takes "smarts" to be witty].*

Teacher responds: "This isn't science ethics" *[mild appropriate silencing to a question not seriously made].*

Roderick responds: "Act like niggers need school."

Teacher: "Niggers don't; but people do."

Roderick: "All school does is keep people down."

He takes his bag and leaves the room as the teacher remarks that a student came to see him yesterday who should have graduated two years ago.

A social worker comes to get a student. Apparently, counseling happens during class time - much to the annoyance of some teachers including this one.

****

With most of the effective or "real" alternative school teachers the classroom interactions with the delinquents were similar in style, tone and form. The main exception to this was that the juveniles were more polite with the female teachers and they used fewer expletives than with male teachers. However, the students were more courteous with older male teachers such as Mr. Sellers, a white male teacher in his sixties. At the comprehensive school, these rules did not apply. Male, or female, young or old, if the students sensed that a certain teacher looked down upon them, they were treated with disregard. The students might totally ignore the teacher, back talk, leave the room, or place their heads on the desk appearing oblivious to the lesson. With teachers who were "real" or otherwise strict, yet caring in their demeanor the students were largely orderly and unlike the delinquents at the alternative school, they rarely used expletives.

Fieldnotes: The Comprehensive High School

The following is a section of my notes from Spring 1999 observing a comprehensive school special education classroom. The teacher a white male, possibly mid-50s in age was sitting in, covering for Ms. Sweeney who was out sick. I had observed this teacher in 1996 in his own classroom. The situation described in the fieldnotes below are typical of those involving "non-real" teachers. Most absent in this teacher was the "unconditional positive regard" for all students. He was not a special education teacher, nor did he want to be and he made this clear to the students. The class was mixed with black and Hispanic males and females *[BM means black male; BF means black female; HM means Hispanic male; HF means Hispanic female]*:

This class took place in early May, about a month before the end of the spring semester. With the regular teacher absent, some of the more deviant (largely those who are very talkative, might have multiple body piercings, decorative contact lens, et cetera) are also absent from class, but not necessarily school. One student BM, came in for a few minutes then left to wonder about the school - socializing.

Teacher writes assignment on the board.

Bossy HF (Marielita) tries to get HF (Conchita) to change seats because her regular seat is taken by girl whom I, (the researcher) have not seen before *[some students who are not in the class seem to take advantage of the regular teacher's absence to visit]*. Conchita does not budge.

Teachers tells student to work in groups. He speaks to BM (Thomas) that he is not a "nun" (?) - therefore, he should join a group.

He then tells HF (Conchita) that he needs to be in a group too.

Then he addresses the other students. He speaks to a HF angrily who responds with a smile: "I'm my own group."

He tells HF (Conchita) not to be a "left-out."

Teacher continues to encourage the students to form groups.

I see no work going on.

Teacher speaks to HF (Conchita) again, this time referring to her as "lady."

Bossy HF (Marielita) snaps at the teacher about taking the books out She then walks over to the classroom lockers containing the textbooks with attitude.

There is a group of HFs to my left speaking with rather foul words (expletives). Three of these girls I have not seen before after being here for weeks.

There is no work going on. A few of the students are passing around an attendance sheet and there is some turning of pages.

HF inquires aloud about the absence of their regular teacher, Ms. Sweeney.
Another responds that she is absent on purpose.

Throughout the class the "new" HF females continue talking - using expletives.
HF (Marielita) shouts at BM (Thomas): "You gotta pen?"
He says "no" defensively.
HM seated in front of him asks if he has paper [BM (Thomas was a rather taciturn fellow, with an exploitable demeanor)].
Teacher walks about the room.
The students who are normally here are working quietly now (perhaps because they care about what Ms. Sweeney thinks of them - having formed a relationship with her).
HF tells teacher that her foul language is connected to her having cramps.
Teacher hands her something, then walks away saying "do the work."

Teacher stands front center in the room with a blank stare looking at the floor.

HF sitting to the rear has been using several four-letter words for a while.

Others are still working.

11:12 a.m. A few are chewing gum.

The classroom door is open and there is much noise coming from the hallway.

Teacher looks through the textbook while standing in front of the teacher's desk.

Teacher comes over and talks to me about some of the places he has taught before (includes juvenile delinquent and higher education settings). He also asked me for clarification on the assignment left to the students.

Group of HFs to the back are still talking. One puts on make-up.

Teacher approaches me again with a question. I defer to HF (Conchita).

Bossy HF (Marielita) says "what?" angrily.

HF (Lisa) snaps about "how hard the assignment may be."

HF (Debra) clarifies the work on the board.

Teacher then defends himself by saying that he teaches honors English therefore, "I'm not slow - I just have to be told" *{Inappropriate implication here that given the context discredits help-seeking behavior--note, this teacher's marginalizing script}*.

HF (Debra) annoyed, continues her explanation of the work.

Bossy HF (Marielita) reads writing on a piece of cloth about "fucking up" some bitch.

Girls in her group have not stopped talking yet. They discuss a conflict between some girls who should be family.

The disengagement that flourished in this classroom and the subtle inferiority with which the teacher held the students was not uncommon at the comprehensive school in special education and mainstream classes. In many of the special education track classes in particular the students were merely equipped to hold secondary labor market jobs upon graduation. Indeed, the school had some "real" and otherwise effective teachers, but these were too few. They were often the ones with college credits beyond a bachelor's degree and licensed. Many of the others entered teaching because it was the available job. Exceptions here included gay persons and theatre-trained persons. Such individuals were more willing to get to know, understand and teach the diverse students before them. There is something positive to be said for those who come to teaching with an open mind.

Self-Concept or Self-Efficacy

Ability versus Effort

Well-adjusted children per teacher evaluations are assertive and they possess a significant internal loci of control and strong self-efficacy (Ollendick et al. 1989). Weiner (1984, 1986) described successful students as possessing: i) a willingness to persist despite difficulties; ii) a sense of success being within reach, ii) a knowledge of the "rules of the game" and iv) a "mental roadmap to reach one's goals" (see "cultural capital" discussed later). In this, parents and teachers are significant socializers.

Their cultures could emphasize one or more of the following related-attribution orientations i) ability; ii) task focus (learning "just because "learning in itself is of value regardless of its material value); or ii) social approval - investing effort to be perceived as "hard working," (Mahr & Nicholls 1980). Often the United States' educational culture is compared to that of Asian countries like Japan with a deep, though sometimes covetous laud of the latter. A major difference in the educational culture of the two countries is the attribution of individual academic success. While Americans often speak of hard work (effort) as the means to success, their daily speech and media images indicate a strong contrary belief – that of the innateness of academic success (Steinberg 1996). In the educational psychology literature this is referred to as the difference between "ability" and "capability." The former relates to a fixed innate trait while the latter refers to competence which may vary with preparation. Indeed, in 1996 Ablard and Mills reported that high school students were more likely to view intelligence as a fixed trait than were elementary school children.

Table 15: Perceptions of the Self

DELINQ.	Parents	Teacher	Friends	Are you a "good boy" Or a "bad boy?"
Russell	Handsome, intelligent, gifted	Bright, going places if mind set		Good
Roger	Handsome, smart, athletic	Handsome, smart, athletic	Handsome, smart, bright	Middle
Vinny	Caring, smart, sometimes hardworking	Joke too much	Funny, playful	In between
Steven	(Grandmother)-"no good"	Smart, but needs to pay attentionh	Don't know	Not perfect, not bad
Malcolm	Don't know	Don't know	Don't know	Alright – just perfect; right
Lunch	Gentleman, nice, good son, could be smart	Good	Cool	Good
Trevor	Good boy	Works hard, has high expectations	Courteous, kind	Good boy
Peter	Reliable	Could do better	Serious person	Mostly good
Player	Annoying, smart, playful	Annoying, smart, playful	Annoying, smart, playful	Good
Jaoquan	Don't know		Different things	
Roderick	Tall, smart, handsom	Don't know	Don't know	Good
Marty	Intelligent, talented, goining somewhere	Borderline genius, focused	Bookworm	Good
Jerome	Hard-headed, smart	Hard-headed, smart	Hard-headed, smart	Sometimes good
Tyrone	Responsible, caring, mature		Funny	
Roshaud	Rude		Black	Whatever I want to be
Mutt	Nice, kind	Clown	Pretty cool, cute thug	In between: varies
NON-DEL				
Bugsy	Quiet, lazy – needs to work harder	Works, but needs to do more	Funny	Good
Mike	Nice, well known	Don't know	Funny, cool	Good
Anthony	Bright	Cleaver	Cool cat	Good
Bobby	Wonderfu;	Smart	Cool kid	Good
Evan	Good, own mind, stubb, goals, active, angry	Calm, cooperative, hardworking		Good
Barry	Hard-headed, but caring	Talkative, but not disruptive	Funny	Good
Ross	Hard-ears	Smart	Nicest guy	Good
Devon				Good

A problem here is that academic success which often translates into primary labor market positions are correlated with larger social structure provisions to that end. Often such provisions are not available to urban students who are so socially isolated that they lack the social and cultural capital for upward social mobility. So, the effort necessary to overcome circumstances of poverty are rarely employed, not because the students are lazy or unambitious, but because they are ignorant of how to proceed. Schools, when they work, should function as "the great equalizers." However, too often, for poor minority students they merely recreate poverty. Katz (1967) rightly noted that the achievement motivation that is realistic for many African-Americans lies in the arena of sports, not academics. He also noted that socioeconomic status has more to do with achievement than ethnic differences. Learned helplessness emerges when students perceive that their circumstances are beyond their control (Weinstein & Mayer 1984). Such has been the lot of many minority children (Weinstein & Mayer 1984: discussing Coleman et al 1966; Nowicki & Strickland 1973; Reid & Croucher 1980).

In response to the question: "What kind of student are you?" the delinquents rendered the following responses indicating a mixture of internal and external outcome attributions. What was surprising about the responses below is that instead of blaming others for their failures the students often blamed themselves. They seemed largely oblivious to the influence of the largely social structure on their circumstances. Often blamed for their own shortcomings, it seemed they had begun to believe that their failings were indeed all their own: The effects of social promotion were also evident. Amongst the most truly disadvantaged (such as delinquents Malcolm and Lunch) passing grades were expected for merely attempting their schoolwork, whether or not they mastered the knowledge.

RUSSELL: A good student.

*****

ROGER: I'm a student that wants to work and does his work and be quiet - don't talk to nobody. I'm a nice person I give respect, show you respect. If you come out of line, I get out of line sometimes.

******

STEVEN: I'm a good student, I get 80s. I've never gotten lower than a 75 in this school.

R: Ok. And at the school before what sort of grades did you get?

STEVEN: I failed.

R: Failed. How come?

STEVEN: I don't know. I just was, you know what I'm saying, I chilled with my friends....whatever my friends did, I just started wilding up. Know what I'm saying?

******

MALCOLM: I'm an awright student; I ain't excellent; I ain't gonna lie; I'm awright.....doing basic.

*****

LUNCH: I'm a good student.

You're a good student, ok. How old are you?

****

TREVOR: Well, good student. I like doing work and stuff.

****

PETER: I go to class. I do my work. Sometimes, I get tired. I slack up a little bit..... But, when it comes down to it. I do my work.

R: Do you work hard sometimes, hardly,....consistently? Would you say that you work hard ....????

PETER: No.

R: When do you work hard?

PETER: When I feel it's necessary to.

R: And what would make you feel that?

PETER: When it's not too many disruptions like the kids talking and being loud whatever. Nobody calling me all the time. If I'm not distracted, I sit down and do my work.

*****

JAOQUAN: I'm a smart student. Unless somebody bothers me I won't, I won't lose my cool.

******

RODERICK: Aaammm I'm a moody student.

R: A moody student? Ok. What does that mean?

RODERICK: Sometimes I feel like doing work; sometimes I don't.

R: Ok. Aaammm what makes the difference? How come you feel like doing work sometimes, not other times?

RODERICK: It depends on how my day is going.

******

MARTY: I was in a couple of honors classes.

******

R: Ok, aammm what kind of student are you?

JEROME: A smart student. I got all 80s and 90s.

****

TYRONE: I describe myself... I think, aaammm I'm a good student.

****

LUNCH: ....the whole thing, overall, is that I try my best. If I try my best they give me a high grade. If I don't try they give me a low grade.

****

ROSHAUD: Hyperactive.

R: Ok. How come?

ROSHAUD: And sticky fingers sometimes.

R: What do you mean by "sticky fingers?"

ROSHAUD: Sometimes I like to go in stuff.

R: Oh. Alright, alright. Aaammm do you like high school so far?

ROSHAUD: No. I like it, but sometimes.

R: Okay, well what do you like and what don't you like?

ROSHAUD: When its a good day. That's it.

R: What is a "good day?"

ROSHAUD: When I don't get in no trouble.

R: What determines whether or not you get into trouble?

ROSHAUD: Fights. Fights get me in trouble. Arguing with teachers gets me in trouble.

R: Muummm...

ROSHAUD: So if I sit down and do nothing, do work, then it'd be alright.

The last subject above, Roshaud was extremely hyperactive - the biological son of a crack-addicted mother. The teachers described him as a very artistic and likable fellow with some real struggles in controlling his behavior. They perceived these troubles to be largely his mother's fault. The teachers had made many efforts to assist him such as seeing to his placement in counseling and on medication.

Nevertheless, the family infrastructure was not there to facilitate the adolescent's consistency in treatment outside the school setting. The juvenile was in a foster care placement with at least six other children and the effects of his medication were being canceled out by his marijuana use.

The descriptions of the non-delinquents to the question "how would you describe yourself as a student" were similar as expected:

BUGSY: In between, so sort of average?

(Later in the interview).

BUGSY: I gotta just apply myself to work harder......Sometimes, I get lazy.

R: And that has changed? What brought about the change?

BUGSY: It's like when you in high school, you always look out for friends, you don't have a lot of friends.

R: Oh, looking out for people when you just start.

BUGSY: When you start high school.

R: Ok.

BUGSY: Junior high. I know friends from elementary school, but, but, you don't know people from here, so you trying to be....

R: Just trying to hang out. Ohhh, okay and so when did you decide not to stop?

BUGSY: Well, I stopped during sophomore year, like 2nd term sophomore year.

R: Ok, and what was it that brought about the change?

BUGSY: Well, I don't wanna graduate when I'm like 20, 21. I wanna graduate now.

R: Ok, so who was it? Did somebody point that out to you?

BUGSY: My mother and my brother.

R: Mother, and brother. So this is an older brother?

BUGSY: Yeah.

*****

MIKE: I'm a, I'm a alright student. I'm lazy though.

(Later in the interview)

R: How come you weren't working hard? What's going on?

MIKE: I don't know. I just was relaxed. I guess just having too much fun, not paying attention.

R: Ok.

MIKE: But I tried to change that around.

(Later in the interview)

R: About how much, how much time do you study?

MIKE: None *(He chuckles)*.

R: None?

MIKE: None, only for finals and midterms.

(Note, Anthony had long been in honors classes. He claimed that he just let his work diminish but he was unable to fully articulate why).
*****
R: Aaammm what kind of student are you?

ANTHONY: Me? I'm a, I'm a ..... C+ student.,

R: C+ student?

ANTHONY: B-

R: Okay what's responsible for that?   How come you're a C+, B-?

ANTHONY: I'm on last minute person. I always do things that the last-minute. I don't know why, it's just always me. I guess I'm comfortable with its cause I'm a senior now. I'm still care, and still going to school.

R: Okay.

ANTHONY: So it don't pretty much hurt me that badly.

******

BOBBY: I'm a bright student.
....
I do my work and I pass all my classes.
......
My average is 75.

R: Ok, so that means mostly what then?

BOBBY: Bs.

(Later in the interview).

R: What's responsible for they grades that you get? Is it...aaammm is it the amount of work that you do or ...?

BOBBY: Behavior.
...
******

EVAN: I would classify myself as a "B" student.

R: "B student" and what's that? What like? What percent?

EVAN: Like 80%, between 80, you know.

(Later in the interview in response to a question about his performance in the last marking period):

R: How many classes did you pass?

EVAN: Aaammm everything except physics.

R: Oh, you passed everything except physics?

EVAN: Yeah.

R: What was the problem with physics?

EVAN: It's like, ok, I don't think it's really hard. It's just, some of the concepts I don't understand.

R: Unnhuh.

EVAN: And it's like, something like in other subjects I get the concepts but physics - it's like math and science mixed together.

R: Ummhuh.

EVAN: So, it's kinda hard you know.

R: Ahhh, is there a problem with the class? Or is it you? Is the teacher helpful?

EVAN: Aaaammm, I not gonna like be the one to point fingers. I mean, first, I gotta start off with myself.

R: Ummhuh.

EVAN: You know. But the teacher she's, she's a great teacher but seems like she has favoritism towards students.

R: Ummhuh.

...

(Later in the interview)

R: Aamm your performance in school what's responsible for it?

EVAN: My performance in school? I think me being like hardworking you know, knowing that..., or put it this way, setting goals for myself. Like making goals and then just trying to reach it.

******

BARRY: Well, my grades are like average or a little above average, but they can be better.

R: What do you call "average" like what A, B, Cs?

BARRY: Like Cs.

(Later in the interview)

R: Aammm would you say that you work hard to get good grades - often, once in a while, or hardly ever?

BARRY: I say I work pretty hard, but not hard enough.

******

R: How would you describe yourself as a student?

ROSS: I'm reasonable.

R: (*I chuckle lightly*), you're reasonable?

ROSS: Yeah...(???) that good. In between there.

R: You're in between there. Ahhh what sort of grades did you get last marking period?

ROSS: Mid-term?

R: Yeah. Did you pass everything?

ROSS: No, I failed two classes.

Ross excelled in gym and music. His was on one of the school's athletic teams and held himself responsible for his performance. He had little time for study because he worked 30 hours per week. He described himself as a star performer at his job and indicated great devotion to it. It was clear that he saw the latter as a more worthwhile use of time than school. The results of employment were more certain, more real. Thus, he was late for school about 15 times out of the month. He frequently studied only a few minutes before tests, and was often sleepy in school. Largely disengaged from anything but the social and athletic part of school life, Ross was also the most deviant non-delinquent in the study - the one cited for both jumping a turnstile and blocking a public staircase.

Regarding his school circumstances, Ross said "ain't nobody help me or anything." It is worth remembering that Ross was a recent immigrant from the Caribbean. As such it may be expected that his views would involve a strong attribution to self for his outcomes because of the strong influence of the "Protestant work ethic" in the Caribbean.

Self-efficacy (or self-concept) is shaped by the attributions orientation of success. Significantly, self-efficacy is different from self-esteem. Self-esteem refers to a "positive or negative regard one has towards the self," (Brookins 1996). Self-efficacy or self-concept speaks to a person's capability or competencies, not to a person's ability. As such a self-efficacy orientation emphasizes effort (over innatenesss) in achievement attribution. Children with a positive self-concept have an augmented motivation to learn, (Ray 1992). These students with a strong sense of self-efficacy invest greater effort to address performance that they or significant others have deemed less than satisfactory (Bandura 1989a). On the other hand, when facing failure, students with a low sense of self-efficacy view failure as a mark of personal deficiency and thus, they become less motivated to achieve (Bandura 1989).

The truly at-risk evidenced a belief that their academic peformance was partly reflective of innate traits and the perceptions or misperceptions that others had of them. There was no significant support for any "acting white" effects. According to Signithia Fordham (1996) the "acting white" effect refers to blacks being secretive about or reluctant to make stellar academic achievement because such would be perceived as imitating whites. Amongst the New York students, the aim was to imitate wealth - color irrespective. Consider the words of Vinny:

> VINNY: Like some people that's smart, they try to hide it, but, I feel that if you got it, hey, show it. You smart, ain't nothing you can do about it - hey you born with the gift.

Nevertheless, in all of this peers mattered as behavior activators. For example, consider the words of the delinquent Lunch below:

> R: Aaaammmm would you say that you work hard to get good grades on a regular basis? Or just sometimes? Or...?
>
> LUNCH: Just sometimes.
>
> R: Just sometimes. How come?
>
> LUNCH: Because, then I get carried away with the playing and everything, but, it's, it's....I'm starting to change. I'm getting my work done more.
>
> R: Alright. And you still don't know why you play?
>
> LUNCH: Not really. I just, just be playing I guess. 'Cause really, I just start to follow the crowd...just wanna be like everybody else, so, that's probably why.

Cause Orientation in Schools

Cause orientation refers to a juvenile's goals in life. Herein, "goals" differ from mere dreams in that goals are expected to actually be accomplished. Both the delinquents and the non-delinquent truly at-risk juveniles had poorly formulated goals. Two-thirds of the non-delinquents and two-thirds of the delinquents held college aspirations. Yet, with the exception of less than a third of the delinquents and a few more amongst the non-delinquents, the subjects were largely clueless about how to realize their aspirations. There was little talk of provisions for higher education, and fantastic goals of wealth and retirement by about 30. Where the students were more informed teachers, older siblings, extended family members, or parents had made the difference. The students like many African-Americans who attend college favor studying business in keeping with a thirst for upward social mobility via material possessions *(see Table 11, pg. 119)*.

Teachers can crucify the ambitions of students by their attributions of success (Dweck 1975). Teachers have had a longstanding history of fostering the death or non-existence of the "American dream" in many African-Americans (Bates & Doob 1999). Thus, not surprisingly 63 percent of the delinquents and 63 percent of the non-delinquents alike expressed a preference for living one day at a time instead of engaging in long term planning. Such supports Cohen's position (1955) of the working class having a short-term orientation. For the truly disadvantaged the present-time orientation reflects a failure on the part of family and teachers to present palatable future time orientations. The present time orientation is not totally unrealistic given the negative outcomes of many black males. For example, the number one cause of death for young black males in America is homicide (Schmalleger 1997). Regarding future prospects the tone of the more at-risk delinquents could be summed up in the words of Vinny and others below. Note the dearth of social capital on the many ways that minorities in the United States might access a college education that is free or subsidized:

> VINNY: If I'm alive I hope I'll be working or something. Like, I don't really think like, I ain't sure if I have plans for college. Only way I'm gonna go to college is like if I have a scholarship. 'Cause I don't wanna keep begging for all this money to go to college.

*****

R: So, you're 15. Ahh 5 years from now, you'll be 20. Where do you see yourself?

STEVEN: College. If I could.

R: If you could? What makes you think that you might not?

STEVEN: I don't know. I just, when I'm mad I just don't care for a while and then I think. I stop and consider then I think "this is your future; it's not theirs" and just do my work. Do what I have to.

R: So you think you will?

STEVEN: Ahh don't know. Yeah, I think I will.

R: Ok which college?

STEVEN: I know I would if I had the, if I had the chance.

If not parents and if not teachers, who will tell and equip the truly at-risk regarding the utilization of higher education for success?

****

R: Don't know. Alright. Now you didn't mention college. Are you thinking of going?

MALCOLM: *[Hisses teeth]*. Naaaw I ain't thinking about that now.

R: Ok, how come?

MALCOLM: 'Cause I ain't got no money for college yet *[slight chuckles]*.

R: So it's a money thing? If you had the money you'd go?

MALCOLM: Ummhuh.

R: Alright, you know that there are loans and grants and stuff?

MALCOLM: I don't like 'em loans though.

R: Don't like the loans. How come?

MALCOLM: Gotta pay them back.

Malcolm's last statement above indicates a youth with a common American trait - self-sufficiency. Later when asked if he had considered grants, he was unaware of such options for pursuing higher education. Significantly, Malcolm was also the delinquent who was most insistent on the point that he should get a passing grade for just effort regardless of material mastery.

Related to cause orientation is a sense of empowerment or sense of control over one's life. Too often, the socially isolated inner city urban black male student has so little cultural and social capital for upward social mobility that he perceives the future with helplessness and hopelessness. Sometimes refusing to accept this bleak picture he may cling fiercely to hopes of success as an athlete. Such was the case with the delinquent Roger, for example. African-Americans males seemed more inclined to aim for a sports career rather than music (unlike some of their Hispanic peers). The preference for sports over the rap music industry in particular may have been because, with practice the former may have seemed more attainable, respectable, and with greater odds of enduring payoffs.

As part of an effort to empower the students by having them exercise more control over their lives, the alternative school teachers emphasized thinking about consequences. They were successful. Consider the words of Steven on this point:

R: ....- do you think you have a lot of control over what happens to you in life or do you...?

STEVEN: No. I don't have no control because, when we have court days we can't go into court, know what I'm saying.

R: Ummhuh.

STEVEN: I don't go to court and just tell the judge what really happened, know what I'm saying.

R: Ummhuh.

STEVEN: ...he ruling off of what, what the people say. Know what I'm saying? I want to go in there and tell him like "no, this don't happen here, this happened" know what I'm saying, I didn't lie about that, I told you, I did lie about that, know what I'm saying.

Paternoster and Iovanni (1989) spoke of some labels within schools as "stigmatizing and exclusionary." The primary labeling effect in the present study was not an overt branding of "delinquent" from the juvenile justice system, but a similarly sinister, yet very subtle social reproduction effect from the labels of academic tracking. Once adopted, some students internalize the limitations inherent in the lower tracks regarding a dampened potential for legitimate monetary success. Of course, nowadays "tracking" has become a dirty word. Thus, the practice continues under the umbrella of serving those with "special needs." The effect of being branded "intellectually inferior" appeared far more debilitating than the label "delinquent" amongst the alternative school students. Indeed the literature indicates that some students will misbehavior so that their misbehavior will be identified as the reason for their academic failure as opposed to some innate intellectual defect (Gutierrez 1998). The students claimed that they had often been misjudged by school authorities.

These schools serving inner city minority students exist within contexts where, if the school does not deliver hope of a better life, little else does. Thus, as Albert Cohen noted in 1955, short-term orientations become more common than any long term ones. With many of the juveniles, their goals were described as ideas as real as the plans people make when they consider winning the lottery. They were largely ignorant about the social capital necessary for realizing their aspirations.

Consider the delinquent Jerome. Jerome often hung out with a marijuana-smoking cousin and he was quick to fight. He thought that he was preparing himself for a life with the Drug Enforcement Administration (DEA). After all, he knew a great deal about local illicit drug operations. He had often pondered how the DEA "don't know anything about all this" - referring to the apparent lack of law enforcement response to the drug dealing in his community. So, who will tell Jerome that his criminal associations are more likely to hurt his efforts to join the DEA than help him? Who will tell him that his juvenile felony record could automatically exclude him from ever joining the DEA? Who will tell him that the DEA probably know more than he does about the drug situation in his New York? Who?

In the United States culture, education is a mere means to an end. Being a good student is ultimately not important, nor are teachers held in high esteem (Messner & Rosenfeld 1997). What really matters is a person's "end." Many African-American males look to sports or the music industry to "make it." Such verbalizations are not from elementary school children but from high school youngsters during a phase of their lives when one might otherwise expect them to hold more realistic career aspirations considering the odds of success in either music or professional sports. Yet, why would they? When the means and ends for accomplishment fail to flow together smoothly (Alexander et al., 1994). Indeed, Hirschi, Liska, Elliott and others who published in the 1960s and 1970s, noted that delinquency was highest when aspirations and expectations were low.

When Teachers and Schools Fail

Schools fail truly at-risk students in many ways besides holding low expectations of them and shortchanging them on the social and cultural capital necessary for upward social mobility. They also fail them in providing well-trained and caring teachers. The manifestations of these include policies and other behaviors that make school unwelcoming. Indeed, schools kill dreams and thwart expectations, such that students may even demand social promotion for effort regardless of academic mastery:

LUNCH: Math class is hard. A 65, I always been getting grades like that in math 'cause math, 'cause I...the only reason they be passing me is because I be trying to do it. Even when test days come and stuff I still be fine and math is hard. I can't really understand that subject.

****

MALCOLM: 'Cause they give it to me. I really don't care what they give me *(said with passion - louder voice rapid pace).* I see...if I'm not doing no work, all right, I expect, a failing grade, but if I'm doing my hardest to get it, good grade, they can at least give me like a 65 or 70 or something.

Of course, such policies have a painful downside as verbalized by Vinny. His words indicated that he got a very clear message that he was not wanted in his school.

VINNY: I was doing the best that I can, but they was... they was passing me along but with failing grades. Every time it was time for me to get promoted, they'd just push me up and I didn't know the work that I was doing. Like 2nd grade - they pushed me to the 3rd. I didn't know what I was doing. They still pushed me to the 4th. They was just moving me up, moving me up and I barely knew. My brother, he started helping me with this, that and all that.

R: Ummhuh, ok, when did this start happening? That you didn't know the work and you just kept getting moved up?

VINNY: Like when I was in public school...

R: Ummhuh.

VINNY: It's just that I was so bad, I'm assuming they just kept pushing me up to hurry up and get me out.

R: Mummm, so how did it feel not knowing the work but being pushed?

VINNY: It was embarrassing. It got to a point where I was in 4th grade and they asked me to read something that was 3rd grade reading level. I was, I was struggling reading that. That made me feel bad. Then the kids in class laughing at me - that made me feel worse.

Vinny's externalization of blame is correlated with a history of academic failure. This goes against the "bootstrapping" notion of succeeding no matter what the odds. The odds here were significantly negative. It involved living in illiteracy. Both Malcolm and Vinny had been identified by their teachers as some of the poorest academic performers in the alternative school. Both students made an effort to take advantage of the alternative school to catch up academically. Nonetheless, even there, many of the teachers thought that their work was so weak, they needed more intensive help. Eventually, the boys got some of this help as their original class was divided into two smaller groups. The division came as a result of some of the weaker students disrupting their peers when, (according to the teachers), those boys seemed overwhelmed by the academic material before them. The result of the class division was amazing. The group that often disrupted their peers became more focused than the original set of focused students. Apparently, the students who had been removed were very concerned that they were being perceived as "slow" and thus, that they had squandered their opportunity to "catch up." As in the classic Hawthorne study, they worked much harder than before. In reality, the academic expectations for them had not changed.

R: Ummm.

VINNY: That, that, I can't even read this and everybody laughing at me - I'm sad now.

R: Mummm.

VINNY: So, I just started going home practicing reading, reading, self, by myself, my brother helping me.

R: Ummmhuh.

VINNY: Stuff like that.

****

Schools also fail students when they fail to provide a challenging curriculum to assist their students in fulfilling their academic potential. Below is how the delinquent Jaoquan described his experience:

> R: What sort of grades were you getting before you came here? Like A's, Bs, Cs?
>
> JAOQUAN: Like Bs and probably Cs.
>
> R: Bs and Cs. What sort of grades are you getting now?
>
> JAOQUAN: When I first came here I was getting As and Bs. And the, this last one since I was behaving a little badly...
>
> R: Ummmhuh.
>
> JAOQUAN: "Cause I was distracted a lot, I passed but I didn't get what I expected.
>
> R: The grade, unhuh. So how does this school compare to the school where you were before? Is it better? Is it not?
>
> JAOQUAN: In a way its better because it's less kids and you can get more attention, but...
>
> R: Ummhuh.
>
> JAOQUAN: It's just that you get distracted a lot.
>
> R: You get distracted here?
>
> JAOQUAN: Here and in other schools.
>
> R: Uummhuh. Distracted by what kind of things?
>
> JAOQUAN: Like the students and al that.

R: Ummhuh.

JAOQUAN: Like when they don't behave and they talk a lot to it distracts you from doing your work and everything.

R: All that stuff. Do you like to being a 9th grader so far?

JAOQUAN: Yeah so far.

R: High school status?

JAOQUAN: But it ain't challenging you or nothing. 'Cause I know basically whatever they are doing, but...

R: So it's not as challenging?

JAOQUAN: No, not yet. But...

R: Okay. All right. Aaammm what's responsible for how you're doing in school? The sort of grades that you're getting? You said distractions are one thing - anything else?

JAOQUAN: Distractions and also like when you're doing the work and it's not challenging you get bored so...

R: Bored?

JAOQUAN: Yeah like, so when you get in trouble it's like you get more excited...??? boreness and stuff.

R: Okay. Was that the case at the school that you were attending before coming here? Was that the same problem- you weren't challenged enough?

JAOQUAN: Yeah that's basically it with, with me.

R: Unhhuh.

JAOQUAN: When the work don't challenge me and I know it, its too easy for me to get bored.

R: Ummhuh.

JAOQUAN: I just can't sit there can be quiet and let everybody... I have to get up and go somewhere else cause this is boring.

******

To impart the social and cultural capital necessary for upward mobility successful teachers must be very active in building a relationship with their students. Below are the delinquents' descriptions of the teachers who had been in their lives. For Russell, there were "no complaints," but for others the story was different. For example, Roger's perception was that the alternative school teachers were often negative characters:

ROGER: Some teachers in here they, they are reminders of like "we're criminals" and like when they think we criminals then they treat us a certain way.

R: Ok, like who? Give me an example of something that somebody would do to let you think that.

ROGER: Moxley sometimes.

R: Really? Like what would he say or do that?

ROGER: He puts us down. He be talk, he always trying to play us like he like "yeah, I didn't teach you guys this" or "you can't do it, I know you can't do it?" How you know I can't do it? How you know I never learn this in my last school? Or the other teacher taught me? He puts us down a lot. *[said with angry passion]*.

R: Ok, but overall, how are the teachers here?

ROGER: Some teachers really care about us.

R:.....ammm...your teachers at your old school - how were they?

ROGER: I didn't even get to know 'em. All I know is they just teaching us.

For the most part Roger's school experiences prior to the alternative school reflected a lack of bonding to the institutions. Evidently, there had been little effort on the part of school personnel to build a relationship with this student from a home with a crack addicted father and a mother who was unaware that her son was a drug dealer. Roger eventually bonded with various teachers and staff members at the alternative school. One of those in whom Roger confided was a recovering addict himself. He was able to spot signs of danger in the teen's life and out of that he spoke candidly with the youngster about changing his life's course. It takes caring and realness to do this. Yet, largely on his own in a household with two parents who were more a risk, than protection, and recently laid off from his conventional part time job, Roger continued his drug dealing.

******

STEVEN: I mean, it's like only a couple of them who really cares.

(Later in the interview).

R: Aaammm, mummm. Ahhh what is it that you find frustrating about school? Is there one thing about school that really bothers you?

STEVEN: Aammm teachers. I can do the work, but the teachers. They just aggravate me, make me go home and then...I'm already mad going home and my brothers and sisters they wanna play with me. I don't wanna play with them.

R: Ummhuh.

STEVEN: Know what I'm saying. Might just...

R: Ok. ahhh... What about the teachers? What would the teachers do that would get you mad?

STEVEN: It's not all the teachers. It's like one or two. I do their work.

R: Ummhuh.

STEVEN: But it's any little thing I do, I just get in trouble, know what I'm saying. They scream on me "why you this and why you that?" "You stop doing this" but, they don't talk to the other person. They gotta talk just to me.

R: Ok. Aaammm well give me an example of one thing that these people would say.

STEVEN: Alright yesterday, T. aaammm, my friend T. he was like he was bothering me cursing at everybody. He playing and Mr .X talking 'bout "T, T, why you this? Why you talking. Do you hear him talking he just cursed at me."
        ****
R: Ummhuh. What about your teachers? What sort of grades do you think they expect of you?

MALCOLM: I don't even know. I really don't care.

****
R: Aammm, the teachers at your school before, how did you get along with them? Would you say you got along well with them? Didn't like them?

JAOQUAN: I don't know about everybody but you bother me...I bother you.

R: Ok. So, that one teacher, what sort of thing happened?

JAOQUAN: What happened was that I went to get my picture, my school pictures but this other person had gotten into an argument with this other teacher ... *[the pictures were yearbook photographs]*.

R: Ummhuh.

JAOQUAN: So, when I went to get my pictures that lady said I couldn't get my pictures 'cause I was arguing with this teacher...

R: Ummhuh.

JAOQUAN: But the thing that got me mad was, I was arguing with that teacher, it didn't concern her.

(Later in the interview)

R: ....what sort of grades do your teachers expect you to get?

JAOQUAN: I don't really know. They always say when I get in trouble that I'm smart, that I can do the work. And they expect a lot out of me but sometimes I disappoint them.

R: Ok. That's the teachers here?

JAOQUAN: Yeah.

R: And what about those teachers before as well?

JAOQUAN: Ummhuh.

****
R: Okay. Is there anything about school life that you really don't like?
[Long pause]. Nothing about the school really bugged you?

MARTY: Not really, 'cept for a couple of teachers. You know what I'm saying. The bad teachers and stuff like that.

****

When asked to compare the alternative school experience to their experiences prior (often in comprehensive settings), the delinquents' most common response was that the alternative school was smaller and this allowed them to learn.

Social / Cultural Capital

"Social capital" refers to how "social structures...facilitate pursuit of various goals" (Kahne & Bailey 1999). James Coleman in his 1988 theoretical model of social capital discussed three areas of capital: 1) social trust, 2) communication patterns, and 3) community norms. The social trust referred to "relationships of trust and understanding from long term commitment, demonstrated capacity to help, and shared experiences," (Kahne & Bailey 1999). Communication patterns addressed a person's ability to access information for achievement. Community norms referred to the system of rewards or sanctions which reinforce various behaviors.

Where social capital refers largely to the social skill necessary for success, cultural capital refers to the actual cultural knowledge necessary for success. This cultural knowledge requires a biculturality whereby those who differ from the mainstream culturally master the mainstream culture. The knowledge involves knowing classical music, drama, and literature (Bourdieu & Passeron 1977). Thus, schools as theoretical equalizing institutions should impart both social and cultural capital by teaching institutionally sanctioned discourses, academic knowledge, navigating bureaucracies including the education and job markets, networking, technical knowledge (such as computing, time management, plus how to study) and problem-solving (Stanton-Salazar 1997).

Many of the parents herein had little capital of any sort to pass on to their children with less than a half of the parents possessing some college (but none with a bachelor's degree). Acquiring the capital does not make acculturation - "acquisition of the cultural patterns of the dominant society," necessary. However, it necessitates significant assimilation where "both groups...regard each other as equals," associating voluntarily with each other (Atkinson et al., 1993).

Table 16 below *(pg. 248-249)* indicates the cultural capital to which the students had been exposed. Students were asked if they had magazines, newspapers, books or a computer at home. "Y" means "yes" and "X" means "no." They were also asked if they had ever attended the ballet, opera or Broadway. In New York City this would indicate exposure to mainstream culture. They were also asked if they read and/or wrote poetry, including rap. Then they were asked to indicate the main types of music to which they listened.

Ogbu (1995) stated that for minorities acquiring the language, knowledge, skills and credentials to compete economically and technologically is very important. Culture refers to a) customary ways of behaving, b) codes or assumptions (e.g. expectations), c) artifacts, d) institutions (e.g. economically, politically, socially, religious), and, social structure (how people relate to each other) (Ogbu, 1995). For example the United States emphasizes individualism, many eastern cultures emphasize dependence or group orientation.

By law and/or custom dominant and subordinate cultures are separated. Nevertheless, certain points in the mainstream culture are important for the latter's upward social mobility beyond the local community (for example, speaking Standard English), (Ogbu, 1995). Ogbu saw cultural assimilation for those who emigrate to the United States as easier for their culture is more readily accepted by mainstream society as different, but not necessarily inferior. This enables the newcomers to more readily retain two cultures. Yet, when mainstream America perceives African-Americans (those who were the descendants of slaves on United States' soil), as culturally inferior the result is subtractive, not additive learning for those deemed "inferior." (Ogbu, 1995). Hence, African-American heritage is not embraced in schools, but is prohibited, shunned, or stereotyped as "bad" except in the arenas of sports or entertainment (areas that are less threatening to many whites (Bates & Doob 1999). The result is a silencing effect in school where teachers avoid discussing "those people's" lives. What follows on the part of minority students is a certain disengagement from a part of themselves as it becomes evident that their lives' customs are somehow taboo. To this some may be fully accepting. For others there may be passive resistance (e.g. various forms of withdrawal). For still others there is active resistance (delinquent behavior, and various forms of school disruptions).

Table 16: Exposure to Cultural Capital in New York

DELINQ	MAGAZINES	NEWSPAPERS	BOOKS	COMPUTERS	BALLET/OPERA/BROADWAY	POETRY
Russell	Y	Y	Y	Y	Opera, broadway w/ family	Y
Roger	Y	Y	Y	X	Opera, broaadway w/ school	X
Vinny	X	Y	Y	X	Cats, Nutcracker	X
Steven	Y	X	Y	X	X	Y
Malcolm	Y	Y	Y	X	X	Y
Lunch	Y	Y	Y	X	Opera w/ school	X
Trevor	Y	Y	Y	X	Cats	X
Peter	Y	Y	Y	X	Opera w/ school	X
Player	Y	Y	Y	Y	Opera, broadway w/ fam. & sch.	X
Jaoquan	Y	Y	Y	X	X	X
Roderick	Y	Y	Y	Y	X	X
Marty	Y	Y	Y	Y	Opera w/ school	X
Jerome	Y	Y	Y	Y	Opera w/ school	X
Tyrone	Y	X	Y	X	X	X
Roshaud	Y	Y	Y	Y	X	X
Mutt	Y	X	Y	X	Cats w/ school	Y
NON-DEL						
Bugsy	X	X	Y	Y	Opera w/ relative	No
Mike	Y	Y	Y	X	Could-but wouldn't pay for it	No-class only
Anthony	Y	Y	Y	X		Yes
Bobby	Y	Y	Y	X	X – No, not interested	No
Evan	Y	Y-sometimes	Y	X	X	No
Barry	Y	Y	Y	X	X	Rap
Ross	Y	Y	Y	X	X – No – don't wanna go	No
Devon	Y	Y	Y	Y	Trying to go to Broadway	Yes

Table 16: Exposure to Cultural Capital in New York (continued)

DELINQ.	MUSIC	NON-DEL	MUSIC
Russell	Hip-hop		
Roger	Rap, reggae		
Vinny	Anything	Bugsy	Hip-hop, R & B, alternative
Steven	Rap, R & B, classical	Mike	Rap, R & B, jazz
Malcolm	Hip-hop, R & B	Anthony	Hip-hop, R & B, classical
Lunch	Rap, R & B, Reggae	Bobby	Rap, reggae
Trevor	Rap, reggae, classical	Evan	All types
Peter	Rap and other types sometimes	Barry	Rap soul
Player	All types except country	Ross	Rap, reggae, classical
Jaoquan	Hip-hop, R & B, some others	Devon	All types including classical
Roderick	Rap, reggae		
Marty	Rap, R & B		
Jerome	Rap, reggae (mother listens to classical)		
Tyrone	Hip-hop, R & B		
Roshaud	Rap reggae		
Mutt	All types		

Materialism

In these subjects' immediate communities, the visions of legitimate success were few. Jay Macleod (1995) wrote in *Ain't No Makin' It,* that the one teacher whom the students respected deeply was an unconventional man, wealthy (having made a great deal in real estate). Additionally, the students knew quite a bit about his life - a mark indicative of the teacher's "realness."

Similarly, the Bronx delinquents at one site admired signs of material wealth as evidenced by their accolades for the gym teacher's lavish car (wealth from auto-trading on the side). As noted in the previous chapter on individual traits, a desire for material prosperity can be a protective individual trait IF legitimate channels for achieving such wealth are available to the juveniles and if the at-risk child knows how to utilize them. Such involves a match in both the means and the ends for seizing the "American dream." But in a city like New York, where the images of wealth are readily available and thus, the desire for material success, the legitimately rich from some communities are athletes. Over 40 percent of the delinquents had pro-athletic expectations (not mere aspirations).

Alternative Cultural Capital: Explaining Violence

If the inner city minority student lacks mainstream social and cultural capital, what exists in their stead? Some alternative social and cultural capital - perhaps. Salt et al (1995) found that when compared to Caucasians, African-Americans report more violence and an involvement in violence at an earlier age. Regarding this point, the present data revealed a most interesting trend. Early in elementary school African-American children became the target of battery from other children. Such was especially the case if the child was male and of a large statue for his age. The physically large African-American delinquents indicated that the attacks were designed to have them prove that they could handle themselves as their size suggested. Oddly, their perceptions reflected Sheldon's mesomorph youth. Jankowski (1991) described the "necessary" acumen for violence as a way of defending oneself in an environment where one is easily prey.

While the large children were the frequent targets of unprovoked fights - no child, male or female seemed immune from this ritual. These experiences were described by delinquents and non-delinquents alike. For the most part the delinquents' stories came from a discussion in a science class. Valuably that day - the teacher, Mr. Vincent, a young black male validated these students' experiences. Having grown up in New York's projects himself he had been through similar experiences and his child (an elementary school female) was presently going through similar experiences. Feeling helpless to protect her in a school setting were the teachers were (for whatever reason) less than vigilant, he resorted to teaching her to defend herself while also emphasizing that non-violent options should still be a primary course of resolution.

The air in the classroom that day is tricky to describe. It was akin to an experience of learning that one was not alone in the world for finally an adult understood the day-to-day realities of a piece of the juveniles' fear. Yes, the sort of fear that might lead a child to bring a deadly weapon into a school for protection when the adults about him fail to protect him. Herein, the delinquent Steven said of the weapons in his school:

> STEVEN: ...the kids there. Yeah, they always talking 'bout they goin' jump somebody. Then, you get something know what I'm saying? You mostly get in trouble for it.

Where was security? At the comprehensive high school, the students stated that it was not uncommon for the security guards to look away when the metal detectors went off. Why have them then? Perhaps there was a good reason for ignoring the metal detector alarms, but the perception of the students was that there was none. They were on their own.

Consider Vinny's experiences described below:
******

VINNY: It's like I don't know my strength and I, when I get so mad, I, I just hit you, so you can feel it, but, it be, I be overdoing it sometimes, I be feeling sorry afterwards.

R: And what would happen?

VINNY: I, I'd get suspended and then when I get home I'd get in trouble because they don't understand.

R: Ummhuh.

VINNY: You know how grown people be, they be like "oh, why didn't you talk it out?" "Why didn't you tell the teacher?" You in school.

R: Ummhuh.

VINNY: You ain't goin' like "oh, he bothering me." First thing you goin' do "oh, you wanna thump, we goin' fight."

R: Ahhh...

VINNY: Nobody really goin' get up like "oh, he hit me,..... he hit me....hit me again." (in mocking childish voice) Ain't goin' do that. You goin' hit the person back.

[At another point in the interview]

VINNY: I wish people would stop telling me that 'cause once somebody tell me they goin' shoot me I take that to the

heart. I feel that you put my life in danger. The next time I
see you that's just forcing me to do something negative to
you. If you don't want that to happen just - the fight is over
it's des...??? you win some, you lose some. I mean, it don't
make no sense like goin' "I'm goin' shoot you," 'cause you
tell me you goin' shoot me; I'm goin' get you first. I mean,
'cause I don't wanna lose my life; I don't wanna get shot. So,
I'm gonna have to do you in first before you get to me.

Consider the following description of violence from Marty, the
only delinquent from a background that might be described as middle
class:

R: Has anyone in your family ever been arrested besides
you?

MARTY: Yeah. My brother got arrested.

R: For what kind of thing?

MARTY: 'Cause, alright 'cause somebody left they dog into
my yard and my brother was like "what's going on?"
(someone's name) he was drunk and he started mouthing off
and my brother punched him in the mouth, cops was called
and stuff like that.

R: What did you think about that?

MARTY: Think about it? My brother did what he had to do.
Not like he did anything wrong.

So what is an inner city parent to do? Jankowski (1991) theorized
that for impoverished persons from a large family - distrust and
competition over meager resources begin at an early age in the home.
These tendencies can flow over into community interactions and may
grow to include violence. But how exactly? The present study offers
insight. The delinquents herein were all in trouble for some violence-
related offense. Significantly, if children exhibit high rates of antisocial
behavior early in life, they are more likely to persist than children

whose initial rates are low, (Sampson & Laub 1997). Additionally, when parents are tolerant of a 10 year-old child's violent behavior they are more likely to see this child manifesting violence by age 18 (Magnum et al., 1995). Children with poor social and cognitive skills are more likely to be aggressive, (Huesmanet et al., 1992). Nonetheless, while both withdrawn and aggressive students are at-risk they are not equally so. For example, in a middle school study of 225 students (note 95 percent of the sample were white students), Ollendick and colleagues (1990) found that 13 out of 65 aggressive children and 8 out of 64 withdrawn children committed at least one delinquent offense.

Also, according to the literature, aggressiveness and peer rejection in middle school are predictive of behavioral problems in adolescence (Coie et al., 1992). Rejected children may then associate primarily with deviants because of their limited social options (Gillmore et al, 1992). But why might an African-American male be rejected by peers? Why might he be aggressive? The literature indicates that for more learning disabled students a weakness in comprehending social queues (a possible symptom of the disability) is one source of problems. The data herein indicate that for African-American males, most are the target of fights especially if they are physically large.

R: Why did they pick? Why did they do that? I don't get it?

PETER: Because I'm not the kid for fighting. I don't like to fight.

R: Ummmhuh.

PETER: I mean when I have to. So they would always try to make me fight because I didn't like to fight so they figured they could just bully me around. But, I fought back. They still didn't care.

How a Youngster May be Motivated to Deviance: The Process of Self-Derogation

Understanding motivation involves understanding the thought-action nexus. The dominant view is that motivation is largely a matter of an individual's thoughts and not innate traits (Ames & Ames 1984). Prior to "motivation" the literature spoke of "achievement theory" when discussing attributions for success or failure. Low effort that brings success is seen as brilliance while low effort that brings failure deflects criticism of one's ability (Covington 1984). Cohen (1955) and Elliott and Voss (1974) spoke of frustration from school failure as leading to school avoidance. Of course, poor performance and low involvement are not in themselves causes of delinquency (Laurence 1985). Nevertheless, these attributions affect "self-evaluations, instructional decisions, help-seeking, problem-solving strategies, emotions and expectancies about future success..." (Ames & Ames 1984).

Cohen (1955) mentioned that failing youths may respond by either i) withdrawing (avoiding school) or ii) by openly rebelling. Gutierrez (1995) took this perspective further describing the opposition as underlife. Interestingly, Stinchcombe (1964) found that middle class boys were more rebellious than working class boys possibly because of their higher aspirations not being realized.

Atkinson & Raynor (1974) also discussed a tendency to avoid achievement in order to avoid failure or humiliation or embarrassment. Maehr & Nicholls (1980) lay the context for such effects in cultural emphases. They mentioned that some cultures emphasize an ability focus ("either you have it or you don't"), others emphasize a task focus ("learning just because") and yet others emphasize a social approval focus (investing effort towards a socially approved label of "hardworking").

On the other hand, Gordon (1978) suggested that delinquency (in particular attacks on property, persons, smoking, truancy and other distracting behavior) was a method of self-enhancement in the face of failure. Similarly, Jenkins (1997: discussing Hanna 1988) spoke of the misbehavior of lower income African-American children as efforts to build self-worth in response to oppressive life experiences.

Rhodes and Reiss (1969) found grades were related to delinquency with social class held constant. Without misbehaving the students labeled "bright" or "dumb" tended to get little attention from teachers otherwise (Laurence 1985). Later Nicholls and Covington (1984) noted that "the desire to protect one's self-concept is culturally learned...it can be protected by either exerting effort and succeeding, leading to an interference of high ability, or by withholding effort (example, procrastinating) and failing, but nevertheless, avoiding an inference of low ability because no effort to succeed was made." Nicholls and Covington (1984) also argued that "competition is debilitating because it places the student in an ego-involved, threatening self-focused...state."

In addition to school performance and personality (self-sufficiency, individualism, sociability, restraint low school involvement is associated with delinquency adjudication (Laurence 1985). How school responds to early deviance affects the likelihood of delinquency adjudication later (Laurence 1985 discussing Schafer and Polk 1967).

Firm discipline rewarding conformity, encouraging involvement and social competence works as opposed to being too punitive, degrading or excluding (Laurence 1985). Laurence (1985) mentioned that students with low intellectual capability (as opposed to "ability") may respond to the frustrations of school with deviance. The students may feel that they have little to lose by acting out and teachers may believe they have little to lose by excluding them from educational activities via punishment (Laurence 1985). On the other hand non-delinquents are likely to be "group-oriented, valuing social approval," (Laurence 1985).

CHAPTER 7

Student Outcomes

Expected Findings Given the Conceptual Model

The study examined five hypotheses:

I. The greater the level of stress in the students' environment outside of school (family and neighborhood) the more likely the student is to be a delinquent.

Hypothesis number one was measured primarily by interviews with the juveniles, *(see Appendix D: 3C, items 27-39 and 44-46, 50, 120).* The questions covered common environmental stressors, often noted in the literature which includes the *Diagnostic and Statistical Manual IV* of the American Psychiatric Association. The items covered matters such as exposure to death, homelessness, illness, re-location and household interactions. Additional information came from more informal interviews with the teachers and staffers. In one case, a parent also rendered a considerable amount of information. The teachers obtained much of their information about the personal lives of their students from the students themselves after the students felt comfortable enough to confide in them. Staff members at the alternative schools also received substantial details from the students. Some of them were even privy to student records and had visited the parents' homes. In many cases they had also gotten to know the parents or guardians at parent-teacher conferences.

Utilizing teachers and staffers as additional sources of information proved quite fruitful in uncovering details about stressors which the subjects omitted in their interviews. The omissions may have been due to social desirability, some embarrassment, or a matter of trust in the researcher.

The responses to the interview items were considered in terms of the implications for each subject as an individual case given the stressors prevalence and cumulative effects. Subject responses were also coded and compared for within and without group differences (delinquents versus non-delinquents).

Amongst the delinquents, for the most part Hypothesis I held true. Those students with the most environmental stressors were the students who embraced delinquent values the most and were amongst the most delinquent (in terms of seriousness of offense, regard for illicit behaviors and indication of a strong likelihood to continue offending). Examples of these juveniles from the most dysfunctional family setting include delinquents - Roger, Steven, Malcolm, Roshaud and Vinny. These individuals were still involved in various forms of delinquency at the time of the study. Indicative of a negative social context amongst them were:

- *An absence of significant positive life experiences* (Roger a drug dealer, dealt to an addict father. Vinny's father had abandoned him years earlier and thereafter, other relatives had done the same. He also experienced the death of his mother and witnessed the incarceration of siblings. He was being raised by a 23 year old brother. Steven lived in poverty. His mother seemed somewhat unstable. His father had been incarcerated. Malcolm had been removed from the custody of a mother who sounded emotionally and otherwise unstable. Malcolm's father forcibly raped his 11-year old sister. Thus, Malcolm dwelt with a cantankerous grandmother who often told him that he would amount to nothing. Roshaud was born to a crack-addicted mother. He had been in foster care amidst a large family where his emotional needs were scarcely met. An extremely hyperactive fellow – life for him had been difficult to date.

- *Perception of their backgrounds as having been difficult.* The students from the most stressful family situations (e.g. having no parents, substance abusing parents, an incarcerated parent, an inattentive parent, or a highly critical and non-supportive guardian) described life as difficult.

- *Little exposure to mainstream cultural and social capital.* All of the most stressed subjects had a desire for wealth, but they were largely ignorant about legitimate avenues to securing it - such as how to obtain a college education). In lieu of legitimate social or cultural capital, the individuals who were "truly at-risk" were well-versed in some alternative social and cultural capital which were reflective of the environments in which they lived. This capital involved a knowledge of how to be a successful drug dealer, not becoming too emotionally attached to anyone in order to avoid emotional vulnerability, not trusting most people and not "squealing" (revealing the illegal activities of others to law enforcement). These traits all support the findings of Jankowski (1991) regarding the effects of poverty on inner city youths who become delinquent.

- *Household composition* (often there was a father involved, but, he was a criminal figure for whom the "truly at-risk" juveniles had little if any respect).

- *Socio-economic status of poverty.* All but one delinquent qualified for free school lunches. Such lunches are free for families with incomes at 1.3 times federal poverty guidelines and subsidized for families with incomes at 1.85 the poverty guidelines (Alexander et al. 1994).

- *Weak formal and informal support systems.* Formal support (towards academic and behavioral success) was available in abundance at the alternative school. Before the alternative school it had been scarce. Informal support towards academic and behavioral success had been inconsistent. For the truly at-risk, it appeared their families held diminished aspirations for them.

- *Family cohesion.* All of the "truly at-risk" juveniles were from families with low family cohesion. An exception was Vinny. He was being raised by a 23-year old brother.

- *Active religiosity.* The "truly at-risk" juveniles all had some history of church attendance. However, by high school age, participation in religious activities was almost non-existent. Exceptions included Roger and others like Trevor and Jerome. These three attended church services more than once per week, largely because their mothers saw to it that they did. Apparently, the religious ideals had not been deeply internalized by the juveniles because it did not stop their delinquency - though by keeping them busy and away from deviant peers, it might have reduced it.

- *Positive parent-child communication.* Positive parent-child communication was scarce for the "truly at-risk" delinquents (Roger, Vinny, Steven and Malcolm). The nature of Roger's communication with his parents was unclear. However, it was unlikely to have been substantial for his mother was ignorant of her husband being a crack addict whom Roger supplied with drugs on occasion. Vinny had a good relationship with the 23-year old brother who raised him, but he had a long history of having a horrible time with relatives who were responsible for him before his brother emerged. Steven stated that his home life was miserable. He claimed the grandmother with whom he lived often belittled him. Malcolm had poor communications with his foster mother. He claimed that she was responsible for so many children implying that this was probably the best that she could do. Less deviant students described more positive relations with their parents. Such communications indicated a significant bonding between parent and child and close, *consistent parental monitoring*. According to the alternative school staff, the most delinquent youngsters led largely unsupervised lives - so much so, that when their parents were informed about their deviance, the parents often refused to believe it. These parents had become so involved in the dramas of their own lives (drug and partner problems)- that they had left their children to form their own lives of chaos.

- *parent school involvement.* The "truly at-risk" delinquents' parents were largely not involved in the juveniles' school. They did not attend parent-teacher conferences with any regularity. The students stated that their parents or guardians were too busy (with work) to render them such attention. The situation was the opposite for less deviant students whose parents managed to take time to attend meetings and to inquire, if only by telephone about their child's performance. The most delinquent students were from families where family gatherings and other activities suggestive of close extended family relations were far less prominent. There was clear support for Jankowski's (1991) theory that often the most disadvantaged persons in the inner city are the least emotionally connected with others beyond a surface intimacy because more than that renders them emotionally vulnerable. Also, in these families that are often large, the competition for scarce resources makes kindred very suspicious of each other.

- *Parents as risk.* With the exception of Marty's mother, all of the delinquents' parents or guardians could be described as agents of risk. Either these parents or others to whom they granted their children significant exposure had demonstrated major deviance to the juveniles. Consider Vinny's incarcerated brother, the alcoholism of Trevor's mother, the incestuous rape by Steven's father and the frequent belittling that he endured from his grandmother. In a number of cases, these boys had seen their mothers beaten by the men in their lives. Often they were themselves their mother's confidants and in that role felt compelled to assume the role of her protector. Nonetheless, when their mothers expected the boys to act as sons, the parental inconsistency seemed a source of   conflict.   This   was especially the case for delinquents Roderick (gun charge), and Jaoquan (violence).

- *High emphasis on materialistic pursuits.* It appeared that both the delinquent and non-delinquent subjects did not have a high emphasis on materialistic pursuits. The most common response to the question on whether having a lot of money was important was "yes." However, when asked to elaborate most of the juveniles indicated that "a lot" meant merely enough to pay all of their bills in a timely fashion – and things like becoming homeowners someday instead of remaining renters. For high school level students, the knowledge of money – for example the earning potential of various jobs was very low - again a sign of a lack of cultural capital. However, there was no indication that a particularly strong drive for an excess of material possessions influenced their delinquency.

-    *Mother's education.* The non-delinquents fared slightly better than their delinquent counterparts. Their parents, older siblings or some extended family member were more likely to have had some college background. Amongst the delinquents, most parents had no college at all. Quite possibly, these students might have done better, had their parents more knowledge to pass on to them. Thus, with the exception of Marty's mother, the educational press was weak. Most of the juveniles (delinquent and non) stated that their parents would be satisfied if they merely passed their classes. In the event of failure, most said that their parents would simply tell them to do better. Of course, this laid back stance towards achievement does not exist in isolation. It reflects the larger American position of merely encouraging students to "try" lest with too much effort they appear to be "nerds" (overly absorbed with academia) or otherwise intellectually deficient.

-    *Attributions of success to effort versus ability.* Most of the delinquents stated that success was a matter of effort. However, at other points in some of the interviews there were statements to the contrary. For example, Vinny spoke of intelligence as a gift – a view in keeping with the common American perspective of the innateness of intelligence.

-    *High neighborhood collective efficacy.* Neighborhood collective efficacy is present when neighbors know each other, look out for the well-being of each other, and take care of their common spaces. Such was not particularly evident amongst the subjects. They noted some sense of community – a familiarity with their neighbors, but these were scarcely friendships. Indeed, it appeared that delinquents were more likely to be familiar with the neighbors than non-delinquents.

Again, the project is not a quantitative one. Thus, the results herein are in no way predictive. Largely, they provide indicators of future qualitative and quantitative research directions.

II. The greater the volume of positive interactions that the student has with teachers (that is the more the student cooperates with the teacher's scripted pact) the less likely the student is to be a delinquent.

This was measured largely by observing the classroom interactions of students and teachers twice per week over the course of at least two-thirds of a semester. The classroom sessions were also audio-taped where permitted and examined for markers of positive interactions. This hypothesis was strongly supported by the findings. The students who most strongly embraced delinquent values were also amongst the most disruptive students in the classrooms. These students included delinquents – Vinny, Malcolm and Roshaud. Many of their alternative school teachers believed that the misbehavior in class was most likely when the class materials proved too challenging for them.

According to the delinquents reports' about their school experiences prior to beginning the alternative school the hypothesis also held true because the delinquents were, for the most part students who had been the ones disrupting class for some time before being expelled from school. Most of the delinquents noted that for their present offense they were other students involved, but they had been the ones expelled (scapegoated) because they had accumulated a record of classroom disruption such that the teachers and school administrators had been awaiting an excuse to expel them. Thus, a history of classroom disruptions had increased the odds that these students would be the ones reported to law enforcement and adjudicated delinquent. Indeed, it is conceivable that if the classroom materials prove most challenging for certain socio-economically disadvantaged students who begin school behind their peers and who continue to lag behind, then, macro variables are most responsible for these micro manifestations of delinquency.

III. If the student performs poorly academically and / or behaviorally early in the semester, the teacher's positive regard for the student (if it ever existed) will ebb for the rest of the semester.

This was measured largely by observations twice per week over the course of at least two-thirds of a semester and by informal interviews with the teachers throughout the semester. Positive regard refers to a positive stance in persisting in an effort to teach each student and otherwise positively impact them. This hypothesis was not supported by the findings herein. Overall, at both the alternative and comprehensive high schools the students before them. Indeed, as the semester progressed the teachers learnt more about the lives of the students before them. Thus, if anything, after learning of many of the students' background the positive regard for students was likely to increase, not ebb. The strongest example of this was Ms. Black at the alternative school. Her compassion for her students grew as she learnt the details of their lives.

The striking difference concerning the less successful comprehensive schoolteachers was that they did not want to concern themselves with the extra details of their students' lives. When such matters came up in the classroom they engaged in silencing, using a desire to complete the curriculum as an excuse. They were also unavailable to students outside of class. According to these teachers the schools had not facilitated such relationships – they had no offices or permanent classrooms to call their own, nor did they have a telephone at the school to readily call anyone.

IV. The weaker the positive regard that the teacher has for a student, the more likely the student is to be disengaged from school.

This was measured largely by observations twice per week over the course of at least two-thirds of a semester. Information also came from interviews with the teachers regarding their perceptions of each student and from listening to the teachers' casual conversations amongst themselves. Student disengagement included various withdrawal behaviors such as truancy, or attending classes with minimal or no participation.

Comprehensive school observation data supported these findings. When the students perceived a teacher looked down upon them many students behaved disrespectfully towards that teacher – ignoring his or her requests, not doing their assignments, sitting with heads on the desk, leaving the room without permission, adjusting make-up and chattering.

Alternative school observation data indicated that the above scenarios need not be. There were some students whom the teachers did not particularly fancy. However, it appeared that those students never knew it. The teachers maintained their positive regard towards them when interacting with them.

V. The trajectory to academic success is very similar to that for non-delinquency (and vice-versa).

This was measured largely by interviews with the students, teachers, and staffers about the students' social contexts, school histories and their present school context *(See Appendix D)*. The responses were then isolated and the most common patterns and themes identified in an effort to describe the common school-related trajectories to: academic success and non-delinquency or, academic success and delinquency, or academic failure and delinquency, or academic failure and non-delinquency. The data support the hypothesis. Thus, students from the most disadvantaged social situations were the most likely to have an on-going record of delinquency. This did not follow in each case. Consider Steven. He was not a particularly weak student but his family situation could scarcely have been more dysfunctional. Removed from the charge of his mother, he lived in foster care with a most discouraging grandmother. His violent father had abused his mother and raped his 11 year-old sister. Steven had been expelled for having a gun in school. Serious? Yes, but he voiced no longstanding embrace of deviance. He claimed the gun was for protection in a school where many other students had guns. He had carried the weapon to school many times (as others also did he said) before getting caught.

The Delinquents' Reflections on Their Deviant Outcome

Regarding their delinquency the juveniles spoke of being misunderstood. Commonly they described themselves as being scapegoated - targeted by teachers for persecution and exclusion as soon as the opportunity presented itself. Indeed, in most cases the delinquents had accumulated a record of minor mischievous behavior prior to the offense that got them suspended.

> RUSSELL: I got sent here 'cause a kid made accusations that I choked him, but it turns like there was a whole bunch a kids and we was all play-fighting. So, he went back and told the dean or whatever that I choked him. So, then Friday came, then they came to my class and they got me. And then they told me I was getting suspended for a year. I got sent here.

+++++++++++

> ROGER: I supposed to have did a robbery but I didn't do it. They found out the other person and I'm supposed to be leaving (states when).

> R: Ok, aamm this was a ... how come? How did that happen?

> ROGER: I was with the person when they took the glasses and had the glasses back before I gave it back to him. And my friend see me then and I was with him, so he's running trying to put (?) it back and my friend ran and I got caught.

+++++++++++

> VINNY: Like, I had gotten into a fight with this kid over some gold teeth. He took the gold teeth from a friend of mine and I had to get it back and they said that I broke his fingers....

> R: Ummmm.

> VINNY: Swelled up his eye, eye and he almost got a concussion, and they sent me here.

> R: Mummm so how do you feel about being here- that whole incident?

VINNY: Really, I wish, I wish that it had never happened. I felt that, that, I could solve the situation in a different way, but, I didn't think about it. I just rushed into it. I got what I deserved.

R: The situation, was it just you who rushed in or were there other people.

VINNY: There was other people.

R: And where are they, where are they - did they go back to school?

VINNY: They went back to school.

R: So, how come you wound up here?

VINNY: 'Cause he say I was the only one who did it.

+++++++++++++

STEVEN: Aaammm gun charges.

R: Gun charges? What did you do? Brought a gun in?

STEVEN: Yeah, gun in school.

R: Aaammm how come?

STEVEN: I mean, I mean like everybody in my school had everything. They had guns, they had blades, they had drugs in the school. I mean that's why when they said the principal got fired at was kind of happy. Because he, he tried to put so much pressure on me because he didn't know how many people was selling drugs out of that school.

R: Ummhuh.

STEVEN: Other people had guns and knives and everything at that school.

R: In this was a junior high or high?

STEVEN: Junior high school.

[Later in the interview]

STEVEN: Yeah, but, he gave me the gun in school. I never had the gun in school and he admitted that, that he had the gun in school and that aaammm know what I'm saying, it's the first time I had the gun in that school. He give it to me outside the school, that, that one day, know what I'm saying.

R: And, but he got to go back?

STEVEN: He got to go back, he got to go back, he got to graduate, know what I'm saying?

++++++++++++++

MALCOLM: Something I didn't do. They said I stabbed a kid.

(Later in the interview)

R: Ok. Aaamm, so how'd you feel about the incident, you said you didn't do it?

MALCOLM: I really don't, I really don't care.

++++++++++++++

LUNCH: Alright, it was over...it was me and my friend, we was aaammm I was going try and let him go in with my program card in lunch room right?

R: Umhuh.

LUNCH: And he aaammm they knew, they knew my name on the program ca..., the program card they see that and they took it from him. But they didn't know that I had given it to him so I was like, so I, so I gave it, so they told me that somebody was trying to get in with my program card.

R: Umhuh.

LUNCH: So, they was like, "Go get it from Officer (person's last name)." That was one of the school safety officers.

R: Umhuh.

LUNCH: And I went over there, I was like "Can I get my program card?" He was like "naaw get out of here. You're not getting it back." He was cursing and stuff. I'm like "can I get my program card back?" "Get the hell outta here." I try to take it out his hand and then we started touching it, we started fighting.

R: Ummmmmm.

LUNCH: He wanted to fight me and then another security guard came and grabbed me from the back. I had throw him over my shoulder and stuff and hit him. And, and mass security guards came in there and handcuffed me and stuff.

R: Hummm.

At the alternative school it was important that all school personnel stay calm when students attempted to escalate situations into serious confrontations. Refusing to take on another's frustration in a situation can diffuse that situation. While observations at the comprehensive school did not include any sightings of teachers acting belligerently towards students, the delinquents reported that such scenarios were not uncommon.

+++++++++++++

R: Six months, ok. And why were you sent here? What happened?

TREVOR: Aamm, they, they said, aamm how you say when you like mess up a classroom? Vandalism?

R: Oh, vandalism?

TREVOR: Yeah, vandalism.

(Later in the interview)

R: Ok, but did you do the vandalism?

TREVOR: No. I didn't do that.

R: Do you know who did? Any idea?

TREVOR: Yeah, I know who did it.

R: And what happened to them? Did they get punished, or...?

TREVOR: They got suspended. But, they didn't get suspended like me.

R: So, they got to go back?

TREVOR: Yeah, they got to go back.

R: So, how do you feel about that? That they got to go back?

TREVOR:I felt that was wrong. That was real wrong.

++++++++++++

PETER: I had got caught in school with a pellet gun.

R: How did that happen? How come you had a pellet gun?

PETER:Play a game..[*manhunting*]..they play up-state too.

R: Uhhhhuh

PETER: ...you put on heavy clothing and that kind of thing so you won't get hurt.

R: Ahhhhuh..

PETER: ...but then I didn't know it was illegal to bring it to school so.

+++++++++++++

PLAYER: I was accused of threatening a girl with a knife.

R: Ahhh, what was that about? How did that happen?

PLAYER: 'Cause really what happened was I was bothering her and she told me to stop but I didn't.

R: You were doing what?

PLAYER: I was bothering her, playing around with her all day long but she told me to stop, leave her alone, but I didn't listen. She was like, "if you keep messing with me, I'll get you in trouble, I'm gonna get you in trouble." So then, I thought, I thought, "hey she gonna get me in trouble when I didn't...???" I didn't think she was gonna say something like that. Then, she got her friend to agree with her, and then....

R: Did you have a knife on you at all? No?

PLAYER: No. They didn't find nothing on me. No weapons or nothing like that and it was just that it was two people who said that I had it and they thought that I passed it to one of my friends or something.....???

R: Ehhh had you ever been in any kind of trouble, any before that?

PLAYER: Yes.

R: For like what kind of thing?

PLAYER: Just interrupting class, talking in class, not listening to the teacher *[active resistance, per Gutierrez 1995]*.

R: Ok, but nothing major?

PLAYER: No. This was the first time this ever happened to me. I was surprised man; I was like leave these girls alone or whatever and from now on I just get out of school and then....

(Later in the interview)

R: Aaammmm....when you got into trouble with this girl, were you with other friends joking around or just you joking around with her?

PLAYER: Actually, the whole class was in there and it had been like, it had been into the period. And then, I was about to leave to go to my next class. The teacher grabbed me and threw me against the wall and it was like: "You got a knife on you don't you?" And I was like "no." So, they just tell me to empty my pockets and everything. They didn't find anything and I still didn't leave the classroom or anything like that, but......

++++++++++++++

JAOQUAN: 'Cause I had gotten into an argument with a teacher.

R: Ummhuh.

JAOQUAN: And I pushed the teacher and they suspended me.

R: Aammm, the teachers at your school before, how did you get along with them? Would you say you got along well with them? Didn't like them?

JAOQUAN: I don't know about everybody but you bother me...I bother you.

R: Ok. So, that one teacher, what sort of thing happened?

JAOQUAN: What happened was that I went to get my picture, my school pictures but this other person had gotten into an argument with this other teacher.

R: Ummhuh.

JAOQUAN: So, when I went to get my pictures that lady said I couldn't get my pictures 'cause I was arguing with this teacher...

R: Ummhuh.

JAOQUAN: But the thing that got me mad was, I was arguing with that teacher, it didn't concern her.

R: Ummhuh.

JAOQUAN: So, she wouldn't give me my pictures, so I went kicking the door and everything.

R: Ummhuh.

JAOQUAN: Some other teacher came out of the way and pushed me.

R: Ummhuh.

JAOQUAN: So when I, she tried to touch me, I like just through my hands off her...

R: Ummhuh.

JAOQUAN: And she went into the wall. And, that's why they kicked me out.

R: Ummhuh. But, other than that you got along with the teachers?

++++++++++++++

RODERICK: 'Cause I had a gun and I don't think I should be here though.

R: Ok, you had a gun on campus?

RODERICK: Naaaw...a block from the school.

R: Aaammm what was that about? Why'd you have a gun?

RODERICK: I just had it.

++++++++++++++

MARTY: Well, I had caught a case at my other school.

R: What was the case about?

MARTY: They say I robbed somebody which was a lie. Guilty, I got guilt by association because I was there.

++++++++++++++

JEROME: I got in a fight with a guy at the school. Me and my friends jumped him.

R: Alright was it somebody from school or....?

JEROME: Yeah, he was in the same school with us.

R: Ok.

JEROME: And then, he came back the Wednesday and then they kicked me out.

(Later in the interview)

JEROME: If I did it, if I could do it again, I would have acted differently. I would a never did it.

R: Aaahh mind if I ask, over what? What was the fight about?

JEROME: Oh, 'cause he was looking at my friend, you know, talking a lot of trash, you know, and because it was in school, the security guard's right there.

R: Ahh..

JEROME: He could talk and talk and talk. So we..??? see him after school.

++++++++++++++

TYRONE: Aammmm I was accused of assault charge aammm with a teacher at my old school which was (name of school). I don't consider that an assault charge. It was an accident, but, she was real old.

R: Uuuhuh. What happened? What did she say happened?

TYRONE: I went to another class to pick up a walkman of mines and the girl was playing around in the classroom, closing the door. It was two sides to the door. So the girl was running to this door, so I closed it, so the teacher wanted to know why I was there, so I was trying to explain to the teacher. But, she wasn't trying to hear me.

R: Okay.

TYRONE: And aamm, so the girl finally came to the door, but the teacher was like holding the door so I wouldn't get in.

R: Uuummhuh.

TYRONE: And aaammm, so I put my like I was in the middle of the door and she was in the middle of me and the girl is in the classroom. So, I went to reach and got my walkman. And, the walkman accidentally dropped on her head and she...

R: She called that "assault?"

TYRONE: Yeah.

+++++++++++

ROSHAUD: I hit a teacher in the head with a bottle.

R: What happened?

ROSHAUD: I hit a teacher in the head with a bottle.

R: You had...oh hit a teacher? With a bottle?

ROSHAUD: Mmmhuh, 24 - liquor bottle.

R: Ahhh, what happened?

ROSHAUD: With the teacher?

R: Yeah. What?

ROSHAUD: All right, in class he always pop jokes (?). He's popping mad stuff saying "sit down" and stuff, and all that, calling me names and then, after school, I had cut school then, he came out and then I was like "what now?"

R: Unhuh.

ROSHAUD: And he was like, "alright, shut up" and then another teacher said "shut up" and I was like "I'm not talking to you; I'm talking to my teacher."

R: Ummhuh.

ROSHAUD: And they would say....both saying "shut up."
So, I went up the block, picked up a big glass bottle and
threw it.

The anecdotes of the delinquents above indicated a stark sensitivity
to injustice that was also manifested in their daily interactions at the
alternative school. Thus, the alternative school teachers often explained
any of their decisions regarding the students that might otherwise
appear unfair. Many students believed that they had been scapegoated
by their previous schools because when they were suspended, their
accomplices were not. Nonetheless, after exchanging stories with each
other, they concluded that their record of largely minor misbehaviors
had counted against them in a most substantial way.

Non-Delinquents

Why do some children become delinquent and not others?   A
comparison of life stories indicated that the lives of the delinquents
were overall more dysfunctional than the lives of the non-delinquents.
Across the board poverty was common. However, having a consistent,
significant, conforming adult figure in their lives, or parents who were
not substance abusers mattered. Of course, the influence of a positive
teacher also made a difference. Through various significant attachments
with positive relations or non-relations the social and cultural capital
towards conforming was imparted and internalized by most of the non-
delinquents in the study. This included alternative ways of settling
disputes besides violence (walking away, or seeking teacher facilitated
dispute resolution), and a knowledge of how to realize their material
aspirations.
    The role of teachers herein, involves building significant
attachments to students in order to mediate against deviance. Such
relationships come via sincere caring and an exchange of information
that the students called "being real." This "realness" involved imparting
the social and cultural capital necessary for the students' success
without looking upon the students as inferior beings. This required an
unconditional positive regard that included communicating that a
promising future was within grasp. When this did not happen, the
trajectory of disadvantage continued towards hopeless and
helplessness. Out of these relationships academic growth was rare.

Many teachers at the comprehensive school believed that discipline had to be in place before significant learning would occur. However, the three semesters worth of observations and the interviews with delinquents and non-delinquents herein indicate that the old navy adage holds truth - "rules without relationship breeds rebellion." With rebellion, exclusion from the school context may occur and thereafter, illegitimate avenues pursued.

The findings herein also indicate that all of the parties involved in the model are important. The macros social context from which the students and teachers came dictated how teacher and students operated in the school context initially. The individual traits that the students brought into the relationship helped to facilitate or aggravate that relationship. Nonetheless, the effective alternative and comprehensive schoolteachers herein demonstrated that regardless of how the teachers or students began school, this course could be affected for the better. Teachers who care for their students and who care to be trained can be. After all, most students did not want to be ignorant. Granted, some students may need to be convinced that education could work to their advantaged (if another message had been communicated to them prior). In such situations the principal should make high expectations the norm, provide teachers support, resources and a voice to help students succeed before holding them accountable for student performance. By being "real" in the sharing of themselves with their students and listening to their students in a caring manner, teachers can build relationships with their at-risk students. Such relationships need to be in place before discipline. Then learning might occur effectively with similarly at-risk or truly at-risk students. When these are in place, the present study suggests that student-teacher interactions have a far less marginalizing texture. Thus, students feel free to speak, to be vulnerable with their ignorance and hence, access the necessary help to catch up academically. With schools as a pleasant experience and a perceived avenue to upward mobility, the embrace of delinquency should weaken. Students cannot aspire to ways of life that are foreign to them. They may merely wish upon them.

CHAPTER 8
What's To Be Done

As previously established, the family is extremely important in determining a child's behavioral outcome and academic success (Hoover-Depsey & Sandler 1997 discussing: Chavkin 1993; Eccles & Harold 1993; Epstein 1991, 1994; Hess & Holloway 1984: Hobbs et al., 1984; United States Department of Education 1994). Also previously established is that the paucity of significant academic achievement amongst most African-Americans is not a function of cultural deprivation but a dearth of cultural and social capital necessary to navigate mainstream society and thus take advantage of all that the dominant culture has to offer. Markedly, parents cannot pass on to their children knowledge that they themselves do not possess.

However, parents may be equipped to assist their children in deciphering life's options. This does not require changing the essence of the family's culture but imparting to parents the knowledge to assist their children effectively. As with the alternative school herein, schools can take the initiative of instructing parents on how to advocate for their children in their educational system – so that each parent may do his or her part to see that his/her child has a shot at getting the best teachers "next year." Beyond teaching parents how to help children succeed, the school personnel may have to also foster in the parents a sense of efficacy in their parenting ability (Hoover-Depsey & Sandler 1997). Such lessons may be taught more easily during the pre-school years (when parents are usually more attentive to matters regarding their children and through home visits supplemented by parenting classes (Wassermann et al., 2000).

What Works and What Does Not

Teacher Development

Developing a professional as opposed to a personal orientation towards students is important. As such teachers may find students in the classroom whom they may not like, but whom they manage to teach effectively regardless, (Haberman, 1995). To develop this skill training in a classroom where mistakes are allowed is important, (Haberman, 1995). Also teachers need to be taught to become change agents with skills of critical self-analysis, self-reflection and culturally relevant teaching, (Carroll, 1990 citing Frank Newman, 1985; Gay, 1993). Clearly, a course, class, workshop, conference, book or article will not change the attitudes and behaviors of everyone (Fereshteh, 1995). However, cultural-content courses supplemented by strictly controlled practicums amongst diverse students might (Gunzenhauser, 1996; Ladson-Billings, 1995).

Immersion in another culture is one of the most powerful ways to create a multicultural perspective. Whether such immersion is foreign or domestic, it should be a common part of pre-service teacher training. These could take the form of internships, practicums, or other fieldwork (Clark et al., 1996; Cannella & Reiff, 1994: Englert, 1997; Payne, 1980; Russo & Talbert-Johnson, 1997; Weiner, 1993). Havas and Lucas (1994) suggested volunteering 15 hours in a community agency as part of one's observations of a community. Such field assignments should include opportunities for reflection on "critical incidents" (Barrett, 1993). This would certainly develop the pre-service teachers' observational and analytical skills on the norms, values and attitudes of others (Clark, 1996; Payne, 1980). It would be a giant step towards the "collective empowerment of a community" instead of a step towards a blossoming, but ineffective teacher with a "messiah complex." Havas and Lucas, (1994) suggested sophomore year for beginning these multicultural field experiences. At this point students are often sufficiently confident with a year of course work behind them.

Parental Inclusion

In communicating with parents, teachers can present themselves in such a manner that parents are more comfortable in approaching them on specific points. Indeed, the literature suggests that students do better when they perceive that teachers and parents are collaborating to ensure a child's academic success. For many urban schools where parents work and thus, find attending school meetings arduous an approach like that of the alternative school herein may be adopted where the venue and time of parent–teacher meeting were rotated to facilitate some parent-teacher contact. Schools could also arrange parent pick-ups where transportation is a problem. Since most students live in the vicinity of their school, such an effort should not be terribly expensive. For more active parental involvement some parents may be given a stipend for encouraging and facilitating the participation of their peers in school programs. As is common in Catholic schools – some minimal service to the school may be required of parents and guardians to increase their input and sense of ownership and comfort with the academic institutions. The present study supports Hsia and Beyer (2000) on the importance of empowering families in similar ways towards reducing delinquency.

Of course, for any of the above measures to work successfully teachers must want such to be the case. It is questionable in present day New York City schools whether teachers like those in the comprehensive one discussed herein want parents to be involved. The context of many of these teachers appears to be a severe divided loyalty to themselves and/or their private concerns (a second job, their own children at home, and the possibility of "escape" from work that they find unsatisfying. The children before them are merely "other people's kids" and parental involvement would be interference. This, of course is not the case for ALL teachers in disadvantaged city schools. There are many who voice a degree of care for their students as if they were their own. Others unwittingly contributed to their students' failure by failing to rid themselves of their sense of helplessness as teachers.

Administrative Responsibility

While caring about children may be the single most important ingredient in educating inner city students, money matters where gaining a quality education is concerned (for example, in hiring quality teachers, using updated teaching aids). Administrators of failing city public schools must admit that their schools have problems and then proceed to fix them. This is admittedly not easy to do – because comprehensive school administrators promptly re-package their failures to look like successes. Consider Michelle Fine's *Framing Dropouts* (1991) a study of a New York City comprehensive high school which proudly touted a high graduation rate – by failing to mention that most of the students who entered the school in each class had dropped out.

Local administrators can also take the lead in making the education of African-Americans and latinos in New York City additive, not subtractive by celebrating the culture, speech and music of people of color. They can also encourage realness, not silencing about ethnic, class and cultural difference evident in their classrooms. Administrators may also be able to make the school grounds ascetically pleasing whether or not the school's external environment is. To further facilitate the bonding of teachers and students to the school active extra-curricular programming should take place. A primary obstacle here is that teachers need to be paid more to do more. Nevertheless, as the alternative school indicated with just a little bit more – such things can happen.

Also, improve juvenile empathy (Hsia and Beyer 2000). At the alternative school the teachers and administrators alike made it a point to bond with the delinquent students because "there are more of them than they are us" (seven teachers to about 32 students attending regularly in each school building). For safety's sake it was important that the students saw each adult at the site as an individual human being. The teachers and administrators accomplished this by taking turns fixing meals and dining with the students at both breakfast and lunch. They also used their opportunities to share details of their personal lives and growing up experiences with the students. Of course, they utilized all possible opportunities to inquire about the students, and to advocate on their behalf when the students had been wronged. Such actions communicate caring to students while also rendering a voice and some legitimacy to the context from which their students come.

Of course, the model alternative school herein enjoyed the luxury of a longer school day such that instruction was not sacrificed when teachers took the time to share with students. Yet, even within a 40-minute class period such steps can be taken – bit-by-bit each day. Indeed in comprehensive schools many of the more effective teachers took time to involve themselves in the lives of their students. Quite possibly this makes a classroom setting more inviting for learning. For indeed, if one cares about the teacher, one is less likely to disappoint him or her.

Addressing Student Issues

Improve anger management and decision-making skills (Hsia and Beyer 2000) through psycho-education, (Wassermann et al., 2000). The alternative school successfully implemented various strategies to this end. The staff made it a theme in their interactions with the delinquents - "think before you act." They placed signs related to that theme at prominent points throughout the school lest, heaven forbid anyone should forget it. The result? For the most part - it worked!

Next, address illicit substance involvement (Hsia and Beyer 2000). For the most part it appears that African-American high school age delinquents might be more inclined to sell drugs than to use it. Yet, the smoking of marijuana (a possible "gateway drug") was common and one alternative school subject was identified as actively using cocaine. The use and "business" of drug dealing are such that it is but a matter of time that one's liberty and or life will be in serious jeopardy. There are other ways to make it and teachers need to communicate this to their students.

Impose immediate and graduated sanctions (Hsia and Beyer 2000). In New Jersey such efforts worked for at least the short term. This involved providing intensive re-entry or aftercare services to ensure juvenile offenders' successful return to their communities. It is a far worthier investment to build on the juveniles' strengths while also involving them with pro-social peers whenever possible (Hsia and Beyer 2000 discussing: Altschuler & Armstrong 1994; Heneggler et al., 1995; Lewis et al., 1994, Umbreit, 1995). In the New Jersey program noted above, the juveniles lived at home while attending their program from 8:00 a.m. to 6: 00 p.m. Similarly, in the New York program the delinquents lived at home and attended school by day. Of course, the students who got these sanctions were the ones expected to comply. Using the least restrictive alternative reduces the stigma of a torrid label that could build deeper self-derogation and thus, foster ties with students determined to stay criminally deviant.

Regarding putting police officers in the school. Such would be recommended only if those officers were of a genteel nature, respectful of diverse ethnic groups and thus, like the officers at the alternative school. Whether the New York Police Department has enough of these people, willing to work in a school setting remains to be seen. Better yet, divert behavioral problem students who need the extra attention to facilities like the alternative school for a limited time - so that others will not see officers on a regular basis.

Foster both student and teacher bonding to the school. Laurence (1985) suggested an increase in the odds of school success via active involvement in classroom and extra-curricular (towards school commitment). Also making the curriculum relevant to the job market. Ogbu (1995) argued for more multiculturalism in education to improve understanding between minorities and whites, closer ties to school and better feelings about the self. Have juvenile personnel, parents and school officials working more closely to avert academic failure and thus avoid delinquency. Also necessary are closer collaborations among social service agencies – the networking of recreation providers, education providers, health practitioners, and mental health counselors (Hsia & Beyer 2000).

Many of the adolescents were unaware of when they had been the victim or perpetrator of certain offenses that they perceived as merely "a part of life." Efforts should be made to disseminate information to both children and their families about activities that may be perceived as "part of life" but which really should be reported to the police. These would include - sexual assaults, being attacked by peers their own age or older, being a victim of theft - even if the odds of recovery are low. In the larger society however, the police have a ways to go in convincing minority communities that they are their servants. Indeed, the question remains - has crime gone down in some communities or are the police grown so distant that it is actually the reporting that has declined?

The public sector in New York is well known for being extremely secretive when it comes to juvenile delinquents under their charge. After a year awaiting permission to proceed, New York's Child Youth and Protective Services denied the investigator's permission to question ask questions on race on the grounds that they believed that they would be too sensitive and the responses likely to be misinterpreted by the press. Apparently, they had been "burnt" by a researcher's work before. They referred the researcher to three private facilities far away in up-state New York. Sadly, even in the juvenile justice system race is being treated like a bad script and silenced. With the over-representation of blacks and Hispanics in the city's juvenile justice system - this is a problem. On the other hand, with a good product to offer, the city's alternative schools were eager to be scrutinized for publicity despite their internal problems.

The criminal justice literature may be enriched by further study on causes of delinquency. The family and the individual have long been examined. However, the influence of schools has not received similar vigorous scrutiny. Students spend much of their lives in school and the authority figures therein may be presumed to have substantial impact especially during a student's early years. Teachers are a significant source of information about life and its options. As such, they are well worth examination especially since schools are philosophically the "great equalizers." For many African-Americans they are not - the reasons and dynamics of this situation should be identified if crime is to be excluded from their life's options. Questions which remain unanswered include: When do African-American children begin to loose interest in school? What triggers this? And how? What larger social structure forces are at play and how in shaping the quality of the product available in various public compared to private educational institutions? And exactly which external factors pull on a student's ability to fully invest in his or her education? What exactly beyond school effects shapes a rejection of legitimate structures for illegitimate structures to material success? Much of these answers will involve a merger of quantitative and qualitative research. For indeed, as Marva Collins would put it – "kids don't fail, teachers fail, schools fail."

Appendix

D: 2B - Questions for the Juveniles about School

Some items adapted from Brody et al., 1996; Cernkovich and Giordano, 1987; Demo & Hughes 1990; Fine 1991; and, Laosa 1982.

*TO BE READ ALOUD TO THE RESPONDENT: *Good day (first name of the subject).................... First let me say "thank you" for taking the time to meet with me today. As you know from the letter that you received about this study, our meeting today is to better understand how different areas of life may lead some folks into delinquency or may prevent delinquency.*

Remember that participation in this study is voluntary. We may stop whenever you like and you do not have to answer every question. Also you may ask me to turn the tape recorder off at any time. Our communication here is anonymous in that your name will not be attached to any of the response sheets. It is also confidential, in that the answers you give will not be revealed to anyone other than my academic advisor. Any reports on this study will not include information that may be traced back to you.

There are two possible exceptions to confidentiality:

1) while it is rare, a court could order me (by subpoena) to hand over the interview materials; and,

2) if you tell me that you or anyone else under 18 years is the victim of abuse, physical or sexual, I will have to report this to the proper authorities for further investigation.

This interview will take less than 1 _ hours. If you would like to take a break at some point - let me know. As we go along I will be making notes. Any questions before we begin?

1. How long have you been at this school?
2. Why are you attending this school?
3. Where did you attend elementary school? Junior high?
4. What kind of student are you?
5. Do you like high school? Why or why not?
6. What sort of letter grades are you getting so far this year {PROMPT: that is, mostly 'As' or 'Bs' or 'Cs' and so on; can you tell me how many of each letter grade?}.
7. What is responsible for how you are doing in school?
8. Tell me about activities available for students at this school?
9. Is there anything about school life that you find particularly frustrating?

10. Is there anything about school life that you find particularly enjoyable?

11. Tell me about your worst school memory.

12. Tell me about your favorite school memories.

13. Has anyone ever said anything to you that you wish was never said?

14. Tell me about your relationship with other students at the school?

15. Why do you think some students do really well in school?

16. Tell me about the students who do poorly in school.

17. If you could change anything about this school what would it be?

18. Tell me about the best teachers in the school. Why are they the best?

19. Tell me about the worst teachers in the school. Why are they the worst?

20. Overall, are you satisfied with this school? Why or why not?

21. Do you get help with your schoolwork outside of the classroom?

22. It seems that you have stayed out of trouble with the law. Tell me what separates you from your friends who got into trouble.

23. Tell me about any times that you may have broken the law. What separates you from those who have not broken the law?

24. Five years from now, let's see, by then you would be about _____ years old. Where do you see yourself - doing what?

25. Ten years from now, you will be_____ years old. What's your life like? {PROMPT: Where do you live; do you live alone (married, children); do you own a car - if so what kind; what do you do for a living?}

26. Describe how you feel most of the time when you know that you will be going to school?

27. What sort of activities do you and your school friends do after school?

28. Describe how your previous school compares to this one?

29. Is there anything about any of your teachers that you would change - anything at all?

30. Can you remember two instances when you got into trouble - any kind of trouble - at school (it does not matter when - maybe this year or last year?) {PROMPTS: What did you do (or not do)? What were you thinking right before you did (did not do) this? Were you punished? How? By whom? How long after this act were you punished? How did you behave when you were caught? If caught by a teacher tell me exactly what happened - what was said between you? Would you show me how you stood or sat during this. Would you show me how the teacher stood or sat during this. Describe your voice and the look you had on your face. Describe your teacher's voice and the look on the teacher's face. Were you with any friends from school at the time? IF 'YES' :Were they punished? State what happened to them.

31. Tell me about the first time you got into trouble with the police (that is arrested or given a warning)? {PROMPT: What did you do? Tell me your reason for doing this? Was this the first time? Were you alone? If not, were you with any students from your school- any classmates? How did you feel about the experience? Would you do it again?

32. How do you think your parent/s (or guardian) expect you to do in school {PROMPT: What is the lowest grade that you can bring home without them getting upset?}

33. What do(es) your parent/s (or guardian/s) want(s) you to become when you grow up? How do you know this?

34. What sort of grades ('As', 'Bs' 'Ds' and so on) do you think your teachers expect you to get? Tell me your reason for saying this.

35. When you do not understand something in class - do you feel comfortable asking the teacher to explain? Why or why not?

36. Do you think that education is important? Why or why not?

37. Do you have responsibilities at home? Chores? If "yes," what? How often?

Date:--------------------------Subject #:---
Location of the interview:----------------------Interview Time (start/end):_____
Okay - all done! Thanks a lot..................................(insert respondent's name)

****

D: 3C - Interview Questions for Juveniles

Some items adapted from Biafora et al., 1993; Braddock III, 1991; Brody et al., 1996; Brown et al., 1993; Cernkovich and Giordano, 1987; Fordham & Ogbu, 1986; Hughes & Demo, 1989; Kaplan, 1975; Wilson-Sadbury et al., 1991) .

*Words in italics indicate instructions, et cetera that will be spoken to the subjects.

Date:.............................Begin Time:.....................End Time:..................

Subject Code:....................Subject Age:...

School Code:..

*TO BE STATED TO THE RESPONDENT :

Good day (first name of subject).................First let me say "thank you" for taking the time to meet with me today. As you know from the letter that you received about this study, our meeting today is to better understand how things about home, school and community may lead some folks into delinquency or may prevent delinquency.

Let me remind you that participation in this study is voluntary. We may stop whenever you like and you need not answer every question. Also, you may ask me to turn the tape recorder off at anytime.

Our communication here is anonymous in that your name will not be attached to any of the response sheets. It is also confidential, in that the answers you give will not be revealed to anyone other than my academic advisor. Any reports on this study will not include information that will allow persons to trace the answers back to you. There are two possible exceptions to confidentiality:

1) while it is rare, a court could order me (by subpoena) to hand over the interview materials; and,

2) if you tell me that you or anyone else under 18 years is the victim of abuse, physical   or sexual, I will have to report this to the proper authorities for further investigation.

The interview will not take longer than 2 hours total. If you would like to take a break at some point - let me know. As we go along, I will be making notes. Any questions before we begin?

*How I ask the questions will change from time to time. For the first few questions, respond freely:

Present Offense(s):...

Demographics

1. How do you define yourself in racial/ethnic terms?

Ethnicity/Nationality:...

2. Where in _____ *(insert the name of the state)* do you live?

3. Who are the individuals living in your household?

4. Do you receive school lunches from your school?

5. Did your mother (or, other primary guardian) complete:

> 1. Grade school
> 2. Middle school
> 3. High School.
> 4. Technical or vocational
> 5. College
> 6. Graduate or professional

6. What do your parents (or guardians) do for a living?

7. Are you employed? If so, why did you become employed? About how many hours per week?

Delinquency
8. Tell me about your last arrest.

9. Describe other times when you have gotten into trouble with the law.

10. Were you alone when you broke the law?

11. Tell me about your friends who also break the law. What are they like?

12. Tell me about the kids who do not break the law.

13. Explain why you broke the law.

* *Next, I am going to ask about religion. For most of these questions I will read you some options from which to choose an answer:*

Religion.
14. How often do you attend religious services?

> 0=Never
> 1=at least once per year

2=at least once per month
3=at least twice per month
4=at least three times per month
5=once per week
6=more than once per week

15. How important are religious services to you?

1= not very important
2= not important
3= important
4= very important.

16. What is the name of the religious facility that you attend?
17. What is the denomination of the facility?

1=Traditional
2=Non-traditional

18. Where is it located?
19. How often does your mother (or other primary guardian) attend religious services?

0=Never
1=at least once per year
2=at least once per month
3=at least twice per month
4=at least three times per month
5=once per week
6=more than once per week

* For the next set of questions, please answer freely:
Cultural Identity

Possible responses
1=very often
2= once in awhile
3= practically never

Do you:

20. Speak Standard English

21. Listen to white music artists (e.g. on white radio stations)

22. Listen to classical music

23. Attend the opera or ballet

24. Work hard to get good grades

25. Read and/or write poetry

26. Has your family given you any special advice about being a black in America? What do you think about being Black in America? Why?

Stressors/risks
*(To affirmative responses in this section the researcher will ask: *Tell me how this has affected you*).
27. Does anyone in your family have a major sickness?
28. Does anyone in your family drink or use any illegal drugs?
29. Does anyone in your family have a mental illness?
30. Has anyone close to you died in your lifetime?
31. Are your parents separated or divorced?
32. Has a parent ever re-married or changed partners?
33. Has your family ever moved? If yes, how often?
34. Do you have any long term illnesses or disorders?
35. Have you ever been sexually or physically abused?
36. How well do you get along with others in your household?
37. Has your family ever been on welfare?
38. Has anyone in your family, including yourself, ever been the victim of a crime?
39. Has anyone in your family ever been arrested? If yes, describe the circumstances.

40. Describe your relationship with other students at your school.
41. Your present classes - are they mainstream, honors or special education? How long has this been the case?
42. Have you ever been held back a grade in school?
43. What sort of grades did you get on your last report card?

44. Have you ever been homeless?
45. Do you feel safe in your neighborhood?
46. Describe your neighbors.

Resilient Families.

47. Describe family goals of which you are aware.
48. How is your family going about achieving these goals?
49. Do you believe that your family will achieve these goals?
50. Briefly describe a problem that your family has had to face?
51. How did your family handle this problem?
52. Are the people in your family proud to be a part of the family?
53. Briefly, tell me about family gatherings - if any?
54. Tell me about some important family beliefs.
55. Do you accept these beliefs?

*For the next set of questions on family I will give you some options from which to choose a response:
Family Caring and Trust.
56. .My parents/guardians often ask about what I am doing in school.

Strongly Agree	Agree	Neutral	Disagree	Strongly Disagree.
1	2	3	4	5

57. .My parents give me the right amount of affection.

Strongly Agree	Agree	Neutral	Disagree	Strongly Disagree.
1	2	3	4	5

58. One of the worse things that could happen to me is to find out that I let my parents down.

Strongly Agree	Agree	Neutral	Disagree	Strongly Disagree.
1	2	3	4	5

59. My parents trust me.

| Strongly Agree | Agree | Neutral | | Disagree | Strongly Disagree. |
| 1 | 2 | 3 | | 4 | 5 |

Family Identity Support/ Parent-Child Fit
60. My parents sometimes give me the feeling that I am not living up to their expectations.

| Strongly Agree | Agree | Neutral | | Disagree | Strongly Disagree. |
| 1 | 2 | 3 | | 4 | 5 |

61. .My parents seem to wish I were a different person.

| Strongly Agree | Agree | Neutral | Disagree | Strongly Disagree. |
| 1 | 2 | 3 | 4 | 5 |

Control and Supervision.

62. .My parents want to know who I am with when I am out with others.

| Strongly Agree | Agree | Neutral | | Disagree | Strongly Disagree. |

63. My parents want me to tell them where I am if I do not come home right after school.

| Strongly Agree | Agree | Neutral | | Disagree | Strongly Disagree. |

Family Conflict

64.How often do you have disagreements or arguments with your parents/guardians?

1= two or more times per week
2= once per week
3= hardly ever or never

65.How often do you purposely not talk to your parents because you are mad at them?

1= two or more times per week
2= once per week
3= hardly ever or never

Instrumental Communication:

66.How often do you talk to your parents about problems you have at school?

1=very often
2= once in awhile

3=never

67.How often do you talk to your parents about your plans for the future?

1=very
often
2= once in
awhile
3=never

Parental Emphasis on Achievement

How often does each of your parents (*ask about the primary guardian, then a secondary guardian after*):

68. Help you with homework when asked

1=very
often
2= once in
awhile
3=never

69. Know how you are doing in school

1=very
often
2= once in
awhile
3=never

70. Go to school programs for parents.

1=very
often
2= once in
awhile
3=never

71.Watch you in sports or other extra-curricular activities.

1=very
often
2= once in
awhile
3=never

72.What is the lowest semester grade that you can get without your parents getting upset?
73. – omitted.
74. How important is it to your parents or guardians that you work hard in school?

Very Important	Important	Somewhat Important	Not Important.
1	2	3	4

Family Educational Resources:

Do you have the following in your home:
75) magazines
76) newspapers
77) books
78) computer(s)

Peers
Please think of your closest friend in this school. Does he or she:

79. Get good grades
Yes = 1; No= 2
What do you consider "good" grades?

80. Interested in school
Yes = 1; No= 2

81. Attend classes regularly
Yes = 1; No= 2

82. Plan to go to college
Yes = 1; No= 2

The next set of questions refer to your school friends only.

83. Tell me about your friends who have been picked up or arrested by the police?
84. Tell me about those who have been suspended from school at some point. What were the reasons?

Parental Disapproval of Peers

85.In general what do your parents/guardians think of your friends?

Strongly Approve	Approve	Neutral	Disapprove	Strongly Disapprove.
1	2	3	4	5

86.In general what do your parents/guardians think of your boyfriend/girlfriend?

Strongly Approve	Approve	Neutral	Disapprove	Strongly Disapprove.
1	2	3	4	5

*Please respond to the next questions freely:

Self-Derogation

87.How would your mother (or other guardian) describe you?
88.How would your friends describe you?
89.How would your teachers describe you?
90.How accurate are these descriptions of you?
91. Would you say that you are a "good boy" or a "bad boy"? Why?

School Involvement

92. Do you participate in sports or some other school activity? Describe.

1= did not participate

2= participated as a member

3=participated as a leader

School Attendance

93. How often have you been absent from school over the past four weeks? Why?

1= none at all

2= 1 or 2 days

3= 3 or 4 days

4= 5 to 10 days

5= more than 10 days

94.. How often have you been late for school? Why?

      1= none at all

      2= 1 or 2 days

      3= 3 or 4 days

      4= 5 to 10 days

      5= more than 10 days

Cause Orientation
95.Where do you see yourself 5 years from now?
96.Where do you see yourself 10 years from now?
97.How important is it to you to someday make a lot of money?
98.What will it take to reach these goals?
99.Realistically, do you believe that you will achieve your goals? Why or why not?
100.How much control do you think you have over things that happen to you?

Protective Response Pattern
101. Is there something that someone has said to you which you wish was not said?
102. Describe your feelings when this happened.
103. When you feel low, how do you cope with your problems?
104. How do members of your family cope?
105. Would your friends say that you have a sense of humor?

Environmental Support
106. Is there an older person to whom you would speak if you had a problem or needed advice? If yes, tell me about this person.
107. Describe your relationship with your teachers.
108. Has anyone ever said that he/she was proud of you? Tell me about these persons.
109. Who would you say are the people who have been most influential in you life thus far? Explain.

Sense of Control
110. Do you think it's better to plan your life a good ways ahead, or would you say life is too much a matter of luck to plan ahead?
111. When you do make plans ahead, do you usually get to carry things out as expected, or do things usually come up to make you change your plans?
112. Have you usually felt pretty sure that your life would work out the way you want it to, or have there been times you haven't been so sure about it?

Racial Mistrust
113. Black parents should teach their children not to trust white teachers.
Strongly Agree   Agree   Neutral   Disagree   Strongly Disagree.

114. Blacks should be suspicious of all white persons who try to be friendly.
Strongly Agree   Agree   Neutral   Disagree   Strongly Disagree.

115. When a teacher talks to a black student it is usually to get information that may be used against him or her.
Strongly Agree   Agree   Neutral   Disagree   Strongly Disagree.

116. White teachers ask hard questions on purpose so that Black students will fail.

Strongly Agree   Agree   Neutral   Disagree   Strongly Disagree.

Effort or innate ability orientation to achievement.
117. My school is a place where hardworking students get good grades.
Strongly Agree   Agree   Neutral   Disagree   Strongly Disagree.

Neighborhood Collective Efficacy
Referring to your neighborhood, would you say that:

118. People around here (*your neighborhood)* are willing to help their neighbors.
Strongly Agree   Agree   Neutral   Disagree   Strongly Disagree.

119.This is a close-knit neighborhood.

Strongly Agree   Agree   Neutral   Disagree   Strongly Disagree.

120.People in this neighborhood can be trusted

Strongly Agree   Agree   Neutral   Disagree   Strongly Disagree.

Neighborhood Images.
121. Think about the women and men in your neighborhood. What are the kinds of thing that they do? What do people expect men to do with their life in your neighborhood? What do you think about these expectations?

****

That's it! Anything that you want to add that I did not ask? Thanks again!

Interview Questions for Teachers

INSTRUMENT FOR THE CONVERSATIONAL INQUIRY WITH EACH TEACHER : Some items adopted from (Brotherton, 1996 unpublished instrument ; Lee et al., 1991).

Good day Ms/Mr.................First let me say "thank you" for taking the time to meet with me for a few minutes. As you know from the letter that you received about this study, our meeting today is to better understand what happens in a classroom from day to day. Let me remind you that participation in this study is voluntary. We may stop whenever you like and you need not answer every question. Our communication here is anonymous in that your name will not be attached to any of the response sheets or revealed to anyone. It is also confidential, in that the responses that you give me will not be revealed to anyone other than my methodologist. This will not take more than an hour. As we go along, I will be making notes. You may ask me to turn the tape-recorder off at any time.

Teacher Code:............................Academic Subject Code:..............................

1. Describe your background:

2. Teacher's sex : Male_____Female_____.

3. Age:

4. Parents occupation/profession:

5. How would you identify yourself ethnically:

      a) White.   b) African-American (or Black).
      c) Asian or Asian-American.   d) Native American.
      e) Hispanic or Latino.   f) Other: _____.

6. 1st or 2nd etc. generation immigrants.

7. Which is the highest degree that you have earned?

a)associates
b)bachelors
c)masters
d)doctorate

8. What grade(s) do you presently teach? ----------------------.

9. What grades have you taught in the past?--------------------.

10. How long have you been teaching?

11. How long have you been teaching here?

12. How did you come to be a teacher here?

13. Describe any changes in your teaching style over the years.

14. Why did you choose teaching?

15. What is your teaching philosophy?

16. _____ is a student in your class. Did you hear anything about him before he *(insert the name of each student in the study who is also in this teacher's class)* became your student? What did you hear?

17. Tell me what separates the students who do well at this school from those who do not.

18. Describe how do you respond to students who are not doing well in your class.

19. Describe the students who create problems in your classroom - if any.

20. Describe some of the strengths of the school?

21. Describe some of the weaknesses or problems at this school.

22. If you had a magic wand and you could change anything about this school - what would it be?

23. What do you know about this area - where the school is located?

24. How do you generally respond to a non-cooperative student - that is, a student who often misbehaves?
25. How would your students describe you?

26. Do you believe that academic performance is related to juvenile delinquency? In what way is it (or is it not)?
Thank you!

Date completed:_____.Location: _____

Endnotes

Chapter 1

[1] "African-American" (A.A.): generally refers to those of African descent, born in the United States of parents who were also born in the United States and who identify themselves as African-American (such eliminates the children of first generation West Indian and African immigrants). However, the data indicate that in New York many who are black or who may identify as "African-American" have recent immigrant roots. The present study specifies the differences as relevant herein.
[2] Property offenses are burglary, larceny, auto theft, arson, vandalism, trespassing, stolen property, et cetera.
[3] Person offenses are homicide, forcible rape, robbery, aggravated assault, simple assault, other violent sex offense, other person offense.
[4] "Social promotion" is an educational policy that requires the advance of students to higher grades regardless of academic prowess for the sake of sparing a child from the psychological pains of being left behind his or her age peers.

Chapter 2

[1] "Race": socially constructed categories of populations distinguished from other categories by phenotypical attributes (usually skin color) (Fiske, 1994). Common race categories are "blacks" and "whites."
[2] "Social capital" informal (from family and friends) and formal (from school and other community sources) support, supervision and information facilitating upward social mobility (Coleman 1988). "Cultural capital" refers to a knowledge areas like fine arts, literature, and language necessary for upward social mobility (Bourdieu & Passeron 1977).

Chapter 3

[1] The "ascribed status" refers to life circumstances which the child does not create, but merely inherits by virtue of birth (Cohen 1955).

[2] "Achieved status": the level of prestige that the student earns himself usually by excelling in academics, sports, and/or peer relations as indicated by unstructured interviews. This differs from "ascribed status" which are circumstances over which the student has no control as defined by the standing of family socio-economic status and values, (adapted from Cohen, 1955).

[3] "Stress": a) major life events (Life Events Checklist) (Johnson & McCutcheon, 1980); b) DSM-IV (1994) list of stressors; and c) daily hassles (as determined by the subject's perceptions).

[4] "Resilience" is both a process and an outcome. As such it is both a protective personality trait which may fluctuate in strength and may be manifest by the outcome it produces – that is, a positive response to risk (stress or adversity be it daily hassles or a major distressing single event [Braddock II 1991]). The outcome may be measured on a continuum: survival – recovery – thriving. For this study, resilience in its broadest sense means academic success and non-delinquency despite adversity. The definition excludes emotional well-being (or happiness) (see Luthar 1991). For this study, broad categories of individual traits that may foster conformity include: high goals or aspirations and a strong sense of self.

[5]"Life-style": "collective actions that characterize an individual's typical behavior pattern" (largely, a person's characteristic work, family, school, religious, and leisure activities) (Zimmerman & Maton, 1992).

[6]"Truly at-risk students" refers to those who are very likely to become delinquents because they lack the means and knowledge of how to navigate legitimate avenues for basic financial sustenance.

[7]"Short vocal back channel": number of single word back channel responses (e.g.. "mhm"," uh-huh" "yes")[Duncan & Fiske, 1977) that the teacher gives to the student while the student is talking or that the student gives to the teacher while the teacher is talking, indicated by classroom observations.

"Long vocal back channel": number of back channel responses longer than one word (e.g.. "that's right" and "I agree") [Duncan & Fiske, 1977), as indicated by classroom observations.

Chapter 4

[1] The center of the concentric zones noted in social disorganization is the core of a city where immigrants first go to work. Crime is highest in this area.

[2] Abner Louima, a young black male Haitian immigrant had committed no crime. While trying to break up a fight outside of a nightclub he was arrested, taken to a police station where he suffered massive injuries from the police including sodomization with the handle of a toilet plunger. Amadou Diallo a young black male African immigrant had been fatally shot by police while on his doorstep reaching for his house keys. He had no criminal record. and was engaged in no crime when shot.

[3] Dorismond was a young African-American male security guard who had aspired to law enforcement. He was fatally shot by police after the police approached him and suggested that he was selling drugs.

[4] Secondary labor market positions are unprofessional and sometimes seasonal jobs offering little or no benefits, and long work hours. From such positions often come "the last hired, first fired."

[5] Homeroom refers to a single class session where the students in a class meet with a teacher assigned to that class as an advisor for the semester.

References

Aaronsohn, E., Carter, C.J. & Howell, M. (1995). Preparing monocultural teachers for a multicultural world: Attitudes towards inner-city schools. *Equity and Excellence in Education, 28,* 5-9.

Agnew, R. (1995). Testing the leading crime theories: An alternative strategy focusing on motivational processes. *Journal of Research in Crime and Delinquency, 32,* 363-398.

Agnew, R. (1985). Goal achievement and delinquency. *Sociology and Social Research, 68,* 435-452.

Alexander, K. & Entwistle, D. & Bedinger, S. (1994). When expectations work: Race and   socioeconomic differences in school performance. *Social Psychology Quarterly, 57,* 282-299.

Ames, Carol, & Ames, Russell (1984*). Introduction. Research on Motivation in Education Volume I,* pp. 1-11. Ames, Carol, & Ames, Russell {Eds.}, New York: Academic Press.

American Psychiatric Association (1994). *Diagnostic and Statistical Manual IV.* Washington D.C.: American Psychiatric Association.

Anderson, E. (1994). The code of the streets. *The Atlantic Monthly, May:* 81-94.

Asante, M.K. (1992). Afrocentric curriculum, *Educational Leadership, 49,* 28-31.

Aspy, D., Roebuck, F. & Black, B. (1972). The relationship of teacher offered conditions of respect to behaviors described by Flanders' Interaction Analysis. *Journal of Negro Education, 41,* 370-376.

Atkinson, D., Morten, G. & Sue, D. (1993). *Counseling American Minorities*. Madison WI: WCB Brown & Benchmark.

Baker, D. (1995). Identifying probationers with ADHD-related behavior. *Criminal Justice, 122*, 33-43.

Bandura, A. (1989). Human agency in social cognitive theory. *American Psychologist, 44*, 1175-1184.

Baumrind, D. (1991). The influence of parenting style on adolescent competence and substance use. *Journal of Early Adolescence, 11*, 56-95.

Berliner, David, C. (1989). Furthering our understanding of motivation and environments. *Research on Motivation in Education Volume III*, pp. 317-342. Ames, Carol, & Ames, Russell, {Eds.} New York: Academic Press.

Biafora, F., Warheit, G., Zimmerman, A., Apospori, E. & Taylor, D. (1993). Racial mistrust and deviant behaviors among ethnically diverse black adolescent boys. *Journal of Applied Social Psychology, 23,* 891-910.

Black, Donald (1976). *The Sociology of Law*. New York: Academic Press.

Borduin, C., Pruitt, J. & Henggeler, S. (1985). Family interactions in black, lower-class families with delinquent and non-delinquent adolescent boys. *The Journal of Genetic Psychology, 147*, 333-342.

Bourdieu, Pierre & Passeron, Jean-Claude (1977). *Reproduction in Education, Society and Culture*. Los Angeles: Sage Press.

Bowler, R., Rauch, S. & Schwarzer, R. (1986). Self-esteem and interracial attitudes in black high school students: A comparison with five other ethnic groups. *Urban Education, 21,* 3-19.

Bowman, P. & Howard, C. (1985). Race-related socialization, motivation, and academic achievement: A study of black youth in three generational families. *Journal of the American Academy of Child Psychiatry, 24*, 134-141.

Brody, G. Stoneman, Z., Flor, D. (1996). Parental religiosity, family processes, and youth competence in rural two-parent African-American families. *Developmental Psychology,32*, 696-706.

Brophy, J. & Good, T. (1974). *Teacher-Student Relationships: Causes and Consequences.* Holt, Rinehart and Winston, New York.

Brotherton, David & Barrios, Luis (in press). *Between Black, and Gold: Politics of the Almighty Latin King and Queen Nation.* .New York: Columbia University Press.

Brotherton, David (1996). Smartness, toughness and autonomy: Drug use in the context of female gang delinquency. *Journal of Drug Issues, 26*, 261-277.

Brown, B.B. (1990). Peer groups and peer cultures. In S.S. Feldman & G.R. Elliott (Eds.), At the threshold: *The Developing Adolescent* (pp. 171-196). Cambridge, MA: Harvard University Press.

Bruno, J. (1995). Doing time-killing time: An examination of the perceptions and allocations of time among teacher-defined at-risk students. *The Urban Review, 27,* 101-120.

Bryan, M (1992). Intervention among children of substance abusers and school success. *Clinical Sociology Review, 10,* 119-129.

Butterfield, Fox (1997). Study links violence rate to cohesion in community. Sept., New York: *New York Times.*

Cannella, G.S. & Reiff, J.C. (1994). Teacher preparation for diversity. *Equity and Excellence in Education, 27*, 28-47.

Celis, William III (1996). Forty years after Brown segregation persists, pp 64-167 in John A. Kromkowski (Ed.), *Race and Ethnic Relations 96/97*, 6th ed. Connecticut: Dushkin Publishing Group.

Census Bureau (1998). Current Population Survey, Washington D.C.: U.S. Census Bureau, March 1998: U.S. Census Bureau, *Current Population Reports,* pp. 20-450

Cernkovich, S.A. & Giordano, P.C. (1992). School bonding, race and delinquency. *Criminology, 30,* 261-291.

Chevalier, M. (1995). Maintaining an ethnic identity in school: A folkloric perspective. *Equity and Excellence in Education, 28,* 26-35.

Children's Defense Fund (1986). *Declining Earnings of Young Men: Their Relation to Poverty, Teen Pregnancy and Family Formation,* Washington D.C.: Children's   Defense Fund.

Clark, R. M. (1983). *Family Life and School Achievements: Why Poor Black Children Succeed or Fail.* Chicago: University of Chicago Press.

Clark, E. R., Nystrom, N. J. & Perez, B. (1996). Language and Culture: Critical components of multicultural teacher education. *The Urban Review, 28,* 185-197.

Coates, D. (1987). Gender differences in the structure and support characteristics of black adolescents' social networks. *Sex Roles, 17,* 667-687.

Cohen, A. (1955). *Delinquent Boys: The Culture of the Gang.* Illinois: Free Press.

Cohen, E.D. & Cohen, G. S. (1999). *The Virtuous Therapist.* Belmont, CA: Wadsworth.

Coie, J.D., Lochman, J.E., Terry, R., Hyman, C. (1992). Predicting early adolescent disorder from childhood aggression and peer rejection. *Journal of Consulting and Clinical Psychology, 60,* 783-792.

Coleman, J (1988). Social capital in the creation of human capital, *American Journal of Sociology, 94,* 95-120.

Coleman, J. (1987). Families and Schools, *Educational Researcher, 16,* 32-38.

Coombs, R. H. & Landsverk, J. (1988). Parenting styles and substance use during childhood and adolescence. *Journal of Marriage and the Family, 50,* 473- 482.

Crouch, J.L. & Milner, J.S. (1993). Effects of child neglect on children. *Criminal Justice and Behavior, 20,* 49-65.

de Kanter, A. Ginsburg, A. L. & Miline, A. M. (1986*). Parental Involvement Strategies: A New Emphasis on Traditional Parent Roles.* Washington, DC: US Department of Education (EDE 293919).

Demo, D. & Hughes, M. (1990). Socialization and racial identity among black Americans. *Social Psychology Quarterly, 53,* 363-374.

Dishion, T. J. (1990). The peer context of troublesome child and adolescent behavior. In P.E. Leone (Ed.), *Understanding Troubled and Troubling Youth* (pp. 128-153). Newbury Park, CA: Sage.

Dodge, K. A. (1983). Behavioral antecedents of peer social status. *Child Development, 54,* 1386-1389.

Dornsbusch, S. M. Carlsmith, J.M., Bushwall, P. L., Ritter, P.L. Leiderman, P.H. Hastorf, A.H. & Gross, R. T. (1985). Single parents, extended households, and the control of adolescents. *Child Development, 56,* 326-341.

Dornbusch, S. M. Ritter, P. L., Leiderman, P.H., Roberts, D. F., & Fraleigh, M. J. (1987). The relation of parenting style to adolescent school performance. *Child Development, 58,* 1244 - 1257.

Elliott, D.S., Huizinga, D., & Ageton, S. S. (1985). *Explaining Delinquency and Drug Use.* Beverly Hills, CA: Sage.

England, R.E., Meier, K.J., Fraga, L.R. (1988). Barriers to equal opportunity: Educational practices and minority students. *Urban Affairs Quarterly, 23,* 635-646.

Englert, R. M. (1997). The university's role in the improvement of inner city education, *Education and Urban Review, 29,* 373-402.

Epstein, J.L. (1984a, April*). Effects of teacher practices on parent involvement for change in student achievement in reading_and math.* Paper presented at the meeting of the   American Educational Research Association, New Orleans.

Epstein, J.L. (1985). After the bus arrives: Resegregation in desegregated schools. *Journal of Social Issues, 41,* 9-22.

Famularo, R., Fenton, T., Kinscherff, Barnum, R., Bolduc, S and Bunschaft, D. (1992) Neuropsychological differences between adolescent delinquents and status offenders. *American Journal of Psychiatry, 149,* 1252-1257.

Farrington, D. (1989). Early predictors of adolescent aggression and adult violence. *Violence and Victims, 4,* 79-100.

Featherman, D. L. (1980). Schooling and occupational careers: Kagan (Eds.), *Constancy and Change in Human Development* (pp. 675-738). Cambridge, MA: Harvard University Press.

Fereshteh, M.H. (1995). Multicultural education in the United States: A historical review, *Multicultural Review, 4,* 38-45.

Figueira-McDonough, J. (1993). Residence, dropping out, and delinquency rates. *Deviant Behavior: An Interdisciplinary Journal, 14,* 109-132.

Fine, M. (1991*). Framing Dropouts: Notes on the Politics of an Urban High School.* New York: State University of New York.

Fine, M. (1986). Perceptions of step-parents: Variations in stereotypes as a function of current family structure. *Journal of Marriage and the Family, 48,* 537-543.

Ford, D. (1992). The American achievement ideology and achievement differentials among pre-adolescent gifted and non-gifted African-American males and females._ *Journal of Negro Education, 61*, 45-64.

Ford, D. & Harris, J. (1994). Promoting achievement among gifted black students: The efficacy of new definitions and identification practices. *Urban Education, 29*, 202-229.

Fordham, S. (1996). *Blacked Out: Dilemmas of Race, Identity, and Success at Capital High*: Chicago: University of Chicago Press.

Fordham, S. & Ogbu, J (1986). Black students' school success: Coping with the "burden" of "acting white." *The Urban Review, 18*, 176-206.

Frisby, C. L. & Tucker, C. M. (1993). Black students' self-perception of self: Implications for educators. *Educational Forum, 57*, 147-156.

Fuentes, Luis (1994). Educating Puerto Ricans in the U.S.: The Struggle for Equity. *Equity and Excellence in Education, 27*, 16-19.

Gallegos, B. (1995). Teachers for Chicago: Ensuring urban teachers with class, *Phi Delta Kappan, 76*, 782-785.

Garcia, J. & Pugh, S. L. (1992). Multicultural education in teacher preparation programs: A political or an educational concept. *Phi Delta Kappan, 74*, 214-219.

Garmezy, N. (1987). Stress, competence and development: Continuity in the study of schizophrenic adults, children vulnerable to psychopathology and the search for stress- resistant children. *American Journal of Orthopsychiatry, 57*, 159-174.

Garner, C.W. & Cole, E.G. (1986). The achievement of students in low-SES settings: An investigation of the relationship between locus of control and field dependence. *Urban Education, 21*, 189-206.

Gay, G. (1993). Building cultural bridges: A bold proposal for teacher education, *Education and Urban Society, 25*, 285-299.

Gillmore, M. R., Hawkins, J. D., Day, L. E., & Catalano, R. E. (1992). Friendship and deviance: New evidence on an old controversy. *Journal of Early Adolescence, 12*, 80-95.

Glass, M., Houlihan, D., Fatis, M. & Levine, H. (1993). Brief report: Compliance in the classroom: Using the "thumbs up" procedure to increase student compliancer to teacher requests.*Behavioral Residential Treatment, 8,* 281-288.

Good, Thomas L. & Brophy, Jene, E. (1990*). Educational Psychology: A Realistic Approach, 4th Ed.* New York: Longman.

Gottfredson, D.C. (1986). An empirical test of school-based environmental and individual interventions to reduce the risk of delinquent behavior. *Criminology, 24*, 705-732.

Grant, C. A. (1989). Urban teachers: Their new colleagues and curriculum, *Phi Delta Kappan, 70*, 777-779.

Greene, M.B. (1993). Chronic exposure to violence and poverty: Interventions that work for youth._*Crime and Delinquency, 39*, 106-124.

Grotevant, H. & Cooper, C. R. (1986). Individuation in family relationships: A perspective on individual differences in the development of identity and role taking in adolescence. *Human Development, 29, 82-100.*

Gunzenhauser, G. W. &_____ (1996). *Assuring an appreciation for diversity: Alternatives to teacher education field experiences.* Paper presented at the Annual Meeting of the American Association of Colleges for Teacher Education, Chicago, Illinois, February 21-24, 1996.

Gutierrez, Fernando (1997). Treating ethnic minority individuals. In Michael O'Connor & Irvin Yalom (Eds.). *Treating the Psychological Consequences of HIV*, pp. 165-193, San Francisco: Jossey-Bass Publishers.

Gutierrez, K.D., Larson, J. & Kreuter, B. (1995). Cultural tensions in the scripted classroom: The value of the subjugated perspective. *Urban Education, 29*, 410-442.

Gutierrez, K.D., Rymes, B. & Larson, J. (1995). Script, counterscript, and underlife in the classroom: *James Brown v.Board of Education.* Harvard Educational Review, 65, 445-471.

Haberman, M. & Richards, W. H (1990). Urban teachers who quit: Why they leave and what they do, *Urban Education, 25,* 297-303.

Harrison, A., Wilson, M., Pine, C., Chan, S. & Buriel, R. (1990). Family ecologies of ethnic minority children. *Child Development, 61,* 347-362.

Hartup, W. W. (1989). Social relationships and their developmental significance. *American Psychology, 44,* 120-126.

Hauser, S. T., Powers, S., Noam, G., Jacobsen, A., Weiss, B., & Follansbee, D. (1984). Familial contexts of adolescent ego development. *Child Development, 55,* 195- 213.

Heath, S.B. (1983). *Way With Words.* New York: Cambridge University Press.

Heath S.B. (1989). Oral and literate traditions among black Americans living in poverty. *American Psychologist, 44,* 367-373.

Henderson, A. (Ed. (1987*). The Evidence Continues to Grow: Parent Involvement Improves Achievement.* Columbia, MD: National Committee for Citizens in Education.

Henry, A. (1994). The empty shelf and other curricular challenges of teaching for children of African descent: Implications for teacher practice, *Urban Education, 29,* 298-318.

Hilliard, A. G. (1992). Behavioral style, culture, and teaching and learning, *Journal of Negro Education, 61,* 370-377.

Hirschi, T. (1969). Causes of Delinquency. Berkeley: University of California Press.

Hoover-Dempsey, K.V. & Sandler, H.M. (1997). Why do parents become involved in their children's education? *Review of Educational Research, 67*, 3-42.

Hsia, Heidi, M. & Beyer, Marty (2000). *System Change Through State Challenge Activities: Approaches and Products.* Office of Juvenile Justice and Delinquency Prevention Bulletin March 2000. Washington, D.C. : National Institute of Justice.

Hughes, M. & Demo, D. (1989). Self-perceptions of black Americans: Self-esteem and personal-efficacy. *American Journal of Sociology, 95*, 132-159.

Hughes, M. & Demo, D. H. (1989). Self-perceptions of black Americans: Self-esteem and personal efficacy. *American Journal of Sociology, 95*, 132-159.

Hurrelmann, K. & Engel, U. (1991). Delinquency as a symptom of adolescents' orientation towards status success. *Journal of Youth and Adolescence, 21*, 119-138.

Ingram-Willis, A. (1995). Reading the world of school literacy: Contextualizing the experience of a young African-American male. *Harvard Educational Review, 65*, 30-49.

Jankowski, Martin Sanchez (1991). *Islands in the Street: Gangs and American Urban Society.* California: University of California Press.

James, R. (1980). The multicultural teacher education standard – challenge and opportunity, *Viewpoints in Teaching and Learning, 56*, 18-25.

Jefferson, T. & Johnson, J.H. (1991). The relationship of hyperactivity and sensation seeking to delinquency subtypes. *Criminal Justice and Behavior, 18*, 195-201.

Jervis, K. (1996). "How come there are no brothers on that list?": Hearing the hard questions all children ask, *Harvard Educational Review, 66,* 546-576.

Kahne, Joseph & Bailey, Kim (1999). The role of social capital in youth development: The case of "I Have a Dream Programs." *Educational Evaluation and Policy Analysis, 21,* 321-343.

Kandal, D.B. & Andrews, K. (1987). Processes of adolescent socialization by parents and peers. *International Journal of Addictions, 22,* 319-342.

Kaplan, H.B. (1978). Deviant behavior and self-enhancement in adolescence. *Journal of Youth and Adolescence, 7,* 253-277.

Keith, T.Z. (1991). Parent involvement and achievement in high school. In S. Silvern (Ed.), *Advances in Reading /Language Research: Literacy through Family, Community, School Interaction (Vol. 5,* pp. 125-141). Geenwich, CT: JAI Press.

Klintenberg, B.A., Andersonnon, T., Magnusson, D., & Stattin, H. (1993). Hyperactive behavior in childhood as related to subsequent alcohol problems and violent offending: A longitudinal study of male subjects. *Personality and Individual Differences, 15,* 381-388.

Krohn, Marvin (1986). The web of conformity: A network approach to the explanations of delinquent behavior. *Social Problems, 33,* 581-592.

Langlois, J. H., & Stephan, C. W. (1981). Beauty and the beast: the role of physical attractiveness in the development of peer relations and social behavior. In S. Brehm, S. Kassin. & F. Gibbons (Eds.), *Developmental Social Psychology: Theory and Research* (pp. 152-168). New York: Oxford University Press.

Laosa, L. (1982). School, occupation, culture and family: The impact of parental schooling on the parent-child relationship. *Journal of Education Psychology, 74,* 791-827.

Lareau, A. (1989). *Home Advantage: Social Class and Parental Intervention in Elementary Education.* New York: Falmer Press.

Laurence, Richard (1985). School performance, containment, theory, and delinquency behavior. *Youth and Society, 17,* 69-95.

Lessard, S. (1994). End discrimination and increase productivity, *The Washington Monthly, Mar.,* 51-52.

Leung, K. & Drasgow, F. (1986). Relationship between self-esteem and delinquent behavior in three ethnic groups. *Journal of Cross-Cultural Psychology, 17,* 151-167.

Lipman, P. (1996). The missing voice of culturally relevant teachers in school restructuring, *The Urban Review, 28,* 41-62.

Loeber, R. & Dishion, T. J. (1983). Early predictors of male adolescent delinquency: A review. *Psychological Bulletin, 94,* 68-99.

Luthar, S.S. (1991). Vulnerability and resilience: A study of high-risk adolescents. *Child Development, 62,* 600-616.

MacLeod, J. (1995). *Ain't No Makin' It: Aspirations and Attainment in a Low-Income Neighborhood.* Colorado: Westview Press.

Marjoribanks, K. (1984). Occupational status, family environments, and adolescents' aspirations: The Laosa Model. *Journal of Educational Psychology, 76,* 690-700.

McGarrell, E. F. (1993). Trends in racial disproportionality in juvenile court processing: 1985-1989. *Crime and Delinquency, 39,* 29-49.

McCarthy, J.D. & Hoge, D.R. (1987). The social construction of school punishment: Racial disadvantage out of universalistic process. *Social Forces, 65,* 1101-1120.

McLoyd, V. (1990). The impact of economic hardship on black families and children: Psychological distress, parenting, and socio-economic development. *Child Development, 61,* 311-436.

Messner, S. & Rosenfeld, R. (1997). *Crime and the American Dream,* 2nd Ed. California: Wadsworth.

Molnar, Alex (1993). Facing the racial divide. *Educational Leadership, 50* (May): 58-59.

Morash, M. & Rucker, L. (1989). An exploratory study of the connection of mother's age at child-bearing to her children's delinquency in four data sets. *Crime and Delinquency, 35,* 45-93.

Myer-Kester, V. (1994). Factors that affect African-American students bonding to middle school._*The Elementary School Journal, 95,* 63-73.

National Criminal Justice Association (May 2000). Racial Disparities Found in the Criminal Justice System. *National Criminal Justice Association Justice Bulletin.* Washington, DC: National Criminal Justice Association.

Nettles, S. & Pleck, J. (1994). Risk, resilience, and development: The multiple ecologies of black adolescents n the United States. In Haggerty, Sherrod, Garmezy & Rutter{Eds.*}, Stress, Risk and Resilience in Childhood and Adolescents.* (pp. 147-181). : Cambridge University Press.

Nicholls, J. & Covington, M. (1984). *In Research on Motivation in Education Volume I,* pp. 1-11. Ames, Carol, & Ames, Russell {Eds.}, New York: Academic Press.

Nieto, J., Young, R.L., Tran, M. & Ooka Pang, V. (1994). Passionate commitment to a multicultural society, *Equity and Excellence in Education, 27*, 51-57.

Oetting, E. R., & Beauvais, F. (1987). Peer cluster theory, socialization characteristics, and adolescent drug use: A path analysis. *Journal of Counseling Psychology, 34*, 205-213.

Ogbu, John (1995). Cultural problems in minority education: Their interpretation and consequences: Part I: Theoretical Background. *Urban Review 27*, 189-205.

Ogbu, John (1990). Minority and literacy in comparartive perspective. *Daedalus, 119* (Spring): 141-168.

Ollendick, T., Greene, R., Weist, M. & Oswald, D. (1990). The predictive validity of teacher nominations: A five-year follow-up of at-risk youth. *Journal of Abnormal Child Psychology, 18*, 699-713.

Ollendick, T. H., Oswald, D. P. & Francis, G. (1989). The validity of teacher nominations in identifying aggressive, withdrawn, and popular children. *Journal of Clinical Child Psychology, 18*, 221-229.

Ooka Pang, V. (1994). Why do we need this class? Multicultural education for teachers, *Phi Delta Kappan, 76*, 289-292.

Patterson, G. R., & Stouthamer-Loeber, M. (1984). The correlation of family management practices and delinquency. *Child Development, 55*, 1299-1307.

Parker, L. & Hood, S. (1995). Minority students vs, majority faculty and administrators in teacher education: Perspectives on the clash of cultures, *The Urban Review, 27,* 159-174.

Peeples, F. & Loeber, R. (1994). Do individual factors and neighborhood context explain ethnic differences in juvenile delinquency? *Journal of Quantitative Criminology, 10*, 141-157.

Peters, M. (1985). Racial socialization of young black children. In H. McAdoo & J. McAdoo (Eds.) *Black Children* (pp. 159-173). Beverly Hills, CA: Sage.

Peters, M., & Massey, G. (1983). Chronic vs. mundane stress in family stress theories: The case of black families in white America. *Marriage and Family Review, 6,* 193-218.

Peterson, K., Bennet, B. & Sherman, D. (1991). Themes of uncommonly successful teachers of at-risk students. *Urban Education, 26,* 141-157.

Puzzanchera, Charles M. (2000). Self-Reported delinquency by 12-year-olds 1997. OJJDP   *Fact Sheet, February 2000, # 3.*

Radke-Yarrow, M. & Brown, E. (1993). Resilience and vulnerability in children of multiple risk families. *Development and Psychopathology, 5,* 581-592.

Reed, R. (1988). Education and achievement of young black males. In J. Gibbs {Eds.}, *Young, Black and Male in America.* New York: Auburn.

Regoli, Robert & Hewitt, John (2000). *Delinquency in Society, Fourth Edition.* Boston, Massachussetts: McGraw Hill.

Reynolds, Arthur, J. & Wolfe, Barbara (1999). Special education and school achievement: An exploratory analysis with a central-city sample. *Educational Evaluation and Policy Analysis, 3,* 249-269.

Richardson, G. & Hawks, S. (1995). A practical approach for enhancing resiliency within families. *Family Perspective, 29,* 235-250.

Rios, F.A. (1993). Thinking in urban multicultural classrooms. *Urban Education, 28,* 245-266.

Roscoe, M. & Morton, R. (1994). *Disproportionate Minority Confinement, Fact Sheet #11,* Washington D.C. : NCJRS.

Rowe, D.C., Rodgers, J.L. & Meseck-Bushey, S. (1992). Sibling delinquency and the family environment: Shared and unshared influences. *Child Development, 63,* 59-67.

Russo, C. J. & Talbert-Johnson, C. (1997). The over representation of African-American children in special education: The resegregation of educational programming? *Education and Urban Society, 29,* 136-148

Rutter, M. (1987). Psychosocial resilience and protective mechanisms. *American Journal of Orthopsychiatry 57,* 316-331.

Sampson, R. (1997). Collective regulation of adolescent misbehavior: Validation results from eighty Chicago neighborhoods, *Journal of Adolescent Research, 12,* 227-244.

Sampson, R. (1986). SES and official reaction to delinquency. *American Sociological Review, 51,* 876-885.

Schorr, L. (1989). *Within Our Reach: Breaking the Cycle of Disadvantage.* New York: Anchor.

Scott, R. (1995). Helping teacher education students develop positive attitudes toward ethnic minorities. *Equity and Excellence in Education, 28,* 69-73.

Seginer, R. (1983). Parents' educational expectations and children's academic achievements: A literature review. *Merrill-Palmer Quarterly, 29,* 1-23.

Shore, R. M. (1996). Personalization: Working to curb violence in an American school. *Phi Delta Kappan, 77,* 362-363.

Sampson, R., Raudenbush, S. & Earls, F. (1997). Neighborhoods and violent crime: A multi-level study of collective efficacy, *Science, 277,* 2-25. NCJ 173119.

Schmalleger, F. (1997). *Criminal Justice Today, Fourth Edition*, New Jersey: Prentice Hall.

Sheets, R. H. (1996). Urban classroom conflict: Student-teacher perception: Ethnic integrity, solidarity, and resistance, *The Urban Review, 8,* 125-

Simpson, S., Swanson, J., Kunkel, K. (1992). The impact of an intensive multisensory program on a population of learning disabled delinquents. *Annals of Dyslexia, 42,* 54-66.

Singer, A. (1994). Reflections on Multiculturalism, *Phi Delta Kappan, 76,* 284-288.

Slavin, R. E., Zkarweit, N.L. & Wasik, B.A. (1993). Preventing early school failure: What works? *Educational Leadership, 50,* 10-18.

Sleeter, C. E. (1995). An analysis of the critiques of multicultiural education. In James Banks & Cherry A. McGee (Eds.), *Handbook of Research on Multicultural Education,* 81-94, New York: MacMillan Publishing.

Smith, L (1995). *Juveniles in jail: Programmatic trends.* Paper presented at the American Society of Criminology 47th Annual Meeting, Boston, 1995.

Snyder, H. & Sickmund, M. (1999). 1999 *Juvenile Offenders and Victims: National Report.* Washington D.C.: Office of Juvenile Justice and Delinquency Prevention.

Spencer, M. (1982). Personal and group identity of black children: An alternative synthesis. *Genetic Psychology Monographs, 106,* 59-84.

Staff, (2000). Black children often mislabeled as hyperactive. *Caribbean Life: Brooklyn / Staten Island Edition, May 2,* p. 52.

Staff (1994). Gender Gap continues to close on SATs, *New York Times* August 25, p. A12.

Stahl, Anne (2000). *OJJDP Fact Sheet, # 4,* March Washington: Office of Juvenile Justice and Delinquency Prevention.

Stanton-Salazar, Ricardo, D. (1997). A social capital framework for understanding the socialization of racial minority children and youths. *Harvard Educational Review, 67,* 2-40.

Steinberg, Laurence (1996). *Beyond the Classroom: Why School Reform Has Failed and What Parents Need To Do.* New York: Simon and Schuster.

Stone, Christopher (1999). Race, crime and the administration of justice, *NIJ Journal,* pp. 26-36 Washington DC: National Institute of Justice.

Swanson, D. & Spencer, M. (1991). Youth policy, poverty and African-Americans: Implications for resilience. *Education and Urban Society, 24,* 148-161.

Taylor, A. R. (1991). Social competence and early school transition: Risk and protective factors for African-American children. *Education and Urban Society, 24,* 15-26.

Taylor Gibbs, Jewelle (1988). *Young, Black, and Male in America: An Endangered Species.* Dover, MA: Andover House.

Thornberry, T., Lizotte, A., Krohn, M., Farnworth, M. & Jang, S. (1994). Delinquent peers, beliefs, and delinquent behavior: A longitudinal test of interactional theory. *Criminology, 32,* 47-79.

Thornberry, T., Lizotte, A., Krohn, M., Farnworth, M. & Jang, S. (1991).Testing interactional theory: An examination of reciprocal causal relationships among family, school, and delinquency. *Journal of Criminal Law and Criminology, 82,* 3-36.

Thornton, M.C., Chatters, L.M., Joseph Taylor, R. & R. Allen, W. (1990). Sociodemographic and environmental correlates of racial socialization by black   parents. *Child Development, 61,* 401-409.

Tikunoff, W., Berliner, D., & Rist, R. (1975). *An Ethnographic Study of the Forty Classrooms of the Beginning Teacher Evaluation Study Known Sample. Technical* Report No. 75-10-5. San Francisco: Far West Laboratory.

Toby, Jackson (1995). The Schools. In James Q. Wilson and Joan Petersilia (Eds.) *Crime,* p. 141-170, Berkeley, CA: Institute for Contemporary Studies.

Tygart, C.E. (1988) Strain theory and public school vandalism. *Youth and Society, 20,* 106-118.

Tygart, C.E. (1992). Do public schools increase juvenile delinquency? *Urban Education, 26,* 359-370.

U.S. Bureau of Census (1992). *Statistical Abstracts of the United States (112th ed.).* Washington D.C.: U.S. Bureau of Census.

Veneziano, C. & Veneziano, L. (1992). A typology of family social environments for institutionalized juvenile delinquents: Implications for research and treatment. *Journal of Youth and Adolescence 21,* 593-605.

Walker, E. & Sutherland, M. (1993). Urban black youths' educational and occupational   goals: The impact of America's opportunity structure, *Urban Education, 28,* 200-220.

Walters, T. S. (1994). Multicultural literacy: Mental scripts for elementary, secondary, and   college teachers, *Equity and Excellence in Education, 27,* 45-52.

Washington, V. (1982). Racial differences in teacher perceptions of first and fourth grade pupils on selected characteristics. *The Journal of Negro Education, 51,* 60-72.

Wasserman, G., Miller, L., & Cothern, L. (2000). *Prevention of Serious and Violent Juvenile Offending,* OJJDP Juvenile Justice Bulletin.

Weiner, L. (1993). *Preparing Teachers for Urban Schools: Lessons from Thirty Years of School Reform*, New York: Teachers College Press.

Wells, L.E. (1989). Self-enhancement through delinquency: A conditional test of self-derogation theory. *Journal of Research in Crime and Delinquency.*

Willis, Paul (1977). *Learning to Labor: How Working Class Kids get Working Class Jobs.* New York: Columbia University Press.

Wilson, P.M. & Wilson, J. R. (1992) Environmental influences on adolescent educational aspirations: A logistic transform model. *Youth and Society 24,* 52-70.

Wilson, W. J. (1987). *The Truly Disadvantaged.* Chicago: University of Chicago Press.

Winfield, L.F. (1986). Teacher beliefs toward academically at-risk students in inner city urban schools, *The Urban Review, 18,* 253-268.

Wittrock, M.C. (1986). *Handbook of Research on Teaching, 3rd ed.,* New York: MacMillan.

Wlodkowski, R.J. & Ginsberg, M.B. (1995). A framework for culturally responsive teaching, *Educational Leadership, 53,* 17-21.

Index